LAB RATS

Dan Lyons is the *New York Times* bestselling author of *Disrupted*. He is also a novelist, journalist, screenwriter, and public speaker. He was a staff writer on the first two seasons of the Emmy-winning HBO series *Silicon Valley*. Previously, Lyons was technology editor at *Newsweek* and the creator of the groundbreaking viral blog "The Secret Diary of Steve Jobs" (aka "Fake Steve Jobs"). Lyons has written for the *New York Times Magazine*, *GQ*, *Vanity Fair*, and *Wired*.

Dan Lyons

LAB RATS

WHY MODERN WORK MAKES
PEOPLE MISERABLE

Atlantic Books
London

First published in hardback in the United States of America in 2018
by Hachette Books, an imprint of Hachette Book Group.

First published in Great Britain in 2019 by
Atlantic Books, an imprint of Atlantic Books Ltd.

This paperback edition first published in Great Britain in 2019 by Atlantic Books.

1 3 5 7 9 8 6 4 2

A CIP catalogue record for this book is available from the British Library.

Paperback ISBN: 978 1 78649 394 1
E-book ISBN: 978 1 78649 395 8

Printed and bound in Great Britain by clays Ltd, Elcograf S.p.A.

Atlantic Books
An imprint of Atlantic Books Ltd
Ormond House
26–27 Boswell Street
London
WC1N 3JZ

www.atlantic-books.co.uk

Once again, with all my love, for my three best friends: Sasha, Sonya, and Paul.

CONTENTS

Every age has its peculiar folly: Some scheme, project, or fantasy into which it plunges, spurred on by the love of gain, the necessity of excitement, or the force of imitation.

—Charles Mackay, *Extraordinary Popular Delusions and the Madness of Crowds, 1841*

PREFACE TO THE PAPERBACK EDITION

O riginally this was going to be a funny book about work. The idea was that I would roam around the corporate world and chronicle the kooky fads (many originating in Silicon Valley) that have seeped into the "new economy" workplace—things that drive employees nuts and make them miserable. Hackathons, Lego workshops, Agile training, moronic mission statements, crazy-making culture codes, goofy gurus passing off New Age bullshit as management science— that's what I would write about. And I have done that. Some of the stories in this book are so far-fetched that you might wonder if you're reading a work of fiction. Trust me, everything is real.

The problem was that when I sat down to write up the material, I realized that some of what I'd wandered into wasn't funny at all. Sure, the idea of unfortunate Dilberts trapped in asylum-like offices, donning silly hats and making stuff out of Play-Doh might be good for a laugh. But it might also deserve a good cry. When I looked at other ways that work has changed—longer hours, lower pay, more stress, no job security—I realized that in pretty much every respect, companies now treat employees worse than they used to. The kooky games were insult added to the injury.

My funny book began to evolve into something more serious, especially as I started to investigate *why* companies were shortchanging workers. In Silicon Valley they call this a "new compact" between employers and employees, and they consider it one of their greatest innovations. In this new compact, companies exist *solely* to benefit investors, and investors relentlessly push for workers to get less. After all, every dollar spent on workers is a dollar that won't go to investors. This trend didn't start in Silicon Valley. The cult of "shareholder capitalism" first took hold in the 1970s, and business schools have taught it as gospel ever since. But since about the year 2000, tech companies (and the venture capitalists who fund them) have pushed the philosophy to new extremes. Investors don't just feel entitled to the biggest slice of the pie; they want the whole thing.

Proponents of the new compact don't worry about shortchanging workers. But maybe they should. Some people warn that this new arrangement, if left unchecked, will produce catastrophic outcomes. "The Pitchforks Are Coming ... For Us Plutocrats," is the title of an essay by Nick Hanauer, a billionaire investor who for years has been urging wealthy people to stop grabbing so much of the loot—if only to save their own hides from the inevitable backlash and economic collapse. I tracked Hanauer down for interview. He painted a terrifying picture of the not-too-distant future, a cross between *Blade Runner* and *Mad Max*—angry mobs, violent uprisings, revolution, civil war, maybe even the end of democracy. Klaus Schwab, founder of the World Economic Forum, has issued similar warnings for years, though in a less dramatic fashion, cautioning that economic inequality represents the greatest threat to global stability.

When the UK unexpectedly voted for Brexit, and the US elected Donald Trump, the catastrophe seemed to be starting. In early 2018 I was trying to write this book, but I was distracted by an acute case of Trump Derangement Syndrome. President Godzilla was smashing everything in sight, and nobody could stop him. In fact, millions of people were cheering for Godzilla. Who were these people? Why were they so angry? One day I realized that the answer was staring me right in the face, in the book I was writing: *these people are angry because of work.*

In the race to create a new economy, millions of people had been left behind, their jobs lost to outsourcing or automation. Worse, when things went wrong for them, the world told them it was their own fault. No wonder they were angry! Those who managed to hang on to their jobs discovered that the new economy brought more stress and anxiety, as well as new rules of engagement. The new compact got dressed up as a radical transformation—*we're hacking the workplace, bro!*—and HR departments championed each change as a tactic intended to protect jobs by making organizations more competitive. The real goal was to strip away as much as possible from rank-and-file workers and give the money to investors and top management. Companies looted pension funds. They wiped out health plans. Jobs were eliminated and replaced with gigs. Middle managers now get "aged out" at fifty and find themselves driving for Uber, making peanuts. The middle class dwindles as its members are shoved down into a new underclass, the "precariat." Hopeless, powerless, fearful and angry, these people are easily manipulated by charlatans who give voice to their grievances. In the UK, that led to Brexit. In the US, we got Trump.

This is not what the new economy was supposed to look like. Twenty years ago, pundits believed the Internet would empower employees and make work better. It would also improve democracy, since more people would participate in elections, and voters would be more informed. Pundits predicted abundance, prosperity, and "a post-scarcity" economy. Ha! Instead, income inequality has soared to record levels, and more people are more miserable than ever before.

This book explains how we got here—and prescribes solutions. The whole thing begins with fixing work. That means scrapping the new compact, and rewriting the rules by which labor and capital engage with one another. Some of the change involves legislating and litigation. But some involves persuading companies to treat workers with dignity and respect, remembering that they are not "human resources" (to be used up and discarded) but human *beings*.

We can't just fix the workplace. We need to fix capitalism itself—and not just by making a few small tweaks at the edges. The whole system needs a major, fundamental reboot. Even some of the people who are reaping the biggest rewards are calling for an overhaul. "Capitalism is basically not working for the majority of people," Ray Dalio, billionaire founder of Bridgewater Associates, the world's largest hedge fund, declared recently. "Capitalism may need modernizing," Paul Tudor Jones, another billionaire hedge fund manager, has said.

Where to begin? Right now companies put investors above employees. We need to flip that upside down so that employees come first. We can do that by changing the incentives given to CEOs and top managers. Instead of compensating top brass based on how well the company rewards investors, we should tie their pay to the well-being of their employees. Instead of shareholder capitalism, we should embrace a form of capitalism that rewards all the other stakeholders—employees, customers, and the community at large.

Shareholder capitalism keeps concentrating wealth into ever fewer hands. That money sits in two big buckets—the swollen balance sheets of giant corporations like Apple, and the bank accounts of billionaires like Amazon CEO Jeff Bezos, the world's richest man. How have these corporations and individuals accumulated such vast fortunes? Apple for years has employed a complex (and according to one Nobel laureate economist, fraudulent) scheme that involves stashing profits overseas to avoid paying taxes in the United States. As a result, Apple now holds more than $200 billion in cash. Amazon over the past two years generated record profits of $16.8 billion, yet paid no federal income tax on those earnings, according to the Institute on Taxation and Economic Policy, a think tank. Amazon boosts its profits by constantly finding ways to spend less on its human beings. Some workers in Amazon shipping centers are paid so poorly that they qualify for food stamps.

This isn't capitalism. It's theft. The billions of dollars that Apple should have paid in taxes—that's our money. Apple stole it. Same goes for wages. When a company generates record profits by ripping money away from workers to line its own pockets, that's stealing. Companies say they're only doing what investors demand. The great paradox is that ultimately, over the long term, shareholder capitalism ends up being terrible for investors. It's "the dumbest idea in the world," former General Electric chief executive Jack Welch once said. Yet investors keep pushing, even as their efforts wreak havoc on the world around them. It's insane, irrational and self-destructive behavior.

Fortunately, there's an easy fix: make the looters give back the money by paying more tax and higher wages. As I write this, in March 2019, a backlash against the super-rich is gathering momentum. "Should Billionaires Even Exist?" the *Huffington Post* wondered. "Abolish Billionaires," Farhad Manjoo declared in a *New York Times* column. "Every billionaire is a policy failure," is the mantra of Dan Riffle, a policy advisor to newly elected Congresswoman Ocasio-Cortez, who advocates a 70 percent top marginal tax rate on people who earn more than $10 million a year. Two months ago, at the World Economic Forum in Davos, Switzerland, Dutch historian Rutger Bregman made news just by speaking a simple truth—that the culprits who caused our mess are rich people who refuse to pay taxes. "Taxes, taxes, taxes. All the rest is bullshit in my opinion," Bregman said. The state of New York is weighing a "pied-à-terre" tax on pricey part-time homes, which many wealthy people use as a way to park money, tax-free. Tech entrepreneur and dark horse 2020 presidential candidate Andrew Yang calls for redistributing wealth via universal basic income, and advocates an economic do-over that he calls "human-centric capitalism." His biggest fans are young people, who are aggrieved about the raw deal they're getting in the workplace.

Union membership has dwindled in the United States, but it's time to revive those unions, or form new ones. Even well-paid white-collar workers and pampered high-tech software engineers have begun to recognize how powerful they can be as part of a collective. Employees at Amazon shipping centers walked out over working conditions. Microsoft workers have protested the company's military contracts.

In late 2018, more than 20,000 workers at Google walked out to protest the company's handling of sexual harassment complaints. Google workers are among the most pampered employees in the world. When *they* walk out, it's significant.

All this stuff about reinventing our system of capitalism seems far removed from the world of silly workshops and hocus-pocus management science. But these are all connected. The frivolous game-playing, the scrumming and sprinting—they're all symptoms of a system that has become dysfunctional. Where do we spend more time than work? What other part of our lives has such a profound effect on our well-being and sense of identity? When we talk about work, we're talking about people's financial situation, their ability to support families, pay for health care, put kids through college, and save for retirement. We're talking about their psychological and physical well-being, the decisions they make, and even how they vote. When we talk about work, we're really talking about society. Over the past two years it has become obvious that bad decisions made in the arena of the workplace can have disastrous consequences. To fix society, we start by fixing work.

That's what this book is about. Sure, you'll get a kick out of the kooky stuff about crazy team-building exercises and ridiculous management gurus. But as you do, remember that the kooky stuff is a symptom of a deeper problem—a form of misdirection, a way to distract employees and keep them from noticing that their pockets are being picked.

At the end of this new paperback edition, I offer Seven Rules for building a sane, healthy, happy culture at work. It starts with giving employees what they want—better pay, great benefits, more stability and job security, day care at work, on-the-job training and career development, mentoring, the chance to learn new skills and work their way up inside the organization. In recent years, some business experts have claimed that Millennials don't care about such things. Yet when I asked twenty-something Millennials what they wanted most from work, these things were exactly what they wished for.

They don't want ping-pong; they want health insurance. They don't care about parties and free beer; they want to save enough money to buy a house.

The first step toward fixing work is understanding exactly what companies have done wrong. On the next page you will find a one-page statement of the new compact that exists in the modern workplace. My version is the one your employer would give you on your first day at your new job if the company dared to be honest with you.

WELCOME TO YOUR NEW JOB

First, you are lucky to be here. Also, we do not care about you. We offer no job security. This is not a career. You are serving a short-term tour of duty. We provide no training or career development. If possible, we will make you a contractor rather than an actual employee, so that we do not have to provide you with benefits or a pension plan. We will pay you as little as possible. We do not care about diversity: ethnic minorities need not apply. Your job will be stressful. You will work long hours under constant pressure and with no privacy. You will be monitored and surveilled. We will read your email and chat messages, and use data to measure your performance. We do not expect you to last very long. Our goal is to burn you out and churn you out. Your managers may not know what they are doing. They also may be abusive. If you are female, there is a good chance you will be sexually harassed. HR will not help you. If you file a complaint, you will probably get fired. If you get pregnant or turn forty, you also will be fired. You may be fired even though you are doing a good job. You may be fired for no reason at all. We do not offer a creche. We do have ping-pong. There are snacks and beer in the kitchen.

INTRODUCTION

MAKE A DUCK

On a Wednesday morning in June 2017, I find myself in Menlo Park, California, sharing a small table in a faux European coffee shop with a woman I'll call Julia—and I'm making a duck out of Lego bricks.

Outside, it's sunny and warm. A late-morning breeze ruffles the big bright-colored umbrellas above the tables in the plaza. Inside, young techies gaze up at the chalkboard menu above the counter and sit at tables clicking at laptops. Django Reinhardt's guitar emanates from hidden speakers. Nobody pays any attention to the two gray-haired people sitting near the window with their plastic toys.

Julia and I have never met before. She's a cheery, round-faced woman in her fifties with a disarming smile and an easy laugh. Julia arrived carrying a big canvas bag filled with Lego bricks, and they're now scattered out on the table. As we're making small talk, she plays with the pieces, idly snapping and unsnapping them. Soon, between sips of my caffè Americano and bites of a remarkably good almond croissant, I start tinkering with them too.

A few years earlier I briefly worked at a Silicon Valley-style startup in Boston, a disastrous experience I chronicled in my last book, before getting a job as a writer on the HBO comedy *Silicon Valley*.

Today, I have returned to the setting of that show—which, while a real place, is also a state of mind—not for fun, but for research. For the last two years, I have made it my mission to speak to as many people as I can to better understand the modern workplace and why work today seems to make so many people unhappy. My theory is that at least some of the unhappiness at work comes from being herded into silly workshops where people are fed a bunch of touchy-feely nonsense about self-improvement and transformation.

That's how I've come to be on this coffee date. Julia makes a living running the weirdest kind of corporate workshops I've heard about so far. In Julia's workshops, she asks people, office workers like I once was, to play with Lego. This is an actual thing now, and the people who teach this take it very seriously. The methodology is called Lego Serious Play, and Julia is one of thousands of people who have become certified to run LSP workshops. Huge companies, including Unilever, Johnson & Johnson, and Google, have embraced it.

When I first heard about Lego workshops I thought someone was pulling my leg. I was talking to a corporate trainer—I'll call him Edward—who said, "You know, you should talk to some of my friends who are certified in Lego."

"Excuse me?" I said.

"I'm serious," he said. He insisted that Lego training really helps people get better at their jobs. "It's powerful," Edward said. "The Lego bricks are a prop. They help get people to talk about how they feel about things, unfiltered. It's like kids who have been abused, and they talk through a doll. People talk through their Lego."

Oh dear God. I closed my eyes and pictured a bunch of poor Jims and Pams talking through their Lego, pouring their hearts out to a team of New Age quacks. This could be either the worst thing or the best thing I might ever see in my entire life. Maybe both.

Edward gave me a name and a number. Soon I was talking to one of the top Lego trainers in the world, a man who lives in Southern California. He put me in touch with Julia, who lives in Silicon Valley, a few miles from where I'm staying.

I'm a little disappointed, because I came here expecting, and actually half hoping, to meet a complete nut job or a shyster. Unfortunately, Julia appears to be neither. She's very bright and really sincere. She has a master's degree in engineering and spent two decades writing software inside some serious organizations. Moreover, I really like her. I don't want to make fun of her. And yet—here we are, in a coffee shop, playing with Lego.

"It gets people talking," Julia says. She tells me about the brain science that supposedly explains how Lego Serious Play works. There is, in fact, a body of scholarly looking research around LSP discussing things like the cerebral cortex and the limbic system. Julia says LSP is especially useful with software programmers, who tend to be introverts, because it creates a "safe space" where they can talk. Lego workshops also help Type-A top executives stop being such over-bearing assholes, and can even be a catalyst for changing an entire organization, she claims. I can see why HR departments go nuts for this. HR people used to be glorified office managers, but now they get MBAs and are called Chief People Officers. They talk about being "strategic talent managers" who "drive corporate transformation" and are "building the workforce of the future." They're suckers for pop neuroscience, and though most wouldn't know an amygdala from an anal wart, they will jump on anything that they think can rewire the brain circuitry of their employees. Lego Serious Play promises to do just that, and comes wrapped in just enough scientific-sounding literature to make it seem legitimate.

To me these sessions sound like a waking nightmare, like a cross between an away day and group therapy, with the added insult of toys. Julia swears it's not like that. Sure, at first, some people are pretty skeptical, but they're quickly won over.

In just the past few years LSP has become a booming industry. There are LSP consultancies and LSP conferences. People write LSP books, LSP white papers, and LSP articles on LSP websites. There's even a Global Federation of LSP Master Trainers. The concept was created in the 1990s by two business professors in Switzerland who drew on research in psychology and educational theory. Over time people started adding in theories about brain science. By one estimate more than ten thousand people have become certified Lego facilitators, and more than one hundred thousand people have participated in Lego workshops.

Lego Serious Play has grown by attaching itself to another corporate training fad: Agile. Agile has become immensely popular in the corporate world and has evolved into something akin to a religion. It's also now a huge industry unto itself, with conferences, consultancies, trainers, gurus, and literally thousands of books devoted to its teaching. A few years ago a lot of Agile trainers started getting certifications in Lego Serious Play, since the concepts behind Lego and Agile are considered complementary. That's how Julia got into this. She began her career as a computer engineer, but about ten years ago she became a programming coach, someone who teaches coders how to code. To do that, Julia needed to get a certification in Agile. Later, she added Lego to her bag of tricks.

That bag also includes a certificate in Neuro-Linguistic Programming. NLP was originally a form of New Age psychotherapy created in the 1970s by Gestalt-loving hippie shrinks at the University of California at Santa Cruz. Critics claim it is pseudoscience, but some people believe NLP can be used for mind control, like hypnosis. You load your language with keywords, study the subject's eye movements, and use a technique called anchoring. Supposedly Tony Robbins uses NLP. A British celebrity magician/hypnotist named Derren Brown, star of *Derren Brown: Mind Control*, makes videos where he manipulates people just by talking to them.

In addition to her Agile, Lego, and NLP training, Julia tells me, "I've also studied hypnosis." I'm ecstatic. When I was in high school I saw a stage hypnotist get four of my schoolmates up on stage, clucking like chickens. I've always wanted to be hypnotized, just so I could see what it feels like.

"Could you hypnotize me? Right now? Could you put me under, right here at this table?"

"Of course," she says. "People go into trance states all the time. Every time you drive a car, you're in a trance state."

"Right," I say, "but I mean the hypnosis where you put me under, like you count backward from three and snap your fingers, or wave a watch in front of my face—that kind of thing."

Julia explains that she would not need to do anything that dramatic. She would just talk to me. "Think about how a mother talks to a child when he scrapes his knee and gets a boo-boo and he's crying, and she's trying to soothe him. The mother uses one of the most powerful hypnotic phrases there is. She gives him a hug, and she lowers her voice, and she says, 'You'll be okay. You'll be okay.' And he stops feeling the pain. The pain goes away."

"So that's hypnosis?" Julia nods. I try not to look too sad. We're sitting at a small table, our faces close. "You'll be okay," she says again. "You'll be okay." Her voice is breathy, her cadence lulling. With each repetition she slightly changes her inflection. "You'll be okay." I look away, but she keeps going. Her voice gets softer. "You'll be okay," she says. "You'll be okay."

"Okay!" I say, a little too loud. I'm incredibly suggestible, and I'm afraid that after another thirty seconds of this she could have me up on the table, clucking. If we were not sitting in a crowded café—if we were alone, in private—I would probably just let her hypnotize me. Instead, I, well, chicken out. "I get it," I tell her. I blink my eyes a few times, as if I could shake off whatever voodoo this woman has put on me.

Of course she might have already put me into a trance. How would I know? She probably started using her NLP mind control techniques on me as soon as we sat down and began making small talk.

That's when Julia produces a little plastic bag and spills out six Lego bricks: two red, three yellow, and then another yellow one that has eyeballs on two sides.

"Make a duck," she says. "You have thirty seconds."

*   *   *

For a moment I sit there just looking at the six plastic blocks. The image that pops into my head is a squeaky yellow bathtub duck, like the chubby rubber duck that Ernie sings about on *Sesame Street*. Somehow I must combine these six rectangular Lego blocks into something that resembles a rubber duck. The head part is obvious. But what about the others? The two red pieces are flat slabs with six knobs. Does one sit on top of the duck's head, like a hat? I hate things like this—Rubik's Cubes, Sudoku puzzles. I hate them because I suck at them, and I never know the trick to solving the puzzle, so I just sit there flailing away. Or I just surrender and sit there staring at the cube, with the same look on my face that my cat has when he looks at the TV, wondering how those little birds got inside the box.

The clock is ticking. I start snapping and unsnapping. I feel frantic, while Julia sits there, calm as Buddha, with a bemused expression. Of course, she knows the answer. She has watched hundreds of people, maybe thousands of them, try to solve this. I wonder what percentage of people succeed. I wonder where I rate among all those people. I suspect I'm near the bottom.

This puzzle might be a kind of IQ test, and if so I'm about to land in a very low percentile. Or it could be a Rorschach test, a puzzle that reveals something about my personality. *Oh, he's one of those*, I imagine Julia thinking. Companies could use the duck puzzle to evaluate workers and separate the wheat from the chaff. The good problem solvers get marked for promotion. The ninnies, like me, get put on the list for the next round of layoffs.

In a panic, I try a new configuration. This too does not work. I break up the bricks and start over. A child could do this, I tell myself. And yet I cannot.

Julia sighs, which I think is the signal that my thirty seconds are up. Quickly I snap together a four-piece duck, leaving two bricks on the table.

"I'm sorry," I say. "That's all I could do."

She picks up my duck and looks at it. In addition to using only four bricks, I've also put the head on sideways. Julia gently unsnaps the head and puts it on so that it's facing the right way.

"I'm sorry," I say again, stammering. "I think I got nervous. I know there must be a way to use all of the pieces, but for whatever reason, I couldn't see it. Maybe if I had more time. I don't know."

"What makes you think you have to use all six bricks?" Julia says. "I never said how many bricks you had to use. All I said was make a duck."

She gives me a little smile, as if to say, *Gotcha!*

It turns out that Make a Duck is the best-known exercise in the Lego Serious Play canon, and this is its lesson—that everyone makes a different duck. The duck is not a puzzle, or a brain-teaser, or an IQ test. The duck is a window into your soul. Why did I assume that I had to use all the pieces? Why did I think it was a puzzle, or an IQ test? Why was I so afraid about failing? I hate to admit this, but in less than a minute, with a half dozen plastic bricks, this woman has gutted me like a fish, and laid bare my neuroses.

But then something else occurs to me.

"Are you telling me I could just snap any two bricks together and call it a duck?"

"Sure," she says.

"Or I could just hand you back a single brick and say, 'Here you go, here's my duck.'"

"Whatever you make, that's your duck. That's how *you* make a duck. And your duck is different from everyone else's duck. Besides, these aren't ducks, are they? They're *representations* of a duck. They're *metaphors* for a duck."

I have to give Julia credit. She has an answer for everything. There's no way to shake her faith in Lego. What's more, she genuinely believes she is helping people. And maybe she is. A lot of people benefit from going to church, and I don't begrudge them their beliefs.

Lego workshops are just one example of the nonsense that is creeping into the workplace. A lot of Agile trainers also do workshops with Play-Doh. In another game, called Six Thinking Hats, people put on different colored hats and role-play. In something called the Ball Point Game, teams compete to find the fastest way to pass tennis balls into a bucket, fire-brigade style. Do a search for "Ball Point Game" on YouTube and you can watch fully sentient adult human beings actually doing this at work.

Why now? Why has the workplace become a cross between a kindergarten and a Scientology assessment center? Why do our offices now have decor that looks like a Montessori preschool, with lots of bright, basic colors? Why does work now involve such infantilization?

I suspect it's because companies are scared. We live in an age of chaos, a period when entire industries are collapsing. We're headed into the Fourth Industrial Revolution, and facing "transformation . . . unlike anything humankind has experienced before," says Klaus Schwab, the head of the World Economic Forum. Even the biggest, most powerful companies in the world are threatened with extinction. To survive, the Big Old Companies must evolve, and recode their DNA. That means replacing or transforming their people, which is why they're digging into our brains and trying to rewire our circuits.

But what does all this psychological poking and prodding do to us? The problem isn't just that these exercises are pointless and silly. For a lot of people this stuff can be really stressful. For older workers—say, people over fifty—these workshops compound the fear they already have about being pushed out of their jobs. But younger workers hate them, too. "It feels like you've joined a cult," says a thirty-something software programmer whose department spent a day doing a Lego workshop. "The purpose seems to be to indoctrinate people to follow orders."

You find yourself being gaslighted, immersed in the kind of shared psychosis and group delusion found in cults. You know these workshops are pointless, and that no one is going to be transformed by

Lego. But to keep your job, you must play along. You must deliver a performance and convince management that you are flexible, adaptable, and open to change, the kind of engaged, dynamic worker who meets the needs of the new economy. Basically the company is conducting a large-scale experiment in organizational behavior. They'd like to test out some theories on you. So you all go into the box, and you are poked and prodded with various stimuli to see how you respond.

Your office has become a psychology laboratory, run by a bunch of quacks. You're not a duck. You're a lab rat.

This coffee date with Lego marked just a single stop on what would become my yearlong quest to figure out how work is changing, and, more important, *why* it is changing. The quest would take me to conferences in the United States and Europe, and to the headquarters of Steelcase, the office-furniture maker, where researchers are trying to figure out how to make offices that are more human-friendly. I'd talk to anthropologists and architects, psychologists and sociologists, management consultants, management coaches and management gurus, economists and engineers, doctors and diversity advocates, lawyers and venture capitalists, business professors and Agile coaches and Lego trainers, and one very frightened billionaire who fears that angry proles are going to launch a violent revolution against people like him.

Over the course of this journey I came to believe that much blame for worker unhappiness falls on Silicon Valley. For one thing, that's where most new office automation technologies are developed. But also, in addition to producing chips and software, Silicon Valley now aims to remake the notion of the corporation itself, by inventing radical new ideas about how to build and manage companies. Unfortunately, many of their ideas are terrible.

In Part 2 of this book I explore four tech-related tendencies—what I call "The Four Factors"—that contribute to worker unhappiness. They are:

- MONEY: We make a lot less today than we did a generation ago. The scale and scope of the robbery that has been carried out on workers in the West amount to trillions of dollars per year—and the heist has been helped along by technology. You'll find the numbers in Chapter 6.
- INSECURITY: We live in constant fear of losing our jobs. That's because employers, especially in Silicon Valley, are adopting a "new compact" with workers. As I explain in Chapter 7, your job is no longer the start of a career, but just a short-term "tour of duty."
- CHANGE: New technologies, new methodologies, kooky new arrangements for where we work and how we work—we are overwhelmed by a workplace that never stays the same for very long. In Chapter 8, you'll find research that shows that being exposed to persistent, low-grade change leads to depression and anxiety. The suffering is akin to what we experience after the death of a loved one or spending time in combat.
- DEHUMANIZATION: Once upon a time we used technology, but today technology uses us. We're hired by machines, managed by them, even fired by them. We're monitored and measured, constantly surveilled. As I explain in Chapter 9, we are expected to become more like machines ourselves.

The good news is that in the course of my journey I also discovered people who are pushing back against these changes that are hurting workers and wreaking havoc on society. In Oakland, Chicago, New York, Boston, and elsewhere, entrepreneurs are forming companies that put the needs of employees first. These companies pay well, sometimes more than they have to. They provide good benefits, and promote work-life balance. Their goal is to provide good, sustainable jobs for as many people as possible. What a shock! You'll find their stories in Part 3 of this book.

I wrote this book because I believe we have reached an important turning point, one where we must make an important decision. We need to decide what the future will look like. Do we want the world to be tech-centric, or human-centric? If we stick with the tech-centric path that Silicon Valley proposes, we will end up with more of what we have now—more misery, ever-worsening income inequality, and potentially catastrophic outcomes. Or we can turn back and embrace a new kind of capitalism. We can create a human-centric future, where employees are treated with dignity and respect, and workers get a fair share of the wealth that their labor is creating. Obviously I'm rooting for the latter.

Before we figure out how to get out of this mess, let's examine how we got into it.

PART I

MISERY IN THE MAZE

CHAPTER ONE

UNHAPPY IN PARADISE

The journey that led to me making ducks out of Lego began in 2013, when at age fifty-two I left the media business—not entirely of my own accord. Specifically, I was laid off from *Newsweek*, the once storied magazine where I had been the technology editor. This happened without any warning. One Friday morning in June my editor called and told me I was done. That was it. I got no severance package. Getting fired sent me into a tailspin. The media business was collapsing. In my darkest moments I worried that I might never find another job. Then what would we do? My wife and I have twins; at the time they were seven years old.

In the months that followed, I decided to make a radical change. I would leave journalism and reinvent myself as a marketing person. I started applying for jobs at tech companies. Soon enough, a software start-up in Cambridge, called HubSpot, offered me a job. I went in with high hopes. The co-founders were a pair of MIT graduates. They had developed a software product that was selling really well. But they were also doing something else that was even more ambitious. They were going to tear up the playbook that corporations have used for the past century and rethink every aspect of how to run a company. The world had changed, and so should companies.

These guys believed they could create a modern corporation that would meet the needs of the new economy.

Thus HubSpot became a kind of experiment in organizational behavior. Part of the experiment involved hiring mostly young kids right out of college and turning them loose, with very little instruction, so they could figure things out for themselves. The average employee was twenty-six years old. They were peppy and energetic, brimming with optimism and new ideas.

The offices boasted all the usual start-up accoutrements—beanbag chairs, Ping-Pong tables, a wall of candy dispensers, refrigerators stocked with beer. We could work whenever and wherever we wanted. One woman spent a year working from trains and hotel rooms as she followed Justin Timberlake as he toured the United States. We had unlimited vacation and first-rate health insurance, completely paid for by the company. One co-founder built a nap room. The other brought a teddy bear to meetings as a prop. We did wacky team-building exercises, like Fearless Friday, where my colleagues spent a day sprawled in a conference room, making paintings.

The organization had evolved into something like a cult. We were told that it was harder to get a job at HubSpot than to get into Harvard. The company had developed its own special language. We were told that we were "rock stars" and "ninjas" who were "changing the world" with our "superpowers." We were told to "make one plus one equal three" and to devote ourselves, with almost religious zeal, to providing our customers with "delightion," a made-up word that meant delighting customers by doing more than they expected. We weren't in the software business; we were in the *delightion* business.

Sure, it was silly, but who cared? The work was easy, the hours light. I liked the flexibility, the free snacks in the kitchen, the hammock in the nap room. Most of all I was relieved to be in a place where I would not have to worry about job security. The company was growing so fast they could barely keep up. They were constantly hiring new workers. For the past ten years I'd been living with constant job insecurity. In the magazine business, the next layoff always loomed. At long last, I could relax. At HubSpot, my job would be secure. Or so I thought. Within a few months, I came to understand that this fast-growing start-up offered even less job security than any of the failing magazines where I'd been working before. Turnover was tremendous, especially in sales and telemarketing.

What's more, the company did not see high turnover as a problem. They were proud of it. They considered it a badge of honor. It demonstrated that the company had a "high-performance culture" where only the best of the best could survive. Weirder still, when they fired someone they called it "graduation." We would get an email saying how "awesome" it was that so-and-so was "graduating," taking their "superpowers" on to a new adventure.

This really messed with people's heads, because you never knew when it might happen to you. Beneath their bubbly exteriors many people were anxious, frightened, unhappy, and massively stressed out. I'd never before had co-workers call me from their cars, sobbing in the parking garage, having panic attacks. Newsrooms have always been pretty miserable places, and they were even more so when business started collapsing, yet never in my journalism career had I seen co-workers in so much pain.

Soon enough I found myself on a trajectory toward "graduation." By the time I left I felt almost relieved. I was, as they say in the startup world, "not a good culture fit." In my final months, my boss had reassigned me to a menial, demeaning job and told me that even at this I was failing. He said I needed to redeem myself, that my coworkers didn't like me. I tried to think of the whole thing as a kind of game. Even so, the psychological stress was tremendous. I slid into anxiety and depression. Sometimes I could not sleep at all. I would lie awake all night, wondering how I had been transformed from a confident, secure, accomplished person into a shivering, quivering, self-loathing wreck. At other times I could do nothing but sleep. I would come home, eat dinner, and go straight to bed.

I hung in for nearly two years and left with my self-esteem in tatters, half-believing that my boss had been right about me, that

I simply did not have what it takes to succeed in the new economy. I had gone into the job with high hopes, deceived by the perks and pampering into believing that these new companies were supportive, progressive organizations inventing a new human-centric approach to work. I came away believing the opposite, that modern workplaces were actually worse than the old companies they were replacing. They were digital sweatshops, akin to the brutal textile mills and garment factories from more than a century ago.

After my own "graduation," I decided to write a book about my experience. I wanted to explain how, after years of writing glowing magazine articles about the new economy, I had ventured into the new economy and found out that most of what I believed was wrong. *Disrupted* wasn't meant to be a book about corporate culture. I just hoped to write a funny memoir about a curmudgeonly fiftysomething journalist trying (and failing) to reinvent himself while working alongside a bunch of effervescent Millennials in the marketing department of a cult-like tech start-up.

But when the book came out, something extraordinary happened. My inbox begin to fill with email after email, hundreds of emotional letters from people who had read *Disrupted* and were desperate to share their stories. Many came from middle-aged people who had been "aged out" of the workforce. But I also got a ton of mail from Millennials, the ones for whom this brave new world of work, with its bouncy castles and beer pong parties, supposedly had been created. These bright young people were as disillusioned with work as their older counterparts.

Day after day, I received letters from people who said they'd laughed at some parts of *Disrupted*, but other parts had hit too close to home. Many came from people who worked in the tech industry, but I heard also from people who worked at design shops, mobile phone carriers, advertising agencies, biotech companies, and market research firms. The letters came from all over the world, even from places where *Disrupted* had not yet been published: India, England, France, Scandinavia, Ireland. A man in Iraq, writing to me while a battle was raging in Mosul, wrote to tell me that he, too, had endured a soul-destroying work experience and that reading my book had been therapeutic.

It was gratifying that so many people were passing my book around, telling their friends about it, and making the effort to track me down and write to me about their own experiences. But it was also depressing. Over time I heard versions of the following stories. People were hired for one job but arrived to find they were doing something else. They sold their home and moved to a new area for a new job, only to get fired a few weeks or months into the new gig. They were hired for a job in which it was unclear what they would be doing, and when they asked for guidance they were told that people who needed direction were not cut out for the modern workplace; they were supposed to be "self-directed." They worked in flat organizations, with no hierarchy and no structure, which drove them nuts.

They worked for managers who were young, inexperienced, and undertrained—or sometimes completely untrained. Their bosses told them that their jobs were not secure, that they were powerless, that they could be fired at any moment without any reason. They were subjected to personality assessments and herded into teambuilding exercises. They were exposed to brainwashing techniques, force-fed notions about "culture," and informed that their success hinged on their ability to fit in with the others, but that the others didn't like them. They were told that they were failing, but not told how or why.

People were surveyed and surveilled, monitored and measured. They experienced bias and discrimination based on their age, race, or gender. They were sexually harassed. Some were shunned and ostracized by colleagues, or coerced into "forced fun" activities, like indoor skydiving, ballroom dancing, or trapeze training, and told they were supposed to be having fun. One young woman had been fired because, as her boss put it, "You're not excited enough." They were exposed to so much psychological pressure that some became physically ill. Some quit. Others soldiered on, only to get fired anyway.

For weeks I couldn't stop reading the letters. Some described a kind of Stockholm syndrome, where they remained in abusive situations even though they knew they should leave. "I still have nightmares about the place, where I'm trying to prove I'm not an idiot—to idiots!" says a woman I'll call Beatrix about her time at a prestigious San Francisco firm that epitomizes the hip new-economy company. Beatrix has an MBA and was in her late thirties when she joined the company, having spent a decade working for both start-ups and multinational corporations. Her previous jobs had gone well, but in her new position she could do nothing right. In a long email (which she has given me permission to use in this book) she poured out her heart to me:

> I would be pulled into windowless conference rooms to have my boss share anonymous team member feedback, where people would discuss my looks ("arrogant and distant") and my IQ ("appears to be very low"). My performance review contained this: "I can't understand whether she doesn't understand our culture or if she's plain stupid." I was told to improve my performance so that "people don't have to write stuff like that." The worst part was when I started to think they were right. Maybe I really was as bad as they said I was. I was freaked out, stressed, crying, self-pitying. All the while, I didn't have the guts to quit. I just kept trying to make it work.

For some reason, Beatrix's boss wouldn't fire her. So they remained locked in a kind of psychological battle, with Beatrix trying to prove her worth and win her boss's approval, and her boss repeatedly telling her that she was falling short. She told no one about this, except her husband. As far as her friends knew, she had landed a cool job at one of the world's hippest companies. When they asked about work, she said it was fine and changed the subject. "It was like an inverted reality. At home I had a loving husband and kids. In my personal life, at home and among my friends, people saw me as a good mother, a good wife, a successful person with a good job. At work I became Gregor Samsa," she says, referring to the traveling salesman in Kafka's *Metamorphosis* who wakes up one day transformed into a giant cockroach.

Beatrix's boss conducted eccentric exercises. One day he called everyone into a conference room and told them they were going to critique each other. He made them stand in a circle, sideways, so each one faced the back of the person to their left. They would write one word about the person in front of them and pin that word onto the back of that person's shirt.

"The person behind you would read the word on your shirt, and then expand on it," Beatrix recalls. "So you're standing there and the person behind you is telling you all sorts of terrible things about you, and you have to just stand there, listening. And this happens in front of all of your co-workers."

This seems amazing, but Beatrix stayed for nearly four years. Toward the end she was suffering panic attacks nearly every day. She still feels panicky if she has to drive near the company's headquarters in San Francisco, so much so that if she needs to go into the city she will plan a route that will let her avoid the neighborhood. She left in 2013, and has not worked since. She is in her forties, which she says makes her virtually unemployable in San Francisco.

A lot of the letters and stories I heard involved managers who played weird, manipulative mind games. Some people were sure they had brushed up against a sociopath. One woman told me she and her colleagues still tracked an ex-boss who had done incredible damage in a relatively short amount of time at their company nearly a decade before. For years they had watched him move from job to job. From people at each stop they would hear stories that he was still engaging in the same sadistic crazy-making and gaslighting and abuse. He was like a serial killer who keeps moving to new cities, seeking fresh victims. A man who lives two thousand miles away from me wrote to tell me that the same manager who had tormented me at HubSpot had tormented him a decade earlier, using the same tactics: "I'm pretty sure I was the beta version of what happened with you," he wrote.

A thirty-something marketing executive (whom I'll call Adrian) told me a story about showing up for his first day of work at a software start-up and being told by his new boss that she already didn't like him. In fact, nobody in the department liked him, she said. "Everybody who interviewed you thought you were arrogant and full of yourself," she told him. "I thought the same thing." She told Adrian they all had voted against hiring him, but the chief marketing officer had overruled them and hired Adrian anyway. "So just be aware that you're starting out here in a very deep hole," his manager told him. "You're going to have to dig your way out of that hole and redeem yourself and win everybody over." Adrian didn't know if she was telling the truth or just playing a mind game with him, trying to knock him back on his heels and motivate him to work harder. In the end it didn't matter. He only lasted nine months.

Martin and Linda, a well-educated twenty-something couple in New York, kept joining start-ups, lured in by perks and a culture that seemed fun, only to find out that, yet again, they were just being packed into digital sweatshops. They were harassed by managers and forced to put in long hours under tremendous stress, doing work that was ultimately pointless and for which they were poorly paid, with no chance of promotion or advancement. "All of my friends who work at tech companies are baseline unhappy," Linda said. "Everyone has one foot out the door all the time."

A fifty-something guy told me about taking a job at a hip Millennial-packed PR agency and having to bail out after only four months, "because I was more stressed out than I'd ever been at any job, and it was affecting my family." One of his equally stressed-out colleagues described the place as "PTSD-inducing." Both had worked in public relations for decades without any ill effects, and could not understand how the job had come to feel like shipping out to the frontlines of war.

Like me, these people didn't just feel that they had taken a rough job or had a bad boss. They felt they had stepped into some kind of alternate reality, where people did bad things to them for no reason. They described feeling helpless, powerless, confused, victimized. They described questioning their sanity or doubting their self-worth. They talked about "what they did to me there." Instead of saying they quit or got fired, they talked about how they had "escaped." They sounded like abuse survivors or people who have been rescued from cults.

Some had even fantasized, as I had during my time in startup land, that their companies weren't companies at all, but rather were part of some long-term psychology experiment, a corporate version of the Milgram experiment at Yale or the Stanford prison experiment. The 1961 Milgram experiment studied obedience to authority figures. Psychologist Stanley Milgram ordered subjects to keep administering ever-stronger shocks to a "learner" on the other side of a wall, and many kept going, even when the learner shrieked, pleaded, and banged on the wall. In the 1971 Stanford prison experiment, twenty-four college students were put into a mock prison, with half role-playing as guards and half role-playing as prisoners, to see what happens when people are given power over others. Within six days the guards were inflicting such sickening psychological abuse on the prisoners that the experiment had to be cut short.

The idea that my place of employment might be a psychology experiment actually made sense to me. This would explain Fearless Friday, and the fact that nobody made fun of the guy with the teddy bear, and the way they pretended to feel good about "graduating" someone. Maybe some group of psychologists from MIT or Harvard wanted to study the limits of obedience and control. How much would people debase themselves, and how much dignity would they sacrifice, in order to continue receiving a paycheck? Would they make a duck out of Lego? Wear funny hats? Keep silent when a colleague gets fired for no reason? How high could you turn the dial? How much silliness and/or cruelty would employees tolerate before they complained or refused to participate? The unlikely juxtaposition of those two seemingly contradictory things—silliness and cruelty—has become a hallmark of the new-economy modern workplace.

That's how I came to think of employees as lab rats. It turns out others had noticed the same thing. "Work is feeling more and more like a Skinner box" is how Gregory Berns, a neuropsychologist at Emory University, put it when he wrote a *New York Times* article about a study he had conducted about how fear impairs decision-making, which involved putting people into an MRI machine and zapping their feet with electric shocks. A Skinner box, invented in the 1930s by psychologist B. F. Skinner, is a cage in which rats learn that pulling certain levers gets them food and that flashing lights might signal they are about to get a shock through the floor.

A NEW KIND OF SUFFERING

When I wrote *Disrupted* I thought my experience had been unusual. But now here were all these people telling me they had experienced something similar. This was taking place not just at start-ups and not just in the tech industry, but in many industries and many countries around the world. Job satisfaction in Britain and Germany has been steadily eroding since the 1980s. In the United States, the percentage of workers who say they are satisfied with their jobs dropped from 61.1 percent in 1987 to 50.8 percent in 2016, according to the Conference Board, a research firm, which adds that it's "very unlikely" that job satisfaction will ever return to 1980s levels. Worldwide, only 13 percent of workers feel "engaged"—meaning enthusiastic at work and committed to their companies—according to Gallup, which has tracked this since 2000. Things are better in the United States, where 32 percent of workers are engaged, but that still means that more than two-thirds of employees are just mailing it in. Worse, Gallup says roughly one in five workers is "actively disengaged," which means they may even be toxic. They're the ones who go around complaining to co-workers and even driving away customers.

In a 2014 survey by Monster, the job-seeking site, 61 percent of workers said work-related stress had made them physically sick, and nearly half said they had missed work because of it. Seven percent said they been hospitalized as a result of work-related stress. The anxiety, depression, and crazy-making that I had experienced at a start-up were becoming a new normal, according to Jeffrey Pfeffer, a business professor at Stanford. Citing his own research into worker unhappiness, Pfeffer declared that "What's missing is a sense of humanity." Companies might offer parties, snacks, and Ping-Pong, but are stripping away things lower on Maslow's hierarchy of needs, like job security. Companies "regularly permit if not encourage management practices that literally sicken and kill their employees," Pfeffer claims in his 2017 book, *Dying for a Paycheck*. "Stress at work . . . just keeps getting worse for almost all jobs, resulting in an ever-higher physical and psychological toll."

In writing my memoir, I realized I had stumbled onto a bigger story. I started reading studies about workplace stress and talking to academics in the field. In recent years these researchers have noted a sudden rise in workplace stress and have been trying to sound the alarm. Gary Rees, a professor at Portsmouth University in the UK, first became aware of the change at a conference in Paris, when he asked a CEO what problem most concerned him, and the CEO replied, "Suicide at work. Suicide caused by work." Rees's own research showed workers were facing so much stress that they were being pushed beyond their limits. "There are companies where suicide has now become an outcome of work," Rees says. "Work has intensified. The expectations are higher. Companies don't want to concern themselves with employee welfare. They just want to employ people who are resilient, and stress-averse, and who will just get on with it."

In 2007, psychologists Mitchell Kusy and Elizabeth Holloway were stunned by what they found when they conducted a survey about workplace bullying and incivility. For one thing, they got a very high response rate (42 percent). But more significant was that many people, unprompted, added long notes about the abuse they had suffered. "We had seventy-two single-spaced pages," Holloway recalls. "People don't bother to do that unless they're using it as a kind of catharsis. I've done research for thirty-eight years, and this was really remarkable."

Equally remarkable was that 94 percent of respondents said they had worked with a toxic person. "That shocked us," Kusy says. "We thought it would be maybe 50 percent. We were really surprised at how pervasive this is and by how little organizations knew about how to handle the problem. If something affects 94 percent of the population you would think there would be systems to deal with it. But there weren't." They wrote up their results in a book, *Toxic Workplace! Managing Toxic Personalities and Their Systems of Power.*

Bullying has become as big a problem for adults at work as it is for kids at school and "is clearly an epidemic," says Gary Namie, a psychologist who conducted a 2014 survey in which 27 percent of respondents said they had been bullied at work and another 37 percent said they had witnessed it happening to a co-worker. The stress of being bullied can cause a host of physical ailments and even brain damage, Namie says. In 2017, researchers from RAND Corporation and Harvard Medical School surveyed three thousand workers and were taken aback to find that one in five reported facing verbal abuse, threats, humiliation, or unwanted sexual advances—*on a monthly basis.* "I was not expecting to see numbers that high," says Nicole Maestas, an associate professor of health-care policy at Harvard Medical School, who worked on the report. "The workplace is a taxing, high-pressure place for a lot of people."

Paradoxically, many of the most stressed-out people are the ones who should be thriving in the information economy. These are coders and engineers, "creatives" and communicators, people who work with their brains instead of their hands, doing high-value tasks that (so far) cannot be performed by machines or outsourced to less-expensive workers in developing economies. They are well-educated and Internet savvy, and often make a very good living. They have what many of us would consider to be *good* jobs. They spend their days in gleaming open-plan workspaces with cool design, ergonomic desks, and gourmet snacks. These aren't the exploited slaughterhouse workers of Sinclair Lewis's *The Jungle*, or seamstresses packed into overcrowded shirt factories, or coal miners dying of black lung. They aren't grinding away on some noisy, dirty assembly line, doing mindless, repetitive work.

But they are suffering nonetheless. However, it's a new kind of suffering, one that is harder to describe and harder to see, because it is psychological. But consider these two statistics:

- In the past thirty years, antidepressant use has grown sixfold in the United States, according to the National Center for Health Statistics.
- In the past twenty years, U.S. suicide rates have soared to record high levels. Recently the biggest increases have been among people aged forty-five to sixty-four, the NCHS says, chiefly because of "rising rates of distress about jobs and personal finances," according to researchers at the Robert Wood Johnson Foundation.

It makes no sense that this is happening now. Global poverty has fallen 50 percent in the past twenty years, according to Johan Norberg, a Swedish economic historian and author of *Progress*. The Internet has unleashed an explosion of new ideas and an unprecedented creation of wealth. Everyday life sometimes feels like magic. Tap your finger on the glowing glass of a smartphone and you can summon a car and driver who arrive a few minutes later. During the ride that same smartphone lets you shop for virtually anything on Amazon, and access all of the world's information on Google. Medical procedures that our grandparents could not have imagined now are performed as a matter of routine. We live 60 percent longer than people did a century ago. We have better nutrition, more clean water, better education. Soon the world will be even more amazing, thanks to breakthroughs in artificial intelligence, robotics, and genomics. In Silicon Valley, techies have vowed to conquer every disease known to humankind. Some even believe we are on the cusp of conquering death itself and achieving immortality.

Yet we are killing ourselves in record numbers and pumping ourselves full of happy pills just to get through the day. Some people opt out entirely. In the United States, opioid addiction and overdose deaths have reached epidemic proportions. In Japan, more than half a million people, predominantly young men, have given up on life and become *hikikomori*, or shut-ins, who refuse to leave their homes and shun social contact.

We tend to focus on the miracles and wonder of the Internet age, the new inventions and advanced technologies that are "indistinguishable from magic," as futurist Arthur C. Clarke once put it. But the tech-driven progress has a dark side. Over the past decade I've watched that dark side take hold in Silicon Valley and San Francisco. A region that once supported a thriving, prosperous middle class has been transformed into something that resembles a Third World banana republic, with an obscenely wealthy ruling class, a vast and growing underclass, and not much in between. San Francisco, once a city full of artists and hippies, with a vibrant gay community, has become overrun with dipshit tech bros zipping around on electric scooters, complaining about the growing ranks of homeless people, seemingly oblivious to the fact that they—the tech bros—are the ones who created the housing crisis that has pushed so many people onto the streets. "San Francisco has become unrecognizable," a sixty-something techie told me, explaining why she had sold her home and fled the city. What didn't she like? "The greed," she said.

Now those same mercenary, clueless tech bros who have ruined San Francisco are gaining ever more power and wielding influence that reaches all over the world. That includes exerting control over how workplaces are reconfigured and operated. But these are not the people who should be inventing the future.

CHAPTER TWO

THE NEW OLIGARCHS

The fifty-mile stretch of land between San Francisco and San Jose used to be a great place to live and work. The best of the lot—the "gold standard in Silicon Valley," as journalist David Jacobson wrote in Stanford's alumni magazine in the 1980s—was Hewlett-Packard. Co-founders Bill Hewlett and Dave Packard created a people-oriented culture known as "the HP Way." HP was informal and casual. Everyone was on a first-name basis. Hours were flexible. There were no time clocks. Bill and Dave believed a company should feel like a family. They trusted employees, treated workers with dignity and respect, and believed a company should be about more than just making money or delivering returns to investors. They valued job security, tried not to have layoffs, and were good corporate citizens in the community. All employees got bonuses and participated in profit sharing. Bosses engaged in "management by wandering around," a practice that struck Tom Peters when he studied HP and raved about the company's way of doing things in his 1982 business classic, *In Search of Excellence*. By the 1970s, HP was a thriving organization that many in Silicon Valley (and beyond) wanted to emulate. Apple co-founder Steve Wozniak, who worked as an engineer at HP in the 1970s, later recalled: "We had such great camaraderie. We were so happy. Almost everyone spoke about it as the greatest company you could ever work for."

The 1970s brought another element to Silicon Valley—the idealistic values of the counterculture. "Power to the people" was the slogan of 1960s, and it was also the motto of the people who led the personal computer revolution in the 1970s. Instead of sharing a mainframe, which was controlled by Big Brother, everyone could have their own computer. This was an incredibly radical idea, with huge implications for society. Wozniak and his Apple co-founder Steve Jobs were long-haired hippie-hackers who built their first personal computers as members of the Homebrew Computer Club, a pack of amateur kit-computer hobbyists. Wozniak was steeped in the people-first "HP Way." Jobs was an LSD-taking, commune-dwelling hippie who often went barefoot and who was influenced by Stewart Brand, a proponent of psychedelic drugs who hung out with countercultural icon Ken Kesey and his Merry Pranksters. Brand created the *Whole Earth Catalog* and co-founded the WELL, one of the first online communities. Its members included John Perry Barlow, who wrote lyrics for the Grateful Dead and co-founded the Electronic Frontier Foundation, an Internet civil liberties advocacy organization. Counterculture values—freedom, personal liberation, civil rights, respect for the individual—shaped the culture of Silicon Valley.

My first encounter with the old version of Silicon Valley came in the late 1980s, when I visited a software company in Santa Cruz where bearded, long-haired engineers wore shorts and tie-dyed shirts and spent evenings lounging in a huge redwood hot tub, drinking wine and smoking pot. "California companies" was the name used to describe this laid-back hippie-hacker approach to work.

But the days of hanging out in the hot tub are long gone. The new generation of tech companies have become pressure cookers. Uber employees have complained about long hours, abusive managers, and sexual harassment. One Uber engineer committed suicide after only five months on the job; his widow blamed the stress of work. Amazon employees have recounted going days without sleep trying to hit impossible deadlines. One "Amabot" (as Amazon office workers call themselves) who had been put on a "performance improvement plan" (a first step toward getting fired) sent a note to his colleagues and then leapt off the building in a suicide attempt.

Tech work has changed because the people have changed. During the second Internet boom, which began a few years after the dotcom crash in 2001, Silicon Valley has attracted a new kind of person. Instead of geeky engineers, the industry draws hustlers, young guys who hope to get rich quick and who in a previous generation might have gone to work as bond traders on Wall Street. Previously, the kings of tech were the wizards who invented new products and built companies, like Hewlett and Packard, or Bill Gates at Microsoft, and Jobs and Wozniak at Apple. But now the power brokers include venture capitalists—like Marc Andreessen of Andreessen Horowitz, Peter Thiel of Clarium Capital and Founders Fund, and Reid Hoffman of Greylock Ventures. They don't actually run tech companies. They're just investors. Nevertheless, their profession is depicted as glamorous, and they rank among the biggest celebrities in Silicon Valley. *Wired* once lionized Andreessen on its cover, calling him "The Man Who Makes the Future." Young guys moving west after college no longer hope to become the next Steve Jobs; they want to be the next Marc Andreessen.

The Valley has become a casino, with VCs and angel investors blindly pumping money into every slot machine, hoping to hit a jackpot. (The difference is that the punter who gets lucky on a slot machine doesn't walk away convinced he's a genius.) Instead of writing about tech, the industry's bloggers now write about venture deals, and who raised how much at what valuation. The Valley has become obsessed with money, and there is a lot of it around. In 2017, venture capitalists pumped $84 billion into start-ups in the United States—that's ten times as much as in 1995, according to the National Venture Capital Association. Where could all that money go?

Are there now ten times as many ideas worth funding? Of course not. But the VCs have to do something with their billions, so they just keep stuffing money into start-ups, fattening them up like foie gras geese. In 2013, when Aileen Lee, a VC, coined the term *unicorn* to describe a privately held company valued at more than $1 billion, she chose the name because such companies were rare. By 2017 there were nearly three hundred of them. Unicorns were all over the place—and wreaking havoc on the Bay Area.

The second Internet boom has created a new caste of American oligarchs, a bunch of socially awkward, empathy-impaired Sun Kings whose influence extends beyond business into politics and culture at large. Techies now dominate *Vanity Fair's* annual "New Establishment" list, a barometer of the zeitgeist, grabbing 40 of the 100 spots on the 2017 roster. Unfortunately many of these new oligarchs seem to possess a decidedly anti-worker, and even anti-human worldview.

At the top of the list was Amazon founder and CEO Jeff Bezos, who is worth $140 billion, the largest fortune (in absolute terms, not adjusted for inflation) ever accumulated. Some see Bezos as a hero, but his fortune has been built on the backs of warehouse workers who toil away in abominable conditions under huge amounts of stress, sometimes earning so little that they qualify for food stamps. In 2018, when Bezos went to Berlin to receive an award, hundreds of his own German workers showed up to protest. "We have an Amazon boss who wants to Americanize work relationships and take us back to the nineteenth century," a union boss told *Reuters*.

Second on the list was Facebook founder Mark Zuckerberg, whose company employs "secret police" also known as the "ratcatching team," to spy on workers, operating what the *Guardian* calls "a ruthless code of secrecy," using legal threats to keep workers from talking about "working conditions, misconduct or culture challenges within the company." The thirty-four-year-old wunderkind runs a social network with more than two billion members, and has become the most powerful person on the planet, Scott Galloway, a professor at New York University's Stern School of Business, told CNN in 2018. Zuckerberg has amassed his $80 billion fortune by plunging into the psyches and private lives of his members so that advertisers and political parties can manipulate them. Even some of Facebook's venture capital investors and employees believe the company has become dangerous. "No one stopped them from running massive sociological and psychological experiments on their users," Roger McNamee, a Silicon Valley venture capitalist and early Facebook backer, wrote in *Washington Monthly* in the spring of 2018, in an article calling for greater regulation of Facebook and other online platforms.

In fifth place on the *Vanity Fair* list was Tesla CEO Elon Musk, whose factory workers complained to the *Guardian* in 2017 about stressful, dangerous working conditions, and overworked colleagues collapsing on the production floor. Also on the list were Uber founder Travis Kalanick and his successor as Uber CEO Dara Khosrowshahi, whose company exploits drivers so badly that they have repeatedly sued the company. In 2016, Uber offered a proposed $100 million settlement for a lawsuit brought by drivers demanding to be categorized as employees, with salaries and benefits.

Exploiting workers is paying off. Many of these VCs and founders are worth billions. But they have driven wealth inequality to insane levels and brought banana-republic economics to Silicon Valley. Awash in money, once-sleepy towns like Los Altos, Los Gatos, Atherton, and Palo Alto now boast Disneyfied downtowns and Michelin-starred restaurants, with Porsches, Ferraris, and Mercedes parked outside. Silent, speedy Tesla sedans have become as common as Camrys, and the hills above the Valley are dotted with Bond-villain compounds belonging to billionaires. Russian venture capitalist and Facebook investor Yuri Milner owns a twenty-five thousand square-foot imitation French château in Los Altos Hills, for which he reportedly paid $100 million in 2011, which was said to be the highest price ever paid in the United States for a piece of residential real estate. Scott McNealy, co-founder of Sun Microsystems, is trying to unload his twenty-eight-thousand-square-foot Palo Alto mansion, which features a climbing wall and a disco, for just under $100 million, the *Wall Street Journal* reports. Both of those pale in comparison to Oracle founder Larry Ellison's twenty-three-acre estate in Woodside, which is modeled after a Japanese emperor's palace. The place took nine years to build, reportedly at a cost of $200 million. Its highlight is Katsura House, a replica of a teahouse from a sixteenth-century royal compound in Kyoto. The replica, which was built in Japan, then disassembled and shipped to California, is 10 percent bigger than the original.

Non-billionaires settle for McMansions priced in single-digit millions, like a "secluded Tuscan estate" that the nouveau riche Chandler Guo, the self-proclaimed "Bitcoin King," snapped up for $5 million in 2018. As for "regular" houses, those no longer exist. In March 2018, a drab, tiny, 848-square-foot house in Sunnyvale sold for $2 million, more than $2,300 per square foot, the highest square-foot price ever recorded on the Multiple Listing Service.

From San Francisco to San Jose, house prices keep soaring. But so do the ranks of the homeless. It is surreal to see so much poverty pressed right up against so much wealth. One day in 2017 I ate lunch on the Google campus with some rank-and-file Googlers who explained that even though they were millionaires, they still felt poor, because here at Google they sat in meetings with people who owned jets and yachts and estates in Hawaii. They seemed not to know how much actual poverty existed all around them. Later, just two miles away, I walked down a street beside Rengstorff Park in Mountain View, where forty or so camper vans lay slumped against the curb. These campers were homes for working-class families who could no longer afford to rent apartments in the Bay Area. Strictly speaking, these campers were mobile homes, but I doubt these rusty, ramshackle old boxes could ever be driven. In the narrow stretch of grass beside the curb, families kept their belongings. Outside one trailer I saw a little kid's bike. I wanted to cry.

A similar mobile home encampment had sprung up in Palo Alto, near the headquarters of Facebook. People in both communities complained to the police, who eventually arrived with tow trucks and dragged the campers away. Santa Clara County is one of the wealthiest counties in the United States, home to Apple, Facebook, and Google, three of the richest companies in the world. Yet in that county there are ten thousand homeless people, many living in makeshift tents and cardboard boxes under highways.

In 2017, Apple, Facebook, and Google had a combined market value of nearly $2 trillion and were sitting on $400 billion in cash. The founders of Google and Facebook possessed personal fortunes worth $175 billion, combined. Noah Smith, a Bloomberg columnist and former finance professor, reckons that for $10 billion a year, we could eliminate homelessness in the entire United States. A handful of tech oligarchs could easily kick in and solve the problem. Instead, tech companies have been doing the exact opposite. For years they have been dodging taxes in the United States by transferring profits through shell companies and parking hundreds of billions of dollars in offshore accounts. Only when Donald Trump got elected and slashed corporate taxes did companies like Apple agree to bring the money back. To be sure, Apple still paid taxes, but the bill was tens of billions less than it would have been previously. Officially, most Silicon Valley oligarchs express contempt for Trump, yet they were grateful for his tax cuts. Meanwhile, all around the Googleplex and Apple's gleaming new billion-dollar spaceship campus, people still sleep in campers and huddle under bridges and freeway overpasses.

In 2017, the *Guardian* published a story about Nicole and Victor, a twenty-something husband and wife who worked in cafeterias at Facebook and earned so little that they were living in a garage with their three kids. Other people rent panel vans outfitted with beds and little kitchens. In 2017 I tracked down a man who has made a business out of converting vans into campers and renting them out. He asked that I not use his name. When he first started doing this, his customers were twenty-something tech guys who worked at companies like Google, which provides free food and plenty of places to shower, so they figured they could save a few bucks by living in a van. But lately things have taken a depressing turn. These days he rents his vans to families, working people who have been evicted or priced out of apartments and are turning to vans as a last resort. "These are people just trying to hang on," he told me.

In San Francisco, home to dozens of big Internet companies like Twitter and Uber, techies grumble about having to step over the homeless people and dodge piles of human excrement as they walk to work. "Every day on my way to and from work I see people sprawled across the sidewalk, tent cities, human feces, and the faces of addiction. The city is becoming a shanty town," start-up founder Justin Keller ranted in an open letter to San Francisco mayor Ed Lee in 2016. "The wealthy working people have earned their right to live in the city. I shouldn't have to see the pain, struggle and despair of homeless people on my way to work every day."

Keller's letter sparked outrage and reminded some of a rant posted in 2013 on Facebook by another start-up founder, Greg Gopman, who wrote that "in downtown SF the degenerates gather like hyenas, spit, urinate, taunt you, sell drugs, get rowdy, they act like they own the center of the city. If they added the smallest iota of value I'd consider thinking different, but the crazy toothless lady who kicks everyone that gets too close to her cardboard box hasn't made anyone's life better in a while." Gopman's post prompted a backlash on social media, and he ended up leaving his own company. He later apologized and vowed to help address the city's homeless problem.

In 2016, a bunch of rich techies came up with their own solution, sponsoring a ballot proposition that would let police forcibly remove homeless people from the sidewalks. Homeless people would get twenty-four hours to either move to a shelter or get a bus ticket out of town. If they didn't comply, the cops could seize their tents and belongings. The problem was that San Francisco had only nineteen hundred shelter beds, but four thousand people were living on the streets. Nevertheless, the proposition passed. In 2017, the cops started sweeping people off the streets.

AYN RAND AND THE PAYPAL MAFIA

One day in May 2018, the police in Laguna Beach, California, published a set of photographs from a car accident: a Tesla Model S sedan, operating in autopilot mode, had crossed the center line and smashed into a parked police SUV. The photos of the Laguna Beach crash seemed like a perfect metaphor for what the new Masters of the Universe are doing to society: turning loose a bunch of half-baked ideas to career around and smash into things, all in the name of progress. Their victims include the world at large, but also their employees. The new oligarchs don't seem to care very much about their community, nor do they show much regard for their workers, or for human beings in general. It's almost as if, having imagined a world in which robots and artificial intelligence can do everything, they resent the fact that for now they still must put up with messy, inferior biological beings.

Tesla's forty-seven-year-old South African-born CEO Elon Musk has become a hero to many, who view him as a real-life version of Tony Stark from *Iron Man*. Yet so far Musk hasn't proved to be very good at making cars or making money. After fourteen years in business, Tesla has lost billions of dollars, and in 2017 the company sold only one hundred thousand cars—half as many as Toyota sells in a week. Nevertheless, Musk is worth more than $20 billion, thanks to Tesla's soaring stock price. Yet he hasn't always been generous to his workers. According to a 2015 biography of Musk by journalist Ashlee Vance, Musk once fired his assistant, a woman who had been with him for twelve years, after she dared to ask for a raise. Even more cruel was the way he did it. Musk told the woman to take two weeks off and he would see if he could get by without her. When she came back, he said he didn't need her anymore. Musk has denied Vance's version of this story.

Tesla's factory workers have it even worse. In 2017 the National Labor Relations Board filed a complaint against Tesla, alleging it had violated labor laws. In the same year, a Tesla factory worker published a blog post complaining about overwork, low pay, and unsafe conditions. WorkSafe, an advocacy group, alleged Tesla's production plant had twice as many serious injuries as the industry average. The United Automobile Workers union claims Musk has fought efforts by workers to unionize and even fired workers who supported unionization. In 2018, Congressman Keith Ellison published an open letter warning Musk that retaliating against workers for trying to form a union "isn't just morally wrong—it's against the law." Tesla has been hit with numerous worker complaints and lawsuits, including three in 2017 by black workers who said they had been subjected to racist behavior and racist slurs. One complaint described Tesla's factory as "a hotbed of racist behavior."

Musk made his first fortune as a co-founder of PayPal, whose alumni, known as the "PayPal Mafia," have since founded other successful tech companies and/or become venture capitalists. Many of them have known each other since their student days at Stanford in the 1990s. In their current roles they exert outsize influence on the workplace culture of Silicon Valley. The problem is some of them don't seem like the nicest people.

One billionaire oligarch, Keith Rabois, a PayPal alum who now works as a venture capitalist, commands start-up founders who take his money to embrace an extreme version of workaholism—they're not supposed to take vacations. Ever. Rabois claims he worked for eighteen years straight without a break, and that others should do the same. In the 1990s, as a law student at Stanford, Rabois became notorious for an incident in which he screamed out homophobic slurs ("Faggot! Faggot! Hope you die of AIDS! Can't wait until you die, faggot!").

Rabois's friends Peter Thiel and David Sacks, who also went

to Stanford and also worked at PayPal, and also have gone on to become enormously wealthy and influential tech oligarchs, in 1995 co-authored a book, *The Diversity Myth*, in which they defended Rabois. Thiel and Sacks decried the rise of "political correctness" and multiculturalism on campus. They argued that women who claim to have been raped might actually have been experiencing "belated regret," and fretted that "race relations have taken a turn for the worse," because "multiculturalists charge whites with more evanescent and intangible forms of racism, such as 'institutional racism' and 'unconscious racism.'" In 2016, Thiel apologized for what he wrote about rape. Sacks also apologized and said he regretted his earlier views.

In 2014, Thiel, the anti-diversity firebrand, published a book, *Zero to One: Notes on Startups, or How to Build the Future*. I suspect that concern for diversity does not play a big role in the future that Thiel would like to build. That suspicion is bolstered by the fact that in 2016 Thiel campaigned for Donald Trump. Maybe it is just coincidence, but in the past two decades, as figures like *Diversity Myth* authors Thiel and Sacks have gained ever more influence in Silicon Valley, the tech industry has developed appalling problems with diversity, with women complaining about sexual harassment and hostile work environments, and people of color complaining that they are shut out nearly completely. I do not think this has happened by accident.

THE NEW COMPACT

Reid Hoffman considers himself a "public intellectual." *Entrepreneur* magazine called him "the philosopher king of entrepreneurs." Like Musk, Thiel, Sacks, and Rabois, Hoffman launched his career at PayPal, then went on to make an even bigger fortune. In 2002 he founded LinkedIn and was CEO until 2006, when he stepped aside, became executive chairman, and began a new career as a venture capitalist. Hoffman is now worth more than $3 billion, and is one of the architects of what he calls a "new compact" between companies and employees.

The new compact says, essentially, that corporations owe no loyalty to workers, and that workers should not expect any kind of job security. This compact encourages workers to view themselves as independent agents, competing against one another for work. Each individual is a start-up—"the start-up of you," as Hoffman once put it in a book by that title. Hoffman describes the new compact in his second book, *The Alliance: Managing Talent in a Networked Age.* The gist is that a job is just a transaction; you'll work here for a year or two, then go on to the next thing. Refer back to this book's opener, Welcome to Your New Job, for my own riff on the "new compact."

The problem with Hoffman giving advice on how to "manage talent" is that he hasn't actually done much of that himself. To be sure, he spent four years at PayPal, and was CEO of LinkedIn for its first four years, but those were relatively tiny organizations at the time. In 2006, Hoffman decided he didn't want to be a CEO and hired someone else to run LinkedIn for him, while he became executive chairman. He says he did that specifically because he didn't like managing people. "I didn't like running a weekly staff meeting," he later wrote in a blog post. "I could do it, but I did so reluctantly, not enthusiastically." He didn't want to spend his time "debating which employees should get a promotion." In other words, Hoffman didn't want to be a manager—he just wanted to write books telling other people how to do the job.

Moreover, LinkedIn doesn't seem to have been particularly well managed. It's true the company grew very rapidly, went public in 2011, and in 2016 was acquired by Microsoft for $26 billion. That sounds like a big win, but in fact LinkedIn started losing money in 2014, and before being acquired its stock had plunged from an alltime high of $269 per share to as little as $101 per share. Microsoft paid $196 per share, a steep premium.

Sure, Hoffman got rich. But it's hard to look at his track record at LinkedIn and see a model for how to manage a company. Howard Schultz or Yvon Chouinard, the founders and CEOs of Starbucks and Patagonia, respectively, have also written books about managing companies. But they're both longtime practitioners who actually ran their companies for decades, and built sustainable, profitable, independent organizations. For what it's worth, neither of them espouses anything resembling Hoffman's tour-of-duty, job-as-transaction philosophy. In fact they urge companies to do the opposite—to invest in employees, treat them well, and try to keep them around.

As an investor, Hoffman has had an amazing track record of picking winners. He and Thiel put early money into Facebook, for example. But in the role of investor Hoffman hasn't always been an ally to workers. He was an investor and board member at Zynga, a company founded by his close friend and fellow Facebook investor Mark Pincus. In 2011, Zynga, which makes cheesy games like FarmVille for Facebook, was getting ready to go public. Just before the IPO, the *Wall Street Journal* broke a story that Pincus had been quietly forcing some employees to give back options that Pincus had granted them when they were hired. Pincus said the company had been too generous. If the employees didn't comply, he would fire them—in which case they would lose *all* of their unvested options. The choice was this: lose a little, or lose a lot. Companies like Zynga use option grants to lure in new employees, often at below-market salaries. Now that Zynga's options were about to be worth something, Pincus wanted them back. This was one of the most egregious cheapskate anti-worker moves in Silicon Valley history—especially since Pincus was about to become a billionaire on the IPO.

After the IPO, Pincus and Hoffman made another controversial move. When the IPO took place, in December 2011, all Zynga workers and management were bound by a lock-up agreement, so they could not sell shares for six months. But as the *Financial Times* explained: "After its December 2011 IPO, Zynga rejiggered its lock-up agreement in early 2012, allowing Pincus and Hoffman, a Zynga director, to jump the line and sell shares before then-current and former employees. Zynga shares collapsed just after that privileged secondary offering."

Shareholders sued, alleging securities fraud and breach of fiduciary duty, arguing that Pincus and Hoffman sold early because they knew the company's financial condition was deteriorating. After a protracted fight, one lawsuit was tossed out and Zynga settled another one, paying monetary settlements but admitting no wrongdoing.

In 2017, Pincus and Hoffman formed a "virtual political party" called #WTF, for Win the Future, to influence the direction of the Democratic Party. The *Financial Times* pointed out that it was "curious" to see Pincus and Hoffman take such an interest in democracy, since in their own companies they had structured corporate governance with different classes of stock, which gave them control even after the IPO—benevolent dictators, basically, who did not have to answer to shareholders or employees.

These are the people who would advise the world on how to "manage talent" in the networked age. Hoffman's new compact is terrible for workers, but great for investors, which is understandable since Hoffman's primary focus these days is on venture investing. The problem is that a venture capitalist writing a book about how companies should treat employees is like Ted Bundy offering dating advice to young women. Unfortunately, in recent years this new compact has become the norm in the tech industry, especially at start-ups. The deal is so awful and exploitative that even Ayn Rand, a hero to many of today's tech libertarians, might gasp a little and ask, "But can you really get away with this?"

They can. They do. My first glimpse of the tour-of-duty ethos came at HubSpot, which celebrated its enormously high turnover with the slogan, "We're a team, not a family," which meant that, just like on a sports team, you might get cut at any moment. When I wrote *Disrupted* I thought this way of treating employees was unusual.

I described my story as a firsthand account of life inside a start-up "during a period when the tech industry had temporarily lost its mind." A few years later, I worry that the insanity I experienced might be permanent rather than temporary, and that it is no longer contained to the tech industry. The disease seems to be breaking out of its container, infecting the rest of the world.

THE TOXIC TRANSFUSION

In San Francisco there is a company called Ambrosia that for $8,000 will give you a transfusion of blood drawn from teenage boys. (For $12,000 you can get the premium package, getting two liters of blood instead of just one.) The company's founder, Dr. Jesse Karmazin, makes the astonishing claim that the new blood does not just *slow* the aging process but can actually *reverse* it, so that you get younger. "You're not going to turn into a twenty-year-old overnight, but theoretically that's possible if we treat someone enough," he tells me. The *MIT Technology Review* quoted doctors and scientists who doubted the treatment will do anything, and questioned whether Karmazin should be offering it. Yet people keep lining up. Karmazin tells me one of his patients is a ninety-two-year-old man who gets a transfusion once a month. Karmazin says the man could live to be one of the oldest people in the world.

Just like that nonagenarian, Big Old Companies are racing out to San Francisco, hoping to become more like start-ups. Some like Walmart open tech labs and incubators in Silicon Valley. Others send executives on two-week tours, known as "silicon safaris," to visit start-ups and learn from them. Local tour guides now sell "innovation tours," shuttling visitors around on buses to visit start-ups. In 2017 on one trip to San Francisco I met a group of German businessmen whose companies had sent them on a two-week safari. When I met them, Zenefits, one of the hottest unicorns, had just booted out its CEO, Parker Conrad, in a scandal that involved allegations of cheating on licensing tests and letting unlicensed brokers sell insurance policies, as well as having an out-of-control frat-boy party culture. (Conrad and Zenefits would later settle charges brought by the Securities and Exchange Commission that they misled investors; they paid a fine but did not admit or deny wrongdoing.) Uber, the biggest unicorn, was on the verge of booting out its CEO, Kalanick, after a scandal erupted over sexual harassment, spying on competitors and on government regulators, and other misbehavior. I asked the Germans, "What could you possibly learn from these people?" They seemed mostly bemused.

Some companies try to instill a little bit of Silicon Valley culture by building miniature start-ups inside their old-company walls, hiring Millennials who fan out across the organization, wearing Converse sneakers and untucked shirts, running hackathons and teaching oldsters how to get "super pumped" and "mastermind some shit" in a "jam sesh," as Uber founder Travis Kalanick once put it. Also, many companies are latching on to faddish Silicon Valley management methodologies, like Agile and Lean Startup, because they are convinced that these tech-spawned ideas will make them as nimble as start-ups.

Basically, they want a transfusion. They want that teenage boy blood. They are old and slow and bloated, with weak hearts and clogged arteries. Most of all, they're scared. They've seen other big old companies get killed off by Silicon Valley, and they would rather not have this happen to them. They seem to believe that some magic elixir exists here, some recipe for innovation that floats in the air and can be absorbed if you drive around with your windows open, smelling the eucalyptus trees. They see people getting rich on things they don't even understand. Blockchain? Ethereum? Initial coin offerings? So they fly out and have drinks at the Rosewood Hotel on Sand Hill Road in Menlo Park, where venture capitalists hang around, as do expensive "companions," many with Eastern European accents. They eat lunch at the Battery, a members-only private club for social-climbing parvenus in San Francisco. They wangle an invitation to a Bitcoin party and rub shoulders with the scammers, hustlers, Ponzi schemers, and obnoxious knobs who are trying to cash in on a modern-day tulip mania based around a cryptocurrency that Warren Buffett describes as "rat poison squared." Buffett's partner, Charlie Munger, was even less polite about Bitcoin mania: "It's like somebody else is trading turds and you decide you can't be left out."

The problem is that when you dig through the bullshit you discover, as Gertrude Stein once said about Oakland, that "there is no there there." Silicon Valley has no fountain of youth. Unicorns do not possess any secret management wisdom. Most start-ups are terribly managed, half-assed outfits run by buffoons and bozos and frat boys, and funded by amoral investors who are only hoping to flip the company into the public markets and make a quick buck. They have no operations expertise, no special insight into organizational behavior.

All they have is a not-very-innovative business model: they sell dollar bills for seventy-five cents and take credit for how fast they're growing. The vast majority of these new companies are losing money. Traditionally, to get rich in business you had to build a company that turned a profit, and then the profits were shared with investors. The new VCs have invented a form of alchemy in which they make a fortune for themselves while skipping the step about building a profitable company. I call it, *Grow fast, lose money, go public, cash out.* You pump millions (or billions) into a start-up, so that it grows rapidly. You generate hype, flog the shares to mom-and-dad investors in an IPO, and scoot away with the loot.

In 2017 I made a list of sixty tech companies that had gone public since 2011. Fifty of them had never made a profit. Some new companies lose incredible amounts of money. In 2017, Spotify lost $1.5 billion, Snap lost $3 billion, and Uber lost $4.5 billion. Yet, as of early 2018, Spotify founder Daniel Ek and Snap founder Evan Spiegel are each worth about $2.5 billion. Kalanick, the founder of Uber, who made such a mess that his own board tossed him out, nevertheless reportedly has a net worth approaching $5 billion. Where else on earth can you run a company that loses billions of dollars—and become a billionaire yourself by doing this?

The money-losing business model helps explain why VCs have invented the new compact and believe in treating employees so poorly. The VC and founders are not trying to build sustainable companies. So why should they care about providing employees with stable, long-term careers, or distributing wealth among the workers? Workers are merely the fuel that generates sales growth. You hire an army of young telemarketers, who hit the phones all day long. You give them impossible quotas and "burn them out and churn them out." Employees can (and should) be underpaid, overworked, exhausted, and then discarded. When the IPO finally happens, a few people at the top get incredibly rich, and everyone else gets little or nothing.

My fear is that in their desire to imitate Silicon Valley tech companies, companies from other industries will adopt its methods and mores, including its new compact with labor and its high-stress, antiworker philosophy. In 2017, Whole Foods Market in the US, which for two decades was known for its fantastic, worker-friendly culture, was acquired by Amazon. Almost overnight, the culture of Whole Foods was destroyed, as Amazon imposed its ruthless number-crunching management style. The danger is what might happen next. Will other supermarket chains known for their worker-friendly culture become equally brutal in order to keep up?

TURNING POINT: THE YEAR 2000

During my research, as I pored over data sets depicting various things related to worker unhappiness, a pattern began to emerge. Curiously, in a lot of charts and graphs, there's an inflection point right around the year 2000. That's when the first dotcom bubble peaked and crashed. It's also when a few technologies that made the Internet actually usable started to become more widely available, like speedy broadband connections via cable modem, followed by Wi-Fi routers. Meanwhile personal computers gave way to mobile devices—the BlackBerry in 2001, followed in 2007 by Apple's iPhone—which have given cheap, ubiquitous Internet access to billions of people.

Social networks arose: LinkedIn in 2002, Facebook in 2004, Twitter in 2006. From 2000 to 2010 the number of people on the Internet grew from 360 million, less than 6 percent of the world's population, to about two billion people, just under one-third of the world, according to Internet World Stats, a website that tracks Internet users. By the end of 2017 there were about four billion people, just over half of the world's population, on the Internet.

Not coincidentally, the year 2000 was when outsourcing really started taking off, thanks to speedy and reliable Internet connections delivered over a global network of fiber-optic cables. Thomas Friedman dubbed the phenomenon "Globalization 3.0" and marked its beginning to the year 2000, in his book *The World Is Flat*. The year 2000 is also a point where the economies of China and India take off; the charts shoot skyward.

Another strange phenomenon related to the year 2000 involves the ratio between the compensation of CEOs and average workers. In 1980, the average big-company CEO earned 42 times as much as the average worker, according to the Institute for Policy Studies. But in the second half of the 1990s the ratio explodes, such that by 2000, CEOs were making 525 times as much as workers, probably due to the enormous windfalls that tech CEOs were reaping during the dotcom bubble. The ratio dropped a bit after the bubble burst, and during the Great Recession of the late 2000s. But here's the curious thing. The ratio never returned to pre-2000 levels. As of 2016, big-company CEOs were still making 347 times as much as regular workers.

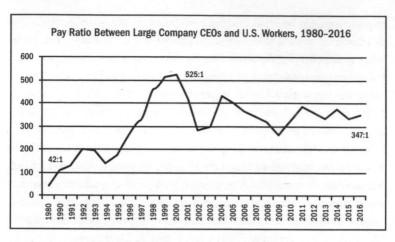

Pay Ratio Between Large Company CEOs and U.S. Workers, 1980-2016

Credit: Institute for Policy Studies

Apparently this is the new normal. Somehow, after the Internet came along, the world decided that CEOs should get paid a great deal more than in the past. This happened just as tech companies were coming to dominate the ranks of the world's biggest companies, when measured by market value—which suggests that somehow the Internet was connected to the rise in CEO pay.

The charts also suggest a connection between the Internet and the increasing levels of worker unhappiness. To be sure, a lot of problems began before the year 2000. But the Internet accelerated those. As outsourcing takes off, manufacturing jobs in the West plunge. Antidepressant usage climbs, as do suicide rates. Income inequality widens. The top one percent takes ever more of the pie.

My sense that there might be a connection between the Internet and worker unhappiness was reinforced by what I saw on the ground in Silicon Valley—the hustlers and tech bros, the greedy VCs, the obscenely rich oligarchs, the new compact with employees, the stress, the insecurity, the suicides and homelessness.

It doesn't seem to make sense that the same idealistic, altruistic wizards who design beautiful products and deliver exquisite user experiences—who create so much *delightion*, as my former colleagues at HubSpot would say—should cause so much misery. Yet that's what is happening. Apple makes terrific smartphones and provides worldclass customer support, but the company also has dodged taxes using a scheme that Nobel laureate economist Joseph Stiglitz once called a "fraud." Amazon Prime is an amazing service, but Amazon abuses workers in its headquarters and warehouses. Customers love Uber, but Uber operates a toxic workplace and exploits its drivers. Tesla makes very sexy electric cars but, by many accounts, Elon Musk behaves abominably toward his employees and has earned a reputation for being less than forthcoming with customers. "I don't believe anything Elon Musk or Tesla says," Apple co-founder Steve Wozniak, a disappointed Tesla owner, said in 2018.

In the past few years I've come to the uncomfortable conclusion that, for various reasons mostly related to greed, the very people in Silicon Valley who talk so much about making the world a better place are actually making it worse—at least when it comes to the well-being of workers.

It would be nice to believe that this is happening because these tech geniuses are a little bit Aspergery and lack the social skills needed to manage people effectively—that is, that they're well-meaning nerds who are clueless about their fellow human beings. But I don't think that's the case. In fact, it's quite the opposite. A lot of these founders and venture capitalists understand a great deal about human beings, and some (especially those in the social media space) have become expert at using psychological tricks to manipulate customers and employees alike. Some even employ teams of behavioral psychologists.

The shabby treatment of employees is not happening by accident. It is happening by design. It is happening because the new economy has been hijacked by a caste of venture capitalists and amoral founders who have taken the notion of shareholder capitalism (the idea that a company's only duty is to provide the biggest possible return to investors) and pushed that caustic ideology to excruciatingly dangerous extremes. But where this leads is nowhere good. This ever-widening income inequality could tear apart the fabric of society. The most appalling part of this is that the oligarchs know this and apparently do not care.

How did we get here? How did progress bring with it such a dark side? In fact, some of what ails us today actually began more than a century ago.

CHAPTER THREE

A VERY BRIEF HISTORY OF MANAGEMENT SCIENCE (AND WHY YOU SHOULDN'T TRUST IT)

Making a duck out of Lego may seem a perfect example of today's workplace zeitgeist, but the exercise I was doing in that Menlo Park café was actually just a new manifestation of an old belief, one that sprang to life in the early years of the twentieth century and came to be known as management science.

The term hinges on the belief that the art of managing people can be reduced to science. Nowadays management science is something you can get a degree in, at places like the Massachusetts Institute of Technology. However, the term barely appeared before the middle of the twentieth century. One early mention in the *New York Times*, on September 1, 1948, came with the headline "New Era Is Seen for Management" and discussed some new ideas about "tightening up methods of quality and cost control, and investigating every means of increasing individual productivity."

The originator of the thinking behind management science was a man named Frederick Taylor, who was born in 1856 in Germantown, Pennsylvania. Like some of the precocious whiz kids of Silicon Valley a century later, Taylor skipped attending Harvard, apprenticing instead to a Philadelphia pump manufacturer, where he quickly rose through the ranks. In the 1890s Taylor claimed he had invented a scientific method that could optimize the efficiency of any process. Taylor was best known for an experiment at Bethlehem Steel, where he boasted that his system had quadrupled the number of pig iron slabs that a group of workmen could load in a single day. Taylor carried a stopwatch and timed everything. He published scientific-sounding papers, packed with equations like this:

$$B = (p + [a + b + d + f + distancehauled/100 \times (c + e)] \, 27/L)(1 + P)*$$

The experiment with the pig iron made Taylor famous. He cited it in books and lectures and during lucrative consulting engagements to big corporations. But as it turns out, Taylor was a quack—or maybe a con man. The story of the pig iron workers never took place, at least not the way Taylor described it. What really happened is that he cranked up the quotas and the workers quit. Bethlehem Steel threw Taylor out, and by some estimates the fees Bethlehem Steel paid to Taylor were greater than whatever savings they achieved through productivity gains. Taylor's methods were flawed to the point of being ridiculous. He fudged his numbers. He cheated and lied. He was at best misguided and at worst a "shameless fraud," as Jill Lepore put it in the *New Yorker* in October 2009. Taylor died in 1915, in a hospital bed, supposedly still clutching his stopwatch.

Despite the debunking, Taylorism became almost a religion, its acolytes described as Taylorites. Taylor had the good luck to be the right person at the right time. In his lifetime the first giant global corporations were taking shape—Standard Oil, Carnegie Steel, U.S. Steel, Sears Roebuck, General Electric—and nobody knew how to run them. Big universities started founding business schools in the early decades of the twentieth century, and the business schools needed something to teach, so they taught Taylorism. Taylor's best-known work, *The Principles of Scientific Management*, was published in 1911 and became the biggest-selling business book of the first half of the twentieth century.

Armed with Taylor's theories, an army of mini Taylors with freshly minted MBAs marched into the corporate world. A century later, the MBA has become the most popular master's degree in the United States, with universities churning out 185,000 of them each year. Business schools also spawned a new profession: management consulting. The corporate world now teems with consultants; there are more than six hundred thousand in the United States alone. Like Taylor, these folks are mostly full of shit but also blessed with the special gift of being able to remain supremely confident even when they have no idea what they're doing. In his memoir, *The Management Myth: Debunking Modern Business Philosophy*, former management consultant Matthew Stewart recalls his first job interview in which he was tested on his ability to bullshit: "The purpose of the exercise was to see how easily I could talk about a subject about which I knew almost nothing on the basis of facts that were almost entirely fictional. It was, I realized in retrospect, an excellent introduction to management consulting." Like Taylor, management consultants get paid a lot of money but don't actually produce anything. An old joke goes that a management consultant is someone who borrows your watch to tell you the time—then keeps your watch.

For the past century these latter-day Taylorites have been creating magical programs and methodologies that can be imposed onto an organization and make the whole machine perform at a higher level. If we workers are the lab rats, management gurus are the mad scientists who stand behind the curtain, concocting new ideas and testing them out on the rest of us to see if they work.

The business world has a seemingly insatiable appetite for management gurus. You probably can't blame CEOs. It may be that no human is really smart enough to run something as vast and complex as a corporation. Yet someone has to do it. Clinging to a system, any system, at least provides the illusion of structure. The system also gives the boss something to blame when things go wrong. Managers grasp at systems the way drowning people reach for life jackets.

Gurus are happy to throw out a line—for a fee. It's almost a new job category, one that lies at the intersection of fields including academics, psychology, consulting, and marketing, and the self-help movement. Practitioners generate income through multiple revenue streams—books, keynote speeches, and consulting engagements. Some are business school professors who dabble on the side. Others make a living as management coaches, private gurus to powerful CEOs.

After Frederick Taylor came Peter Drucker, an Austrian-born intellectual whose thirty-nine books, including *Concept of the Corporation* (1946) and *The Practice of Management* (1954), established him as "the father of modern management." Drucker was a trained economist and respected academic who coined the term *knowledge worker*. He loved Taylor and ranked him above all other business thinkers. He shared Taylor's love of quantification and data gathering. "If you can't measure it, you can't improve it" is perhaps Drucker's most famous quote.

Later came Michael Porter, a Harvard business professor who claimed to have developed a methodology that would enable companies to create sustainable advantages using his Five Forces Framework. Porter launched a consulting company, Monitor Group, which raked in enormous fees from corporate clients—until, somehow, in 2013 the bottom fell out and the group went bankrupt. After Drucker and Porter came Clayton Christensen, a Harvard professor who achieved business guru status with a 1997 book, *The Innovator's Dilemma*. Gary Hamel wrote *The Future of Management* and talked about Management 2.0. Jim Collins explained how to go from *Good to Great*. Renée Mauborgne and W. Chan Kim wrote *Blue Ocean Strategy*. If you work in the corporate world you've undoubtedly heard of these books. Combined, they have sold tens of millions of copies.

Those gurus mostly offer advice on strategy. But over the course of the last century there also emerged new twists on Taylorism, nuts-and-bolts methodologies for speeding up production lines, reducing defects, boosting quality, and getting more work out of fewer people. During the Second World War, the U.S. Department of War created a methodology called Training Within Industry to help overburdened defense contractors. Just like Taylor with his pig iron lifters, the idea of Training Within Industry was to get factory workers to crank out more stuff in less time. After the war, Japanese companies refined Training Within Industry into what came to be known as the Toyota Production System, which then evolved into Lean Manufacturing and just-in-time manufacturing. In the 1980s, two engineers at Motorola, the American consumer electronics giant, dreamed up a manufacturing system called Six Sigma, which big companies around the world spent the next two decades adopting.

And so it goes. For the past hundred years, since the days of Frederick Taylor, companies have been latching on to new management fads, and each new fad runs its course, and then everyone leaps onto the next one, believing that this time things will be different.

MANAGEMENT SCIENCE MEETS THE INFORMATION AGE

Twentieth-century Taylorite methodologies like Six Sigma, Lean Manufacturing, and the Toyota Production System were developed for manufacturing physical things—cars, airplanes, lawn furniture, whatever. But now we're in the Information Age, and most of us work with our brains, not our hands. Of course, with the rise of the Internet, clever management consultants started wondering if you could create a system that would optimize the productivity of knowledge workers and impose rigor and discipline on tasks like writing software code. And hey, if you could develop a scientific system for writing software, why not apply that to every aspect of running a company?

Two new forms of Taylorism attempt to do that. The biggest is Agile, a management fad that has swept the corporate world and morphed into what some call a movement but is more like widespread mental illness. The other is Lean Startup, which has its own cult-like following but is less popular. Taken together, these two methodologies represent an enormous global experiment in organizational behavior, in which millions of poor Dilberts are being turned into unwitting lab rats, sometimes with terrible consequences. Just like Taylor, proponents of Agile and Lean Startup believe with almost religious fervor that they can make organizations more efficient. They are probably well meaning but almost certainly dead wrong.

Significantly, both Agile and Lean Startup originated in Silicon Valley, and both were invented by computer scientists. Both use the metaphor of the organization as a kind of machine, a computer that can be reprogrammed, rebooted, and updated with new businesses processes. Metaphorically speaking, the processes are the software. As with actual software, you can write a version of a program, see how it runs, then tweak it, optimize it, and keep iterating.

The big drawback with the metaphor of company-as-computer is that in a computer you're dealing with chips, which are made to be reprogrammed—but we humans are not. Oddly enough, Agile, the most popular new methodology, used at thousands of companies ranging from IBM to Barclays Bank, was not originally created as a way to run a company or manage people—it began, quite literally, as an attempt to solve a computer problem.

NINETY PERCENT BULLSHIT: AGILE RUINED MY LIFE

In the late 1990s the world of software development was facing a crisis. Corporate programming projects kept failing, and some of these disasters were costing companies millions of dollars. Banks and insurance companies would assign hundreds of coders to write enormous software programs containing millions of lines of code. The coders would work for a year or two, falling so far behind schedule that by the time they finished the project, the company didn't need it anymore. They would start a new project and maybe hire more coders, hoping to speed things up, only to discover that extra hands actually slowed things down.

In February 2001—less than twenty years ago but in a move that feels absurdly quaint—seventeen veteran software gurus met at the Snowbird ski area in Utah to launch a revolution. The whole field of software development needed to be blown up and reinvented. Out with the old! Toss out all the assumptions and models and methodologies! Wipe the board clean and start again! Give power to the programmers! These revolutionaries were like Lenin and Trotsky and the Bolsheviks, dreaming up the rules for a new world, except they were holed up at a posh ski resort, high up in a remote, secluded canyon and surrounded by craggy, snow-capped peaks that rise eleven thousand feet above sea level.

Over the course of three days, the rebel alliance leaders hammered out a simple one-page document, which they titled "Manifesto for Agile Software Development." The manifesto comprises twelve principles to speed up the software development process. The essential idea is that it's better to break up a big job into little pieces and to crank out working code in shorter time periods—a few weeks, if possible.

Note, in the above title, that *agile* is used as an adjective, not a noun. Well, agile somehow evolved into the noun *Agile*, with a capital *A*, and those simple rules for how to write software evolved into something akin to a religion for how to run every part of a company. The religion spread, and forked, and wandered in different directions, escaping from software departments and creeping into other parts of the organization. In the great tradition of management science, a priesthood arose. By the mid-2010s there were Agile conferences, Agile certification programs, Agile engagements sold by management consulting firms, and Agile alliances, one of which claims forty thousand members. Over the past decade Agile has spread like wildfire through corporations. "Why Agile Is Eating the World" is the grosssounding title of a recent essay by an Agile proponent. A search of Amazon's catalog turns up more than four thousand books about Agile. The *Harvard Business Review* urges companies to "embrace Agile," "make Agile work for the C-suite," and "bring Agile to the whole organization."

A methodology that began as a one-page list of commonsense principles for software coders—*Deliver working software frequently; Simplicity is essential*—has morphed into a miracle elixir with the power to do everything, including an alleged magical ability to transform entire organizations. The disrupted can become disruptors. Slow, sludgy, sclerotic old manufacturing firms can become nimble, fleet-footed sprinters. There are Agile lawyers, Agile marketers, and Agile HR people. After all, who doesn't want to be agile? The religion has some common ideas, and they all make sense. Agile is about working in small teams, keeping projects short, and collaborating more. But as Agile spreads, its meaning keeps getting diluted. There are many different versions of Agile. Some of them directly contradict each other. Nobody seems to agree on what Agile actually is, or how to do it, including all those experts who write all those books.

Despite all this confusion, your company is probably still going to adopt Agile, so, buckle up. You are about to become a lab rat. What's in store, you ask?

Get ready to spend months learning an entirely new way to do every part of your job. You will attend workshops, take online courses, and participate in role-playing exercises. Maybe you'll play with Lego and make a duck, or wear a funny hat, or play the Ball Point Game. You'll learn a new language and a dizzying alphabet soup of acronyms. You'll talk about antipatterns, heartbeats, information radiators, and timeboxes. You'll work out Given-When-Then formulas. At the end of the day you'll describe your mood by drawing a smiley face or an angry face on the *niko-niko* calendar. If you work in IT you'll learn about pair programming, mob programming, and extreme programming. You might get a new title and a new role. Or you might be fired by some Agile-drunk boss.

When your training is complete, you'll start each day with a "stand-up meeting" and work in a "scrum" with a "Scrum Master," and you'll pick tasks from a "backlog" of "story points." You'll work in "sprints," and at the end of each sprint you'll do a "demo," and a "retrospective," and then you'll start a fresh sprint. Instead of a scrum, you might have a "kanban," which is more or less the same thing, or you might have a "scrumban," which combines the two—and I am not just making that up. The groups must coordinate with each other, so in each morning meeting the team will nominate an "ambassador," and that poor bastard will have to attend a second meeting, called a "Scrum of Scrums," which keeps the scrums humming.

Similarly, the Scrum Masters need to meet with other Scrum Masters, and they all report up to an Agile Coach, but each coach can only manage a few Scrum Masters, so you may need a bunch of coaches, and they will need their own dedicated Agile Practice department. So-called Agilists now have their own career path, climbing the ladder from Agile Coach to Agile Evangelist to Enterprise Agility Coach and finally to the top of the mountain: Agile Practice Leader. At some point you will likely become aware that a methodology that purported to make your organization more agile and nimble has instead added an extra layer of management to your company—it's like trying to make your car go faster by hooking it up to a second car filled with a team of car-speeder-uppers.

Agile becomes your second job. Now in addition to all of your regular, awful meetings you will have Agile meetings where you talk about Agile and debate various aspects of Agile dogma. Some may kvetch in private about Agile, but probably no one will dare to protest publicly, because doing that—defying the cult—means you risk being marked out as an Agile skeptic and therefore an obstacle to progress. The pressure is extra high on older workers, who are experienced enough to realize that this is bullshit, and that Agile usually fails, but wise enough to realize that the real point of Agile may be to create an excuse to fire older workers, and so the smart thing to do is to shut up and go along. God forbid you should be deemed to be insufficiently Agile, or not enthusiastic enough, or unable to adapt to the new way of doing things.

In Finland, there's a bird called the tawny owl whose feathers can be either dark brown or pale gray. For a long time, the pale grays had an edge over the dark browns, because Finland was snowy and cold and the pale grays could blend in during the winter. Their light feathers helped them hide from predators and sneak up on voles, which is what owls like to eat. Thus there were a lot more pale grays than dark browns in Finland. But then came global warming, and the winters in Finland became milder, and there was less snow, and guess what? Scientists noticed the pale gray owls were disappearing. They no longer had an advantage. Instead of blending in, they stuck out. Fewer of them lived long enough to reproduce. Now the dark browns are thriving, while the pale grays dwindle away.

You there, sitting there in your Agile workshop, fifty years old, playing with a lump of Play-Doh or a bag of Lego—are you a pale gray? In the old ecosystem you thrived. You had an advantage. You got promotions and raises—you ate all the tasty voles and avoided the predators. But the climate has changed. Now things are Agile, and you're sticking out like a pale gray owl in a dark brown tree. But you want to keep that job! For you, the pale gray, every day becomes a fight for survival, one that involves overcoming the disadvantages of your genes. The games with the Lego and Play-Doh aren't just harmless fun; they scare the shit out of you.

At some companies people end up doing "kabuki Agile," meaning they all pretend to be adopting Agile practices, like the stand-up meetings and the scrums, but really they're still just doing things the way they always did. In some companies, Agile slowly fizzles away, but is never officially dropped. Few companies dare to throw in the towel and openly declare that the experiment was a waste of time, that Agile did not improve productivity and might even have slowed things down—because nobody likes to admit they've made a huge and costly mistake. In any case, by the time the Agile frenzy has come and gone, some good people will have left the company, either because they couldn't take the shitshow or because their managers thought they were pale grays.

It's easy to laugh at Agile and write it all off as just another nutty fad, except that in some places this is really causing harm. The original version of Taylorism, where Taylor stood with his stopwatch barking at laborers lugging slabs of pig iron, drove men to physical exhaustion and injury. Modern-day Taylorism takes an even bigger toll but on the psyche.

"This is destroying people's lives," says Daniel Markham, an Agile consultant who in 2010 published a widely shared essay titled "Agile Ruined My Life" in which he ranted about the nutters who were taking over the field. In 2017 I tracked him down and asked if maybe things had changed since he wrote the essay. "It's gotten worse," he told me. Markham said Agile began with good intentions and good ideas, but morphed into a monster. He now makes a living as a kind of Agile mop-up man. He gets hired to fix things at companies where Agile has gone off the rails. "I drive the ambulance, so I see all the bodies on the road," he tells me. "It's bad."

Even the software gurus who authored the original Agile manifesto back in 2001 say they can't make sense of Agile anymore. In 2017, I met one of them, Martin Fowler, for lunch. "I'd say about 90 percent of it is bullshit," Fowler told me. Fowler, a fiftysomething Englishman with a broad Midlands accent and a penchant for tweeds and cravats, was one of the seventeen gurus who co-authored the original Agile manifesto in Utah. He has authored eight well-regarded books about software programming and is considered something of a legend among computer scientists. Talking to Fowler about Agile is like meeting Saint Paul to talk about Christianity and having Saint Paul tell you that most of modern Christianity has nothing to do with what he envisioned when he wrote those epistles back in the first century AD.

But that's to be expected, Fowler said. "It's like a game of Chinese whispers," he told me. "One person tells the next person, and the next, and the next, and by the time it gets to the end of the line it's all garbled up."

"We've lost our way" is how another manifesto author, Andrew Hunt, put it in a 2015 essay titled "The Failure of Agile." Hunt tells me the word *agile* has become "meaningless at best," having been hijacked by "scads of vocal agile zealots" who had no idea what they were talking about. Agile has split into various camps and method-ologies, with names like Large-Scale Scrum (LeSS) and Disciplined Agile Delivery (DAD). The worst flavor, Hunt tells me, is Scaled Agile Framework, or SAFe, which he and some other original manifesto authors jokingly call Shitty Agile for Enterprise. "It's a disaster," Hunt tells me. "I have a few consultant friends who are making big bucks cleaning up failed SAFe implementations."

SAFe is the hellspawn brainchild of a company called Scaled Agile Inc., a bunch of mad scientists whose approach consists of a night-mare world of rules and charts and configurations. SAFe itself comes in multiple configurations, which you can find on the Scaled Agile website. Each one is an abomination of corporate complexity and Rube Goldberg-esque interdependencies.

For Agile's many critics, the methodology's biggest problem is simply that most Agile implementations fail—and it doesn't matter which flavor you choose, because they're all pretty much dog shit being passed off as chocolate ice cream. A programmer in London who went through Agile training told me he suspects companies adopt Agile hoping to drive down salaries, because part of the Agile philosophy is that everyone should be a generalist, rather than a specialist, which means they can be more easily replaced and thus can be paid less. He fears some companies adopt Agile as a way to get rid of older, better-paid workers—getting rid of the pale grays by saying they could not adapt to the company's new way of working.

Another problem is that Agile is often adopted in an ad hoc fashion, by managers who have no real training. Some manager reads a book about Agile and decides to give it a shot—he's the mad scientist, and you, the people who work for him, are his lab rats. Imagine your next-door neighbor doing an emergency appendectomy on you, using a Swiss Army knife and reading the instructions from a website, and you get the idea.

Agile is not limited to the corporate world. It's even infiltrating tra-ditional public sector employers all over the world. In 2013, the NHS issued a document entitled "Agile Working: A Guide for Employers", which promised to give information on how to "empower" staff by "giving more flexibility and reducing constraints". Similarly, London's Metropolitan Police has fallen prey to the same organizational sickness.

Cries for help abound on Internet forums, like this one posted in 2013 on Hacker News, a website popular among coders: "I can't take this Agile crap any longer. It's lunacy. It has all the hall marks [sic] of a religion. A lot of literature, a lot of disciples, hoards [sic] of money grabbing snake oil selling evangelists, and no evidence at all that it works. In fact, as far as I can see, there's more evidence that it *doesn't* work."

Researchers keep doing studies trying to find empirical evidence that Agile actually works, but they have mostly come up empty-handed. When Agile proponents tout success stories, they're mostly anecdotal. If you go looking for real numbers, they're hard to find. Yet big organizations keep latching on to Agile.

IT'S NOT EASY BEING LEAN

As Agile morphed and evolved and seeped into every crevice of the corporate world, a rival methodology was also taking shape in Silicon Valley. In the mid-2000s, a young entrepreneur named Eric Ries embarked on a radical experiment in organizational behavior, which developed into a methodology known as Lean Startup.

Ries studied computer science at Yale and graduated in 2000. During his college years he launched a start-up, which failed. After graduation he worked for a Silicon Valley company that developed an online virtual world. In 2004, he and four others split off and built a new virtual world, a place where people create avatars to socialize and play games. They called the company IMVU. Ries was the chief technology officer.

Ries stayed at IMVU for four years, and during his time there he became fascinated with the Toyota Production System and Lean

Manufacturing. He theorized that you could take the principles that Toyota uses to assemble a Corolla and apply them to developing new software products, or even to the process of building a company. IMVU, his start-up, provided a real-life laboratory for testing his theories.

In 2008, after leaving IMVU, Ries started writing a blog and giving speeches, laying out his theories. These served as the basis of his 2011 book, *The Lean Startup*, which became a huge bestseller. The second Internet boom, also known as Web 2.0, was starting to take off, and suddenly people were launching start-ups all over the place. But most of these people had never run companies before. Some had never even had jobs before. They had no idea what they were doing. Ries provided them with a road map.

Like Agile, Lean Startup has its own lingo and acronyms, like "minimum viable product" (MVP), "leap of faith assumptions" (LOFA), and a process called "Build-Measure-Learn." Just as Agile evolved from being a few ideas about how to write software into a magical methodology that can be used for almost anything, including transforming entire organizational cultures, so Lean Startup has been embraced by disciples who have imbued the methodology with near-supernatural powers. Like Agile, Lean Startup has become a global phenomenon, and an industry unto itself. Ries formed a consultancy, Lean Startup Co., to sell engagements, run conferences, and offer education programs. Other consultancies have built Lean Startup practices as well. Despite its name, Lean Startup is not aimed just at start-ups. Ries says any organization, big or small, can use the principles. People inside big companies can behave like entrepreneurs; Ries calls them "intrapreneurs."

GENERAL ELECTRIC: A PARABLE

One would-be intrapreneur was Jeffrey Immelt, the CEO of General Electric, who read Ries's book in a single day and said it struck him like a thunderbolt. GE is a sprawling, century-old conglomerate that at that time generated about $150 billion a year in revenue. Immelt's empire employed three hundred thousand people, who were arranged into so many divisions that even Wall Street analysts struggled to understand how all the pieces fit together. In other words, GE was about as far from being a start-up as any company could be.

Yet Immelt wanted to be more like a start-up. He aimed to transform GE into a tech company. He opened a software development center in Silicon Valley and set out to hire one thousand software engineers. As Immelt saw it, this was a matter of life or death. As Immelt recounted in an essay for *Harvard Business Review*, he told his managers, "Guys, if we don't become the best technology company in the world, we're doomed. We're dead. There's no Plan B."

Ries became key to Immelt's plan. Immelt brought him into GE to preach the Lean Startup gospel inside the company's far-flung divisions. Back at headquarters, Ries and Immelt launched a program that GE calls FastWorks, which is based on Lean Startup. Over the past few years more than sixty thousand GE employees have received Lean Startup training.

Unfortunately, it wasn't enough. GE's revenues stalled. The stock price languished, even as the overall stock market was surging. In 2017, the board booted Immelt. Soon after that, GE announced huge financial problems and a giant loss. The Securities and Exchange Commission launched an investigation into GE's accounting practices. The stock collapsed, losing half its value. Immelt's successor started talking about breaking up the company and selling off the parts.

Instead of a shining example of how to reinvent a big corporation in the digital age, GE became a cautionary tale of what *not* to do. To be sure, Lean Startup did not cause GE's problems. But nor was it able to save the company. The problem is not that GE chose the wrong methodology and should have gone with Agile instead of Lean Startup. Nor is it that GE failed to implement Lean Startup correctly. The lesson, if there is one, might be something even scarier—that maybe there is no silver bullet, no magical miracle methodology that can transform an organization with three hundred thousand employees into a start-up. You can't make an aircraft carrier zip and leap like a Jet Ski.

THE AGE OF FEAR

Even some people who have made a living selling "management science" say this stuff is snake oil. "The modern idea of management is right enough to be dangerously wrong and it has led us seriously astray. It has sent us on a mistaken quest to seek scientific answers to unscientific questions. It offers pretended technological solutions to what are, at bottom, moral and political problems," Matthew Stewart declares in *The Management Myth*, in which he debunks the work of management gurus from Taylor to the present day.

So why do companies keep searching for the fountain of youth, grasping at miracle cures? Right now most of them are scared to death. Their size used to be an advantage, but now it works against them. They've seen other companies that once seemed invincible get destroyed by the Internet—Blockbuster, Tower Records, Borders Books. They fear they will be next.

"Software is eating the world," venture capitalist Marc Andreessen once famously said, meaning that tech companies were no longer content to sell computers and software to other industries and instead intended to replace them. The media business has been nuked. Brick-and-mortar retailers are being wiped out so fast that people call it the "retail apocalypse." Toys "R" Us bit the dust in 2018. Sears is circling the drain. A quarter of the malls in the United States will be out of business by 2022.

Next on the menu are Hollywood, Detroit, and Wall Street. Fintech companies want to kill off the banks and manage your money. Amazon and Netflix are making movies and TV shows. No matter what business you're in, some VC-funded techie is scheming to destroy your company and steal your business.

Big companies have good reason to be scared, but their anxiety is making them crazy. Like the old guy who starts dyeing his hair and wearing skinny jeans and cowboy boots, or the ninety-two-year-old man who shows up once a month for his blood transfusion at Ambrosia, they become frenetic and foolish. They do things they would never have done in the past. They forget who they are. They have an identity crisis.

In the fall of 2016, I got to see this fear up close, when I traveled to Dearborn, Michigan, to the headquarters of the Ford Motor Company.

CHAPTER FOUR

WHO'S AFRAID OF
SILICON VALLEY?

I should begin by confessing my bias: I love Ford. It's a big, brawny, no-bullshit manufacturing company, an organization that for decades has occupied a spot near the top of the Fortune 500 list, with one of the world's best-known brands. Ford has two hundred thousand employees and sells six million vehicles a year, generating $150 billion in annual revenue and keeping $8 billion in net profit. Ford is the corporate equivalent of an aircraft carrier. Operating something of this scale is a monumental task.

The company's world headquarters building is an enormous twelve-story glass-and-steel fortress that embodies the broad-shouldered swagger and confidence of America in the 1950s, when it was built. Inside, the lobby exudes the same kind of quiet power: reserved, professional, almost serene. In places it looks and feels like a museum, with classic Mustangs and pickup trucks on display behind ropes that keep visitors from touching them or jumping inside. There's no kooky start-up decor. There's lots of dark wood. This is a serious place, where serious grown-ups do big, serious things.

Except today is different. On this day, a Monday in September 2016, an idiot is riding up and down a hallway on a forty-pound hoverboard, teeter-tottering and waving his arms for balance, zigging and zagging and endangering his own life and the lives of others, including loads of startled Ford employees who are returning from their lunch break. The idiot is me. I'm here because Ford is holding a two-day event, and they have hired me to give a brief talk about disruption and to interview a Ford exec onstage. Ford has invited three hundred journalists to travel to Detroit and learn about the company. There's also a hackathon, and the hoverboard is one of the finalists, so a PR guy has talked me into taking it for a ride.

Why are these guys running a hackathon? The answer, I suspect, lies two thousand miles to the west, in a set of bland buildings on a windy road in the barren foothills outside Palo Alto, California—the headquarters of Tesla. Tesla is a mess, but when it comes to sex appeal, nothing in Ford's lineup can keep up with Tesla's sleek, speedy Model S sedan. Though Ford generates thirteen times as much revenue as Tesla and sells sixty-six times as many vehicles, Tesla's stock market valuation is about the same as Ford's.

Tesla's soaring stock is held up mostly by hype. CEO Elon Musk is a masterful marketer, a genius at generating buzz. But Tesla also has raced ahead of Detroit in developing the two biggest new car technologies: electric motors and autonomous vehicles. Tesla is not the only Silicon Valley company that threatens Ford. Google and Uber are working on self-driving cars. Apple is rumored to be operating a secret automotive laboratory. The Silicon Valley guys realize that transportation is becoming a technology business. Self-driving cars depend on artificial intelligence, which means sensors and lots of software, stuff they know how to do. To them, a car is just a container for an AI computer, a bunch of software that happens to have wheels attached. In ten years, people won't buy cars based on which model has the most horsepower or the nicest leather seats. They'll care about which one has the best software, the most reliable autonomous-driving system, the smartest navigation computer, the coolest add-on services delivered through the dashboard.

Google and Apple have a huge advantage. They employ armies

of software developers and AI engineers. They also have hundreds of billions of dollars. Their resources are virtually unlimited. That doesn't mean they will ever be able to build millions of cars a year, the way Ford does. Techies in Silicon Valley tend to underestimate how difficult it is to manufacture things, especially products as complex as automobiles. Ford has been doing it for more than a century. In fact, in 1917, when Ford was the same age as Tesla is now, the company cranked out seven times as many cars as Tesla does today— and that was without robots or computers or software.

But lately Ford has gone wobbly. Sales aren't growing very much. The stock has been sagging for years. Ford CEO Mark Fields has been in the top job for only two years, but the board is already getting impatient. He's supposed to be turning things around. Fields has announced plans to bulldoze parts of the drab old Ford campus and build a new campus that looks like the Googleplex. Ford has been hiring artificial intelligence engineers, built a tech lab in Silicon Valley, and struck a deal with a San Francisco software company whose engineers will teach Ford's coders about Agile development.

Ford wants us to know that it's in the midst of a huge transformation, and that it's not falling behind. Earlier, we all took turns going for rides in Ford's prototype self-driving car, which Ford vows to have in production by 2021. Now we've come indoors for an event that is meant to evoke the atmosphere of a big Silicon Valley conference, or an Apple product announcement. Tim Brown, the head of IDEO, a cooler-than-thou Silicon Valley design shop, hangs out in the hallway. The Ford execs wear jeans and give casual talks about coping with change and disruption. Dan Ariely, a famous TED Talk guy, gives a TED-style talk. A journalist interviews Fields on stage, and I conduct a similar interview with Ford's chief technology officer.

At last we get to the hackathon. As a host explains, months ago Ford challenged all of its two hundred thousand employees to dream up their wildest, craziest, most ambitious inventions. From all of the ideas submitted, Ford chose the best three. Those are the ones we will see today. To create an air of drama, Ford has turned it into a competition, with a format like *Shark Tank*, the TV show where entrepreneurs pitch business ideas to investors.

I'm hoping for something big, like a flying car, or an engine that gets three hundred miles to the gallon, or an AI-powered robot that looks like Henry Ford. Instead we get the hoverboard that I rode on previously, presented by three engineers from Germany who built it as a way to travel into crowded city centers. Next comes a Ford engineer with a smartphone app that can control the radio and climate settings in a car, and someday might do language translation on the fly. Finally comes an engineer from Ford's powertrain division with a system he calls On-the-Go H_2O. This guy has attached a cooking pan to the bottom of his car, so it captures droplets of condensation from the air-conditioning system. Up in the passenger compartment he has affixed a tap, like the one you see at the dentist's office, to the side of the cup holder. Water collected from the condensation pan gets pumped through a filter up into the passenger compartment and into a plastic bottle. Just like that, you've got free drinking water.

That's it. I feel certain that no journalist will leave this event feeling more confident about Ford's chances against the giants of Silicon Valley.

"So what d'you you think?" a Ford PR guy asks me afterward, as he walks me out to my car.

"I liked the self-driving car," I tell him. I keep my opinion of the hackathon to myself.

The truth is, I feel bad for these guys. I understand why they want to look hip, but holding a hackathon only makes them look scared. Sitting in the audience, I was having PTSD flashbacks to my last few years at *Newsweek*, when the magazine was dying and we all knew we were doomed, but we didn't want to admit it. We could not stomach the fact that shitty websites like Huffington Post and BuzzFeed were the hot new thing, and we were yesterday's news. Every few months our CEO would get up at a company meeting and pretend that things were getting better, and we would pretend to believe him. Many of us loved *Newsweek*. We were proud to work there. We hated to see it fade away. I'm sure a lot of Ford employees feel the same way about Ford.

At *Newsweek* we made two big mistakes. First, we waited too long to build up an online business. Second, when things got tough, we invested loads of money into hype and marketing—like Ford, holding this hackathon—trying to create a new image for ourselves, to convince people we were "reinventing" the company and carrying out a radical transformation. What we should have done was forget about marketing, forget about trying to get followers on Facebook, and just invest in our core business, which was journalism. We should have just kept doing what we did best.

What I want to tell my friend at Ford is this: To hell with hackathons. To hell with trying to be a tech company, or generating hype. Just be Ford. Build the best cars you can build. Make electric cars, and self-driving cars, whatever cars people want. Develop the technology you need, or acquire start-ups that can do a better job than you can. But don't stop being Ford, because Ford is great.

A few months after my visit, Ford fired 10 percent of its whitecollar workers. Then the board fired Fields, the CEO. The chairman, Bill Ford Jr., said Ford had canned Fields because the company was facing "unprecedented change" and needed "transformational leadership." The subtext: we're terrified. A year later, in early 2018, Ford's new CEO, Jim Hackett, announced that Ford would stop selling most of its car models in the United States, focusing instead on SUVs, in order to save money. The message: now we're even more terrified.

In fact, fear was everywhere. Fear was at every conference I attended, in the eyes of every CEO and consultant and expert. Three months after my trip to Ford, in December 2016, I attended an invitation-only Yale CEO Summit at the Waldorf Astoria in New York—and here, too, the scent of fear hung in the air. The event was off the record, so I can't tell you what happened or who attended, but the crowd included billionaire CEOs, a former CIA director, and various high government officials, think tank analysts, professors, people from big trade associations, and a few famous journalists you would recognize from TV.

"Delight and Despair over Disruption" was the title of the event. Donald Trump had just been elected but had not yet taken office. There was a feeling that we were standing at one of history's inflection points, not just because of Trump but because of the Internet. Digital technology had already transformed great swathes of the economy, but even bigger and more momentous changes lay ahead. Everyone was trying to figure out what those would look like, but nobody had any idea, not even the CEOs from the big tech companies who had unleashed the whirlwind. Throwing Trump into the mix added even more chaos and uncertainty. What if he started a trade war? Or a real war?

It was difficult enough to be grappling with complex issues like growing income and wealth inequality, and the potential impact of robotics, artificial intelligence, and automation—but now we would have a man-child president whose obsessions included arming schoolteachers, banning Muslims, and building a wall at the Mexican border. At a time of unprecedented social and economic change, at the dawn of the Fourth Industrial Revolution, the American people had elected a chimp with a machine gun. Everyone looked scared, disruptors and disrupted alike.

"NOBODY IS SAFE"

Then came 2017, the year of corporate bloodbaths. "CEOs are dropping like flies" was how TheStreet.com put it. Lands' End, Ralph Lauren, and Tiffany booted their CEOs. So did toy maker Mattel, which brought in an executive from Google, because so much business has moved online that Mattel believed it needed "a leader with digital experience."

Target, under attack from Amazon, booted a slew of top executives, including the chief innovation officer and chief digital officer, who ran the company's e-commerce business. Kellogg, Mondelēz, Coca-Cola, and General Mills all lost CEOs (or pushed them out) as the packaged food business endured what *Fortune* called "the most disruptive and challenging period they've ever seen in the industry." All over the place, in every industry, big blue-chip companies were fumbling and flailing, getting tossed around like toy boats trying to ride out a tsunami.

Even Millard "Mickey" Drexler, the CEO and chairman of J.Crew, a man whom many people considered the greatest living retailer, proved to be no match for the Internet. In 2017 Drexler stepped aside from J.Crew, saying he had failed to recognize how profoundly the Internet would disrupt the retail industry. "I've never seen the speed of change as it is today," Drexler told the *Wall Street Journal*.

"Nobody is safe," the president of a global consulting firm told me over dinner—and apparently that included him, because a few months after we met, he got booted, too. And the phenomenon was not confined to US corporations. In the UK, 2018 heralded a crisis for its high streets: several familiar chains were met with demise or near death, including House of Fraser, BHS, Mothercare, and Poundworld.

Fear pervades the workplace, from the CEO suite down to the ranks of regular workers. Kae Lani Palmisano, a twenty-eight-year-old social media and editorial producer, tells me she lives with constant fear of being laid off. "It's pretty scary. It feels like any day now the rug could be pulled out from underneath me and I'd have to scramble to get a new job. It's really stressful."

For the past fourteen months Palmisano has had a contract gig making food and travel videos for *USA Today*. But she keeps her LinkedIn and personal website up to date, just in case. "Every Millennial I know is constantly bracing to be laid off," she tells me. "Especially if they work in tech, digital marketing, or journalism." In the past seven years Palmisano has had five jobs. "Every two years you have to find a new job. You get flung from one thing to another." Recently married, she'd like to have kids, but she doesn't dare start a family yet because her work situation feels so precarious.

WHAT FEAR DOES TO YOUR BRAIN

A decade ago, Gregory Berns, a neuropsychology researcher and director of the Center for Neuropolicy at Emory University, wanted to find out how fear affected people's abilities to make decisions.

To do that, he constructed an experiment that was downright shocking.

He put people into an MRI scanner and made images of their brain while giving them painful electric shocks through electrodes attached to the top of their feet. Berns says it was basically a human version of a Skinner box. Berns, you may recall from Chapter 1, was the guy who once wrote that "Work is becoming more and more like a Skinner box."

Thirty-two people signed up to let Berns and his colleagues turn them into lab rats. He let each person set the maximum amount of pain they could tolerate, then gave them jolts, while using the scanner to see what was going on inside their brains. The shocks didn't come at regular intervals, so subjects didn't know when they were going to get zapped. They just had to lie there, waiting. The intervals ranged from one to thirty seconds.

Soon Berns noticed something: once people had received a few jolts, their brains started lighting up *before* the jolt arrived. It turns out the *dread* of the pain was as bad as the pain itself.

Berns added a twist by giving subjects a choice. They could get a big shock right away—meaning they could control the timing. Or they could wait and not know when the shock would come, but get a milder shock. Most chose to get the big shock right away. That was obviously a bad decision. More pain is worse than less pain.

Berns concluded that people who are scared basically can't think straight. "Fear—whether of pain or losing a job—does strange things to decision-making. Fear overtakes our brains and makes it impossible to concentrate on anything but saving our skin. When the fear system of the brain is active, exploratory activity and risk-taking are turned off," he wrote.

I tracked Berns down at his lab in Atlanta and asked him whether his experiment might teach us anything about what happens to people when they live in fear of losing their job. He said it did, and that during the economic downturn after the big crash in 2008 he saw this happening all the time. People were afraid of losing their jobs, afraid of having their life savings wiped out in the stock market. Because of their fear they were making "suboptimal" decisions.

"If you're living in fear of losing your job, then all of your decisions and actions are geared to preserving your job rather than taking risks," he told me. But that's actually the exact wrong thing to do. In a time of uncertainty, "taking risks and trying new things would actually be in your best interest," Berns said. "But that's difficult when you're afraid of losing your job."

Berns said that for a lot of people, the workplace really does feel like a Skinner box, where you wander around like a rat in one of B. F. Skinner's cages trying to figure out how to get rewards and how to avoid punishment. "It's like you're in a box, and you have no control over what's happening to you," Berns said. "It's controlled by experimenters outside. You learn to associate certain places in that box with good and bad things." Fearful rats can only think about one thing—how to get out of the box and stop getting shocked.

The Berns MRI experiment might explain why the CEOs of big corporations, who fear that their organizations are on the verge of being put out of business and fear that they will be blamed for the collapse, might start doing crazy things, like staging hackathons, or making huge acquisitions, or imagining that a company with three hundred thousand employees could turn itself into a "start-up," or making people learn Agile, even though there's no empirical evidence that Agile actually works.

Fearful companies make bad decisions. Somehow CEOs must find a way to respond to threats without being driven by fear. The same goes for fearful employees. People who live in fear cannot do their best work. The most obvious lesson of the Berns experiment is that if companies want to boost the productivity of their workers and encourage people to engage in the kind of creative thinking that generates amazing ideas, they first need to make people feel safe. Spend more on training. Pay a little better. Offer health benefits and job security. Remove the fear that a job might disappear at any minute.

But as I explain in the next few chapters, many companies are doing exactly the opposite.

PART II

FOUR FACTORS OF WORKPLACE DESPAIR

BUILDING THE WORKFORCE OF THE FUTURE (OR: SORRY, YOU'RE OLD AND WE'D LIKE YOU TO LEAVE)

How do you make a lab rat feel depressed? That sounds like a setup for a joke, but it's actually a question scientists needed to answer. Their ultimate goal was to test out new antidepressant drugs on these rodents before trying the concoctions on humans. But to test an antidepressant you need a depressed test subject. It turns out there is a simple, guaranteed-to-work method for making an animal depressed: just put it under a bit of low-grade stress and maintain the stress for a little while. Voilà—you've manufactured depression.

Scientists call it the unpredictable chronic mild stress (UCMS) protocol. The process involves making small changes, like putting a rat in a new cage, maybe one that previously was occupied by another rat. Scientists might also tilt a rat's cage, change the cycle of light and dark, or give rats wet bedding or sawdust that has been used by other rats and still contains their urine and feces. They might play recordings of predator birds for ten minutes, or put a rat into a tight restraint tube for fifteen to thirty minutes, and then set it free again. The changes are randomized and altered frequently, so the rats can't get used to a new condition.

The rats are not deprived of food or water or subjected to any physical pain. Nothing life-threatening occurs, and there is no real danger—just some environmental changes and some mild stress. That's all it takes.

Within weeks the rats slide into a state that looks a lot like clinical depression in humans. They become apathetic and lethargic. They stop grooming themselves. Their coats get matted and dirty. They won't build nests, they lose interest in running in their exercise wheels, and they become less motivated to seek out treats like cookies. (Scientists call this *anhedonia*, the inability to feel pleasure.) The rats gain weight. They show signs of despair, have difficulty making decisions, and experience sleep disturbances. They exhibit immune system dysfunction, problems in the hippocampus and amygdala, and higher levels of cortisol, which in humans has been linked to heart disease and depression.

When I heard about this rodent stress testing, I was taken aback. It all sounded to me eerily similar to what work is becoming for more and more of us humans. Ther's no danger to our physical safety. But there are constant, random changes. Loss of privacy or familiarity. Dealing with bad, disturbing technologies creeping into our environment.

A new study on rats at West Virginia University suggests that chronic stress diminishes blood vessel function, so much that animals whose weight is normal end up with blood vessels that look like what you find in obese animals. One of the researchers tells me these findings have direct implications for workers. Stressed-out workers could have "an increased risk of cardiovascular disease, high blood pressure, stroke, heart attack, and cardiovascular mortality," said Evan DeVallance, now a postdoc at the University of Pittsburgh.

Consider how big companies are rushing around adopting Agile and Lean Startup, changing where and how people work, forcing employees to embrace new routines, and crowding workers into stressful new environments like noisy (and sometimes even smelly) open offices. Think about how we're working longer hours, but also less predictable hours. Or how we now worry more than ever about losing our jobs and whether we will be able to retire. Think about how often you hear someone at work say, "Change is the only constant."

Squint your eyes a little bit and the whole thing looks a lot like a human version of the unpredictable chronic mild stress protocol. Could the rising antidepressant usage and suicide rates we discussed in Chapter 1 be related? Could other health problems?

Here in Part 2, I'm going to take a deeper dive into the four factors that contribute to worker unhappiness: money, insecurity, change, and dehumanization. Also, I will explore the ways in which Silicon Valley and the Internet have contributed to those four factors.

Why do we now have so much tumult and upheaval, and this sudden flurry of activity, all this talk of reinvention, accompanied by constant "change initiatives," with their workshops, and classes, and role-playing games? Some of this comes from fear. Companies are scared of getting killed, so they start racing around in a kind of frenzy, trying to tip things upside down and transform themselves.

I wonder whether all of this sound and fury is also a form of distraction, a sideshow created to keep us so busy and so scared that we don't notice how companies keep eroding the terms of the bargain that once existed between workers and employers. Distract workers with Lego workshops, put them in new offices, ply them with snacks and Ping-Pong and meditation rooms, bombard them with rhetoric about mission and purpose and "changing the world," and maybe they won't complain that their pay has gone down, their benefits have been pared back, the pension fund was raided, and their jobs are no longer secure. Maybe it is all just sleight of hand, a form of corporate misdirection. Focus on the cards in the magician's hand, and you don't even notice that he's stolen your watch.

Consider what's going on at IBM, which is putting all of its 366,000 worldwide workers through Agile training—but has also spent the past two decades screwing its workers. IBM's massive Agile campaign began in 2015 and will take four years to complete, costing hundreds of millions of dollars. So far more than two hundred thousand IBMers have been trained. IBM's goal is far more ambitious than just teaching software programmers to crank out code faster. IBM wants to completely rewire its corporate DNA, by applying Agile to every part of the business—sales, marketing, and so on. Agile will become "an engine for business transformation," Sam Ladah, vice president of human resources, wrote in a July 2017 blog post, adding that Agile will help IBM build "a workforce of the future."

That last bit about the "workforce of the future" was a canny bit of corporate doublespeak that covered up something else that IBM was doing with Agile—using it to get rid of workers. As part of its "business transformation," IBM opened new offices called "Agile hubs" in six cities in the United States, with groovy decor and desks jammed into pods, in what Quartz described as "a sitcom version of an 'Agile office.'"

Then IBM told thousands of employees who had been working from home that from now on they would have to work out of one of these Agile hubs. Or they could quit. It was their choice. The problem was that many of these people lived hundreds of miles from the nearest hub. To keep their jobs, they'd have to sell their homes and move. It's not clear how many quit instead of relocating. In his blog post, Ladah said about five thousand employees would return to working from an office instead of working at home. By some estimates, 40 percent of the company's employees don't work from a traditional office, the *Wall Street Journal* reported.

The reason IBM had so many remote workers was that for years the company *encouraged* employees to work from home, so that IBM could save money on office space. Now IBM is reeling people back in and taking away the "work from home" perk, but announcing the decision using the happy-face mendacity that big companies love: "It's time for Act II: WINNING!" read the subject line on a message that Michelle Peluso, the company's chief marketing officer, sent to the company's five thousand marketing people when she announced the end of the work-from-home policy. Workers were not cheered by all the WINNING! Many were devastated. The announcement reportedly sent shock waves across the company.

IBM's Agile campaign comes after two decades in which IBM has slowly but steadily robbed its workers while enriching top executives and Wall Street investors. In the 1990s, under CEO Louis Gerstner, IBM gutted its employee pension fund and used some of the money to boost its earnings, as former *Wall Street Journal* reporter Ellen Schultz details in her 2011 book, *Retirement Heist*. IBM also slashed retiree health benefits, which "generated a fresh pool of accounting gains that the company added to income over a period of years," Schultz reported. In 1993, Gerstner presided over the biggest layoff in corporate history, nuking sixty thousand workers.

Nine years later, in 2002, Gerstner waltzed away with a severance package worth $189 million. His successor, Sam Palmisano, IBM's CEO from 2002 to 2012, walked out with a package worth $270 million, according to Footnoted.com, a stock market watchdog website. IBM's current CEO, Ginni Rometty, earned $33 million in 2016.

For the past few years Rometty has been busy slashing jobs, especially targeting older workers. From 2014 through 2017, IBM fired thirty thousand American workers, and twenty thousand of them were over age forty, according to a March 2018 investigative report by ProPublica, which said IBM had "flouted or outflanked U.S. laws and regulations intended to protect later-career workers from age discrimination." ProPublica later reported that the U.S. Equal Employment Opportunity Commission had launched an investigation.

The thing is, from 2012 to 2017, when IBM was firing all those workers, the company was turning hefty profits and in fact generated $92 billion in cash. Where did the money go? IBM delivered most of the loot—about 80 percent—to investors, via dividends and stock buybacks, according to Toni Sacconaghi, an analyst at Sanford Bernstein, a Wall Street firm. Sacconaghi said IBM could have used that money to acquire other companies. IBM also might have launched new products and business lines. Instead IBM used the money to prop up its stock price. By buying back its own stock, IBM reduced the number of shares outstanding. That increases earnings per share, since there are fewer shares. Higher EPS tends to boost the stock price. That's great for investors in the short term. But, for the long term, companies are better off trying to build new lines of business to replace the ones that are fading away. Devoting money to buybacks often means management is just throwing in the towel, admitting they have no good ideas.

Where did IBM get the cash for buybacks? In part by laying off tens of thousands of workers. In effect, IBM used their wages to buy back shares and pump up the stock price. Why do that? Because the executives' own compensation is tied to the stock. The trick didn't really work; IBM stock has shed a third of its value from 2013 to 2018, plunging from $213 to $141. But who knows how much worse things could have been without the stock buybacks? As for management, the ploy worked out great. In 2017, the board awarded Rometty, the CEO, with a pay package worth $50 million, according to Institutional Shareholder Services, which advises big investors. This wasn't the first time. "IBM's CEO writes a new chapter on how to turn failure into wealth" was how Michael Hiltzik in the *Los Angeles Times* put it in January 2016 when Rometty raked in a $4.5 million bonus. But hey! Let's talk about Agile, and the workforce of the future! Let's talk about how we're turning IBM into a start-up!

You see how the trick works.

IBM is hardly alone in the way it has abused its workers. Loads of big companies, including household names like GE, Verizon, and AT&T, raided their pension funds in the 1990s and "managed to take hundreds of billions of dollars in retirement benefits that were intended for millions of workers and divert them to corporate coffers, shareholders, and their own pockets," Schultz writes in *Retirement Heist*.

In the UK, the infamous retail tycoon, Sir Philip Green, was pushed into agreeing to pay £363 million into the coffers of BHS's pension scheme after he had sold the company for a nominal figure to avoid the firm's retirement liabilities in 2015. Under Green's tenure, the firm's pension scheme had gone from a surplus to a significant deficit. Frank Field who was the politician in charge of the Commons work and pensions select committee at the time responded to a regulator's report by saying, "[this] confirms that Sir Philip Green stripped BHS bare and then left it for dead, with contemptuous disregard for the pensioners."

In 1999, near the height of the dotcom bubble and after years of soaring stock market valuations, many big companies were sitting on enormous surpluses in their pension funds—more than $250 billion dollars combined, including $25 billion in extra assets at GE and $24 billion at Verizon. This meant those companies could pay the pensions of all their employees for decades to come, without ever putting in another penny. Companies were supposed to keep the pension money in those funds, but instead they found ways to siphon money out of the pensions and apply it to their earnings. By 2011, Verizon's $24 billion surplus had vanished and its plan had a shortfall of $6.5 billion. GE's $24 billion surplus became a $13 billion deficit by 2011, Schultz reports. And that was just the beginning. By 2017, GE had a pension deficit of nearly $30 billion. That was a swing of more than $50 billion!

Where did the money go? Some funds lost money in stock market crashes in 2011 and 2008. But companies also started using pension fund money to pay for things like retiree health benefits, which previously came out of their operating budgets. (Using pension fund money meant they saved that expense on their income statement, which boosted their quarterly earnings.) Another way to get hold of supposedly untouchable pension fund money was to sell off a business unit and package surplus pension money into the deal; in exchange, the buyer paid a higher sale price. Thus the transaction essentially let the seller convert pension money into cash it could apply to earnings.

Siphoning off the surplus money was just the beginning. Companies also started cutting back on pension benefits—basically finding ways to renege on the promises they had made to employees about how much they could expect to receive after retirement. One trick was to change the formula used to calculate how much pension an employee would get in retirement.

Schultz's book offers a sickening look at how big-company executives conspired with benefits consultants to slash benefits to employees while lying about it, using tricks like switching to new plans that were so complicated that most employees couldn't understand how they were being swindled. "It is not until they are ready to retire that they understand how little they are getting," an actuary from Watson Wyatt, a benefit consultant, declared at a 1998 conference. The comment got a big laugh from the audience, Schultz reports.

IBM used a bunch of tricks. First it changed the formula used to calculate benefits. Next, in 1995 IBM cut more by changing to a "pension equity plan." In 1998 IBM slashed again by changing to a cash-balance plan. Later, Big Blue saved by offering its retirees lump-sum payments when people retired or were let go. Along the way, IBM was using money from its pension fund to pump up its earnings, Schultz reports. Back in 1999, IBM enjoyed a pension fund surplus of $7 billion, Schultz says. By the end of 2017, IBM announced it would contribute $500 million to the plan, but that its assets would still be less than its obligations.

Robbing people of their pensions was just one tactic in the wider strategy of disempowering workers. In the next four chapters, I move on to four factors of workplace despair: money, insecurity, change, and dehumanization.

I begin with money, because if you want to know why people are miserable, it's usually a good idea to start by looking at their wallets. What you find there is depressing.

CHAPTER SIX

MONEY: "GARBAGE AT THE SPEED OF LIGHT"

One day in February 2018, a sixty-one-year-old New York City livery driver, Doug Schifter, parked in front of City Hall and shot himself in the face with a shotgun. A few hours earlier Schifter had posted a long essay on Facebook explaining his reasons. He said that he had once made a good living driving a limo in New York, earning enough to buy a house outside the city. But then came the onslaught of new drivers working for services like Uber and Lyft, and rates plummeted for everyone, so low that nobody could make a living as a driver anymore. Schifter was putting in seventeen-hour days, sometimes earning as little as $4 an hour. He fell into debt. He missed a mortgage payment and was in danger of losing his home. "I have been financially ruined," he wrote. "I will not be a slave working for chump change. I would rather be dead."

Silicon Valley promotes the gig economy as an innovative new industry that is creating jobs for millions of people. But the jobs being created are mostly bad ones. Meanwhile, gig-economy companies threaten established industries. Airbnb steals business from hotels. Uber and Lyft have hurt business at car-rental companies like Hertz and Avis, and have utterly decimated the taxi and livery business. Pundits like to talk about "creative destruction" as if it were an abstract concept, but the sight of a driver parked in front of

City Hall with his head blown off served as a reminder that all this change and so-called progress is coming at a very high cost to actual human beings. As the *New York Times* reported, Schifter "was not a participant in the gig economy; he was a casualty of it."

There are many others. In New York, cabbies and limo drivers are going bankrupt, losing their homes or being evicted from apartments. From 2013 to 2016, the average New York cabbie's annual bookings dropped 22 percent, and the value of a New York taxi medallion plunged 85 percent from more than $1 million to less than $200,000, according to the *New York Times*. London now has over 40,000 registered Uber drivers and the effect on the traditional black cab has been stark. The number of people seeking to study "the Knowledge" (the famously difficult test of London's streets which is a prerequisite for a license) dropped from 3,326 in 2012 to 2,159 in 2014. Steve Albasini, a black-cab driver told the BBC that "the cab trade is facing its biggest challenge in 300 to 350 years."

Twenty years ago, pundits believed the Internet was going to make the world better in all sorts of ways, from perfecting democracy to saving the planet. Best of all would be the financial impact. During the heady days of the first dotcom boom, when stocks were soaring and people were mooning over the magical powers of the web, *Wired* founding editor Kevin Kelly declared the Internet would usher in decades of "ultraprosperity," with "full employment . . . and improving living standards." We were entering "the roaring zeroes," as he called it, while declaring, "The good news is, you'll be a millionaire soon. The bad news is, so will everybody else." Bill Gates would become a trillionaire, Kelly predicted, perhaps as soon as 2005. By 2020, average U.S. household income would be $150,000. Regular people would have personal chefs and take six-month sabbaticals.

A more accurate prediction came from curmudgeonly business guru Tom Peters, who fretted, "I'm concerned that this global economy will in fact be garbage at the speed of light." Peters was right. Even people who helped build the Internet economy, and have benefited from it, now fear they created a monster. Chris Hughes, a Facebook co-founder, says the new economy "is going to continue to destroy work," and in a 2018 book, *Fair Shot*, he argues for providing universal basic income—essentially handouts to unemployed adults—paid for by taxing the top 1 percent.

The first of the four factors boils down to this: twenty-five years after the dawn of the Internet, we haven't all become millionaires. In fact, quite the opposite. Almost everyone is doing worse than they were a quarter century ago.

Income inequality in the United States has reached a level not seen since 1929, just before the Great Depression. Technology may not be entirely to blame for that widening gap between haves and have-nots, but it certainly has played a crucial role. If nothing else, the Internet sped up anti-worker practices that were already in place, acting like a turbocharger for bad behavior, becoming "the greatest legal facilitator of inequality in human history," Silicon Valley venture capitalist Bill Davidow wrote in a 2014 essay for *The Atlantic*.

Real wages (adjusted for inflation) have been flat or down for decades. Millennials earn 20 percent less than their parents did at the same stage of their lives, according to a 2017 study by Young Invincibles, an advocacy group. The economy has been growing, but almost all of the benefits of that growth go to the highest-income Americans, leaving the rest with scraps. In 1970, middle-income households reaped 62 percent of aggregate household income in the United States. By 2014, their share had fallen to 43 percent. The share going to upper-income households grew to 49 percent from 29 percent over the same period, according to a 2015 Pew Research Center report. From 2000 to 2014, the median income of middle-income households actually declined by 4 percent. Their wealth (assets minus debts) dropped 28 percent from 2001 to 2013. As a result, the middle class itself is shrinking—from 61 percent of Americans in 1971 to 50 percent in 2015, according to Pew.

A similar picture appears through much of the developed world. In the UK, in 2017, The Resolution Foundation predicted that by 2021, the richest 10 percent would earn more than six times the poorest

10 percent after housing costs. If they prove correct, this will be the highest ratio on record (compared to a ratio of approximately 3:1 in the 1960s and 1970s). Median wages actually fell by 10 percent in the UK from 2008 to 2014, with the poorest hit to an even greater degree.

It took the election of Donald Trump and the rise of populism to really wake elites up. In January 2017, a few months after the election but before Trump actually took office, attendees at the exclusive, annual World Economic Forum in Davos were all talking about income inequality. The WEF itself cited widening income inequality as a threat to the global economy. Some saw the election of Trump as a warning that the victims of the Information Age were lashing out. "People around the world have become aware they are part of the bottom class, and they're angry. Trump could be just the beginning," British economist Guy Standing declared. Standing uses the term *precariat* to describe a new class of people who lack secure employment or predictable income, and suffer psychologically as a result.

While economists and government ministers wring their hands, some billionaires and tech leaders have taken matters into their own. But instead of trying to fix the situation, they are making plans to escape whatever calamity might arise from the forces Trump has unleashed—civil war, a proletariat uprising, a collapse of the power grid, an economic meltdown. According to a 2017 article in the *New Yorker* by Evan Osnos titled "Doomsday Prep for the Super Rich," the loaded have taken to stockpiling guns and food, gold bars and Bitcoin. Others have been building "boltholes"—armed compounds in places like New Zealand, where they can ride out a catastrophe. Tech oligarch Peter Thiel owns a hideaway there and has even obtained Kiwi citizenship. "Saying you're 'buying a house in New Zealand' is kind of a wink, wink, say no more. Once you've done the Masonic handshake, they'll be, like, 'Oh, you know, I have a broker who sells old ICBM silos, and they're nuclear-hardened, and they kind of look like they would be interesting to live in," billionaire VC Reid Hoffman told Osnos. Hoffman estimated that "fifty-plus percent" of Valley billionaires had built some kind of doomsday hideout. In

Kansas, an entrepreneur converted an old underground missile silo into a survival bunker. He put apartments on the market priced at $3 million each. They sold out in a heartbeat.

THE $2 TRILLION SWINDLE

Nick Hanauer was born rich, thanks to a family-owned business in Seattle, and then he made an even greater fortune in tech. In 1997 he founded a company called aQuantive which he sold a decade later to Microsoft for $6 billion. But an even greater part of his wealth comes from a single investment that might turn out to have been the single smartest bet of the last hundred years. In the early 1990s, Hanauer met a nerdy young guy named Jeff Bezos and became the first person to put money into Amazon.

Instead of normal billionaire hobbies—starting a space exploration company, purchasing a private island—Hanauer became an unlikely advocate for the working class. He says he had a kind of epiphany one day in 2008 when he was poring over Internal Revenue Service data (how's that for a hobby?) showing how the share of gross income had been shifting over time. In 1980, the top 1 percent of earners raked in 8.5 percent of all income. By 2008 that figure had climbed to 21 percent. Over the same period the share going to the bottom half of earners dropped from 17 percent to 12 percent.

For Hanauer, that was a wake-up call. "All I did was take that data and put it into a spreadsheet and assumed that the current trends would continue for another thirty years," he told me. "It does not take a genius to see that this is unsustainable."

He urged his fellow one-percenters not to ignore the problem or run away from it, but instead to try to fix it. That was only fair, since they had created it. Hanauer started writing books and essays, giving speeches, and lobbying politicians to enact policies—like raising the minimum wage—that could reverse the widening gap between haves and have-nots. In a blistering 2014 essay, titled "The Pitchforks Are

Coming for Us Plutocrats," Hanauer warned that if we continued on the same path, eventually millions of people in the precariat would launch a revolution. "You show me a highly unequal society, and I will show you a police state. Or an uprising. There are no counterexamples," he wrote.

What's more, Hanauer believes the people rising up would be completely justified, for they have been the victims of one of the greatest swindles of all time. They have been robbed of $2 trillion a year that should be flowing to working people and instead has been siphoned off by the rich, he says.

Here's how he does the math. First, companies managed to slash wages paid to workers and keep that money for themselves. Forty years ago, wages represented 52 percent of the gross domestic product. Today, wages represent only 46 percent, according to the U.S. Bureau of Economic Analysis. With the U.S. GDP now at $17 trillion, that 6 percent swing represents $1 trillion a year that has been stolen from workers.

Over that same time period, corporate profits *rose* by 6 percent, to 12 percent of GDP today from 6 percent of GDP in 1980. Basically, companies vacuumed up 6 percent of the economy that used to go to workers and moved it to their bottom lines.

That's only the first trillion. Another trillion vanished because not only did the portion of the pie that goes to wages decrease but regular workers also now get less of that smaller portion. Four decades ago, regular workers (meaning the bottom 99 percent of wage earners) collected 92 percent of all wages. Today, regular workers get only 78 percent. That 14 percent drop represents another trillion dollars per year.

Where did that money go? The top 1 percent of wage earners now reap 22 percent of all wages, up from 8 percent four decades ago.

"If you add it up, it is $2 trillion a year that used to go to normal people and now goes to rich people," Hanauer says.

That $2 trillion, if divvied up among the 125 million full-time workers in the United States, would amount to $16,000. For the average full-time employee, who earns $44,000 a year, an extra $16,000 would represent a 36 percent raise. For minimum-wage workers, the windfall would more than double their pay. It's a big deal.

This amounts to a robbery in broad daylight. But it all happened slowly, and so most of us missed it. But most people do know that it's harder to pay the bills and harder to get by. Some chalk it up to individual luck and career decisions. But it turns out their misfortune is systemic. And that is making people angry. "We are in a cycle of immiseration," Hanauer says. "People are pissed, and they have a right to be pissed."

How did companies get away with such an outrageous smash-and grab looting of workers? The story begins nearly a half century ago, in 1970, when the economist Milton Friedman published an essay in the *New York Times* magazine titled "The Social Responsibility of Business Is to Increase Its Profits."

That's a pretty boring title. But few documents have inflicted so much harm on so many people.

MILTON FRIEDMAN STOLE YOUR PENSION

Friedman was an economics professor at the University of Chicago and probably the most influential economist of the late twentieth century. He was a libertarian and free-marketeer, and he admired the ideas of Ayn Rand, the nutty novelist who wrote *The Fountainhead* and *Atlas Shrugged*. He served as an adviser to President Ronald Reagan, Margaret Thatcher, as well as other world leaders. In 1976 he was awarded a Nobel prize. He trained generations of economists who spread his ideas to other universities and business schools.

In his famous essay in the *New York Times* magazine, Friedman argued that people who manage companies should have only one goal, which is to make as much money as possible for their investors. CEOs should not worry about "providing employment, eliminating discrimination, [or] avoiding pollution," Friedman wrote. The top executives of a corporation were not free to do whatever they wanted.

Those executives were employees of the shareholders. If they wanted to do charity work in their spare time, with their own money, that was fine. But at work they were duty-bound to do nothing but generate the biggest possible return for investors.

By then Friedman was already famous, because in 1962 he had published *Capitalism and Freedom*, a global bestseller in which he argued that governments should stay out of the way and let the free market work things out for itself. Now, with his essay in 1970, Friedman was taking things a step further. Not only should governments leave corporations alone, but corporations should not feel bound to do anything good for society.

In truth, companies have multiple stakeholders—customers, employees, and society. The opposite of shareholder capitalism is stakeholder capitalism, which argues that companies should serve all of those constituents, not just investors. In a 2014 essay, Robert Reich, the former U.S. secretary of labor, points out that in the era before Friedman, stakeholder capitalism had been seen as a good thing. "Johnson & Johnson publicly stated its 'first responsibility' was to patients, doctors, and nurses, not to investors," Reich wrote. Reich cites Frank Abrams, the chairman of Standard Oil of New Jersey, who in 1951 declared that "The job of management is to maintain an equitable and working balance among the claims of the various directly interested groups . . . stockholders, employees, customers and the public at large." But here was the legendary Milton Friedman, soon-to-be Nobel laureate, saying CEOs need no longer worry about employees or the community. Those who did were "preaching pure and unadulterated socialism," he wrote. Socialism! *Gasp!* The horror! Friedman's doctrine quickly became accepted as the correct way to run a business. Indoctrinated with this ideology, a new generation of MBA students roared into the corporate world and became foot soldiers in the junk bond, leveraged buyout, hostile takeover craze of the 1980s.

Naturally, Wall Street loved the Friedman doctrine, since according to Friedman they were the only ones who mattered. For CEOs the Friedman doctrine also made life simpler. All they had to worry about was hitting quarterly targets and boosting the stock price. What's more, CEOs quickly figured out how they could benefit from this arrangement. All they had to do was tie their compensation to the stock price, and then find ways to goose the stock.

There were many ways to do that. Many, unfortunately, involved screwing workers. You could raid the pension fund, depriving people of money they had planned to live on in retirement. You could slash benefits. You could lay off workers and outsource their jobs to India and China.

Another tactic was simply to slash pay. Since 1970, the year Friedman published his essay, hourly wages for the average worker have grown only 0.2 percent per year, according to the *Harvard Business Review*. Normally, you'd expect wages to rise in lockstep with productivity. That's what happened in the United States from the end of the Second World War until Friedman declared his doctrine. Since, productivity has grown 75 percent, but wages have grown only 9 percent, according to the Economic Policy Institute. Middle-wage workers have seen even less of a bump, gaining only 6 percent. Hardest hit have been low-wage workers, whose wages have declined 5 percent, even as productivity has been soaring.

Unions at one time protected wages, but, beginning in the 1980s, unions went into sharp decline, partly because of legislative changes. Today, only 11 percent of U.S. workers belong to unions, about half as many as in the early 1980s. In the UK, union membership has fallen from a high of 13.2 million in 1979 to barely six million today. The labor movement was "the institution most responsible for working- and middle-class prosperity," labor historian Raymond Hogler says. There has been a cultural shift away from the collectivist instinct that fostered the labor movement. In a 2017 Gallup poll nearly half of the people surveyed said they expect unions to become weaker and less influential in coming years.

Then came the Internet, and everything sped up. It was like those scenes in *Star Wars* when the spaceship makes the jump to light speed. Companies that were already sold on the Friedman doctrine and committed to exploiting labor and pushing down wages now found themselves armed with an incredibly powerful new weapon: outsourcing. By the year 2000, we had speedy global connections, software that enabled free communication, and computers whose power was doubling every eighteen months. Information technology and back-office work shifted to India. Manufacturing moved to China. From 2000 to 2016, India's GDP quintupled. China's GDP grew from $1 trillion to $11 trillion. In the United States, over the same sixteen years, GDP grew 33 percent.

As it happens, I got an early glimpse of the outsourcing trend as it was taking off. In 2001, Jeffrey Immelt had just been named the CEO of GE, and *Forbes* magazine sent me to interview him. In those days, the Web was still in its toddlerhood. Websites were ridiculously primitive, and most people relied on sluggish dial-up modems. Yet Immelt could look a few years into the future and see how the Internet would improve, and how that would let him move jobs overseas. He told me with great enthusiasm about his plans to boost GE's bottom line by shifting most of GE's IT and back-office operations to India. "The Web is going to let us do a big redeployment of resources," he told me. "It's a big deal." We did not talk about where all of GE's laid-off workers would go. But over the next fifteen years, GE shed sixty-five thousand U.S. workers. The company seems to have especially targeted union workers, who made up about a third of the jobs cut. Today, GE's global workforce is almost the same size as it was in 2000, with about three hundred thousand people. But the mix has changed. In 2000, more than half of GE's employees were Americans, while today Americans make up only one-third.

As I mentioned in Chapter 2, the year 2000 once again marks an important turning point in a lot of ways. The number of people employed by the U.S. Postal Service peaked in 1999, at just under eight hundred thousand. Since then the headcount at the post office has dropped 36 percent, to about five hundred thousand, meaning today the organization is about the same size as in 1967. Manufacturing also took a weird turn after the year 2000. Jobs in manufacturing had been declining since the 1980s, but after 2000 the numbers plunge, with the U.S. shedding five million manufacturing workers, a drop of 30 percent, from 2000 to 2016.

YOU LOST YOUR JOB—HERE'S A GIG INSTEAD

Where did all those laid-off factory workers and clerical workers and middle managers and postal workers go? Some went into service-sector jobs, where employment grew 17 percent, from 108 million in 2000 to 127 million in 2017, according to the Bureau of Labor Statistics. But lately many have ended up in the gig economy, driving for Uber or running errands via apps like TaskRabbit. The gig economy is the second way in which Silicon Valley has helped drive down wages. Instead of hiring employees, companies use the Internet to assemble a workforce of contract employees. The shift to gig work was helped along by the Great Recession, which put 8.7 million people out of work in the US between 2007 and 2010—just as companies like Uber and Airbnb were being formed. The problem is that the jobs people lost had provided them with health insurance and some kind of retirement plan. Gig work pays almost nothing and provides no benefits. Apps like Uber might feel like magic for consumers, but the gig economy is not so magical for the people trying to make a living in it.

Nevertheless, gig-economy jobs represented 34 percent of the U.S. economy in 2017 and will hit 43 percent by 2020, according to software company Intuit, maker of TurboTax. Consulting firm McKinsey estimates there are sixty-eight million gig-economy "freelancers" in the United States, and that twenty million of them, or roughly 30 percent, have resorted to gig-economy work not because they find it appealing, but in desperation, as a last resort, because they can't find real jobs with better pay.

The gig-economy model is coming for white-collar workers, too. Gig-economy lawyers get hired on short-term contracts or by the project. WorkMarket, a New York start-up, runs online "on-demand labor clouds" of graphic designers, copywriters, editors, and computer technicians who get hired as contractors to work for big companies like Walgreens and are paid by the gig. Presto! These companies save money by carrying fewer full-time employees.

WorkMarket drives wages down by forcing workers to compete with each other for each gig; it's like a real-life version of *The Hunger Games*. There is huge appetite for this. More than two thousand companies hire contract employees through WorkMarket. The company has enlisted several hundred thousand workers and is growing at an 80 percent annual rate.

WorkMarket CEO Stephen DeWitt says his service helps companies operate more efficiently. "There will be a huge purging of old-model inefficiencies," he said in a 2016 interview. Who will suffer? "A lot of people. It's carnage," DeWitt conceded. But that's just how things are going to be. "If philosophically this scares you, I'm sorry," he said.

That *does* scare me. What some people think of as "inefficiencies" are known as paychecks and health insurance to workers. Just because the Internet makes it easier to replace full-time workers with piecemeal contractors does not mean we should do it.

THE RETAIL APOCALYPSE

A few chapters earlier I invoked the crisis in retailing, citing the demise of Toys "R" Us. It's hard to believe this now, but in the late 1980s and early 1990s, Toys "R" Us so completely dominated the toy-selling business that it was considered a "category killer," a retailer with such depth and breadth, and such overwhelming market power, that no new upstart could enter its market and compete. Toys "R" Us was a corporate Godzilla, smashing through local markets, putting little toy shops out of business, and bullying toy manufacturers into withholding products from its rivals, according to a 1997 ruling by a Federal Trade Commission judge.

But supermarkets started chipping away market share, and then came Amazon, a company that nobody seems able to compete against. By 2013 Toys "R" Us was losing money. In 2017 the company filed for bankruptcy protection, apparently hoping to restructure and carry on. Six months later management announced the company would shut down its remaining seven hundred locations in the United States—and put thirty-three thousand people out of work. Shortly after, all 106 shops were closed in the UK with over 2,000 redundancies.

This is what analysts call the "retail apocalypse." The first wave of Internet destruction targeted companies like Blockbuster (DVD rentals), Tower Records (music CDs), and Borders Books, as well as the media business, as readers ditched print newspapers and magazines for online publications. But that wave was nothing compared to the typhoon that hit the retail industry, starting in about 2010.

The thousands of workers who lost jobs at Toys "R" Us come on top of ten thousand workers who got cut from Macy's, and sixteen thousand who lost jobs when Sports Authority went bust. All told, more than one hundred thousand retail workers lost jobs in 2017, as chains closed more than eight thousand locations, according to *Business Insider*. As I previously mentioned, this has been a global phenomenon with a host of international casualties as well.

As bad as that is, things soon might get even worse. "If today is considered a retail apocalypse, then what's coming next could truly be scary," Bloomberg reported in November 2017, predicting that by the time the storm ends as many as eight million people in the US, most of them low-income workers, could be put out of work.

Where are those millions of laid-off retail workers going to go? People in Silicon Valley like to talk about "creative destruction," a term popularized by economist Joseph Schumpeter. In the happy-face version of how this works, technology kills old jobs, but it also creates new and better ones. Factory workers lose their jobs to robots, but then go to work at the company that makes the robots.

But millions of displaced retail workers are not going to get absorbed into Amazon. The online retailer employs five hundred thousand people worldwide, which sounds like a lot but is actually remarkably lean. Amazon generates about half as much revenue as Walmart, but does it with only a quarter as many people—which means Amazon generates roughly twice as much revenue per employee as Walmart does.

Even if newly unemployed retail workers could get jobs in Amazon shipping centers, they might not want them. You might imagine that since Amazon makes so much money with (relatively) few employees, the company probably pays those workers exceedingly well. Especially since Jeff Bezos, Amazon's founder and CEO, is the world's richest man, worth $140 billion. Can you imagine the kind of holiday bonus you must get when you work for the world's richest man?

Bah, humbug. Bezos is a modern-day Ebenezer Scrooge.

AMAZON, THE SILICON SOCIOPATH

Amazon's warehouse workers earn on average about 15 percent less than other warehouse workers, according to a study by the Institute for Local Self-Reliance, a Washington, DC, advocacy group. In Ohio, seven hundred Amazon workers are so poorly paid that they are receiving food stamps, according to Policy Matters Ohio, an advocacy group.

Bezos is not just frugal, or cheap, or a tightwad. He runs what many have called modern-day sweatshops, where human beings are pushed beyond their limits in ways that make Frederick Taylor and his stopwatch seem like Mother Teresa. Bezos loves data, but when it comes to actual human beings, he seems indifferent at best.

In 2011, a Pennsylvania newspaper reported that workers at the local Amazon warehouse were toiling in a building that lacked air conditioning, in temperatures that climbed above one hundred degrees. Amazon stationed ambulances outside, with paramedics to treat workers who keeled over. In June 2018, an investigation by a trade union in Britain found there had been six hundred ambulance calls to Amazon's UK warehouses in the past three years. One site alone, in Rugeley, received 115 ambulance calls, making it "one of the most dangerous places to work in Britain," a union officer said. "Amazon should be absolutely ashamed of themselves." The union said pregnant women had been forced to stand for ten hours a day and do physically demanding work, and that one woman suffered a miscarriage while working. Amazon insisted it was "not correct to suggest that we have unsafe working conditions," *Business Insider* reported.

Amazon employs various stratagems to drive down labor costs, like hiring through subcontractors and forcing workers to be "permatemps," rather than actual employees. The company also has squeezed down the cost of deliveries. It did this by adopting the gig-economy model, signing up part-time drivers who use their own cars and pay their own costs, just like Uber drivers. Amazon drivers get paid based on how many packages they deliver.

Amazon skins its white-collar workers at headquarters, too. Most tech companies grant workers options (or, if the company is already public, restricted stock units) and dole them out over a four-year period, so workers get 25 percent each year. But as journalist Brad Stone reports in his book *The Everything Store*, Amazon back-loads the grant so that workers get 5 percent after year 1, 15 percent at the end of year 2, and then 20 percent every six months for the next two years. You might say Amazon back-loads the stock grants to create an incentive for employees to stay at the company. The other explanation is that Amazon knows most people can't survive for long in its brutal culture, and back-loading means the company will pay out less. In 2013, Amazon had the second-highest turnover rate of any company in the Fortune 500, with the average employee lasting only one year, according to a study by PayScale, a company that tracks compensation trends.

As bad as the warehouse wages are, the conditions are reportedly even worse. Bathroom breaks are monitored and limited. Flat-screen TVs display images of workers who have been caught stealing or breaking rules, with TERMINATED or ARRESTED next to their silhouettes—"a weird way to go about scaring people," one worker told Bloomberg. "It's just letting people know that you're being watched," another said. Workers are surveilled and pushed to reach such high quotas that there have been reports that some resort to peeing in bottles to save time. In 2015 a British labor union complained that constant stress was making Amazon employees physically and mentally ill. Workers were pressured to be "above-average Amazon robots" and were "chewed up and spat out by a brutal culture," a union rep told the *London Times*.

Some Amazon workers in Britain were so badly paid that they resorted to living in tents beside a highway. One day in December 2016, just before Christmas, Craig Smith, a newspaper reporter in Scotland, was driving his Honda Civic on the A90 motorway when he noticed a few tents in a field, about a half mile from a big Amazon facility in Dunfermline. *Who would go camping in December,* Smith wondered, *when temperatures dropped below freezing, and in such a weird place?*

Smith pulled over and tramped down into the woods. "I turned up first thing in the morning, and basically 'knocked' on the side of the tent to see if anyone was home," he told me. The occupant told Smith that he worked in the nearby Amazon shipping center. He was camping out because he lived thirty miles away, and although Amazon provided transportation, the company also charged workers to ride the bus. The fare took such a bite out of his paycheck that he had decided to rough it instead.

"Obviously he wanted to hold down the job, and you can't blame him, though the harsh conditions would have stopped me," Smith told me.

Smith's front-page article in the *Courier* about the Amazon worker who lived in a tent quickly spread around the world, and sparked outrage in the UK. One Scottish politician calculated that after charging for transportation and imposing unpaid lunch breaks, Amazon was paying sixty pence below the minimum wage. "Amazon should be ashamed," he said. Smith's article quoted an Amazon spokesperson saying the company had created thousands of jobs and was paying "competitive wages."

Amazon could easily do better. In 2017 the company booked $3 billion in profit on sales of nearly $180 billion. The company can afford to pay warehouse workers enough money to live a middle-class lifestyle and enjoy a financially secure retirement. But it doesn't.

Amazon is not a scrappy, struggling start-up that has not yet turned a profit. Nor is it a fly-by-night tech sensation whose founder hopes to cash out quickly and scoot away with the loot. Amazon is twenty-four years old, and Bezos seems intent on building for the long term. The company is already one of the most important companies of the century, with boundless ambitions for gobbling up new markets.

Maybe Bezos reckons that eventually Amazon will operate without human beings, at least in its warehouses, so there is no sense in treating them well today. Still, there's something chilling about his relentless push to drive down labor costs, and his apparent lack of regard for human dignity.

When Amazon announced plans in 2017 to build a second headquarters, Bezos did not ask where he could do the most good or how he could help the most people. Instead, he invited American cities to compete for his business, asking who would do the most for him. More than two hundred cities, among them some of the poorest in the United States—Detroit, Cleveland, Cincinnati, Milwaukee—submitted plans. Hoping to land Amazon in the benighted city of Newark, the state of New Jersey offered $7 billion in tax incentives.

And so we were treated to a hideous spectacle: here were some of the poorest people in the United States offering to pay the world's richest man so that he might bless them with an office complex.

WAITING FOR THE END OF THE WORLD

Hanauer, the billionaire-turned-activist, was at one time close to Bezos. I asked him if he had ever talked to his old friend about paying workers better and treating them more humanely. "I took a crack at getting him to care about it," Hanauer said. Apparently Bezos wasn't persuaded. In recent years, "I have lost touch with Jeff," Hanauer said. He was reluctant to say more.

For years Hanauer has been trying to convince legislators to raise the minimum wage to $15 an hour, more than double the current minimum wage of $7.25. Even that $15 wage would not be enough to make things square, but it would at least be a start.

"If the minimum wage had tracked the growth of productivity since 1968, it would now be $22," Hanauer says. "If it tracked the top 1 percent, it would be $29."

The reason to give back the money, he says, would be so that the 1 percent can save their own skins. As Hanauer sees it, the election of Donald Trump might be only the first step toward something much worse. "People were hurting, and they lashed out—by voting for the guy who was lashing out, too."

If we don't shift wealth back toward workers and just keep carrying on the way we are now, Hanauer predicts we will end up in a real-life *Mad Max* movie: "If you don't give it back, things are not going to get better. Oh, dude, we are in for a bumpy ride. This is going to get way worse before it gets better. I think the country is in trouble. The West is in trouble. We have institutionalized a set of dynamics which benefit the few and immiserate the many.

"People are not going to get less pissed. People's lives are going to get worse. People are going to be even more angry and more polarized. The talk will get even crazier. Plan on violence. Plan on it. People do stupid shit when they're angry. It's not going to be good. I think we're going to have a lot of civil unrest."

CHAPTER SEVEN

INSECURITY: "WE'RE A TEAM, NOT A FAMILY"

On August 1, 2009, the founder and CEO of Netflix, Reed Hastings, published a PowerPoint presentation on SlideShare, a hosting website for slide decks. The presentation was a kind of manifesto, created by Hastings and his director of HR, Patty McCord, which explained, in 128 slides, the corporate culture of Netflix. Hastings and McCord figured the slide deck might serve as a recruiting tool. Instead, it changed the nature of work in Silicon Valley and shaped the way tech companies have treated their employees ever since.

One of Netflix's big ideas, and the one that has become the most famous, is contained in this line: "We're a team, not a family." With that line, Netflix ripped up decades of conventional wisdom about how to treat employees. The notion of company-as-family has become so widely accepted that it is almost trite. Treating workers like family might seem hokey, but it was the essence of the "HP Way," the culture developed at Hewlett-Packard, which for decades had been the Silicon Valley gold standard.

But here was Netflix, poster child for the Internet revolution, saying to hell with that. We're not your family. We're not your friends. We're a team. We bring in the best players we can get. If you get cut, too bad. The meaning of "team, not a family" is completely brutal: at Netflix you have no job security. Your boss can fire you at any time. You can be fired even if the company is doing well—and even if you're doing a great job.

The only thing worse than a diminishing paycheck is none at all. But this is the second of the four factors—insecurity. It's the new notion, part of the new compact, which decrees that no matter where you work, and no matter how well you're doing, your job is never secure. You might get fired because the company doesn't need what you do anymore and can't be bothered to train you to do something else. You might get fired because your boss thinks you are a bad fit with the culture. One way to be a bad fit is to "value job security and stability over performance," the Netflix code says. People who cherish job security "feel fearful at Netflix," and the company engages in a process of "helping [them] realize we are not right for them." In other words, the more you fear losing your job, the more likely you are to lose your job.

When you do get fired you're not supposed to get upset. In an interview on NPR, McCord recalled being flabbergasted when a woman she was firing burst into tears. "You're crying?" she scoffed at the woman. To McCord and to others who share her vision, a job transition, even an involuntary one, is simply a fact of life—a transaction, like switching banks, or changing from Verizon to Comcast for your cable TV.

Of course that is hopelessly unrealistic. The inconvenient truth is that most people, no matter how accomplished or how resilient, find it incredibly painful to get fired. Shrinks say that when we get fired we experience emotions similar to the ones we feel after the death of a friend or a loved one.

You know what's even worse? The fear that you *might* lose your job. People who live with the uncertainty and dread of losing a job end up suffering even more psychological harm than people who just get fired. Low job security correlates with all sorts of problems, including higher rates of depression and suicidal thoughts. Unfortunately, nearly half of us now live with that gut-wrenching, depression-causing, anxiety-inducing fear, according to Conference Board, a research group, which has been tracking workers since 1987 and found job insecurity on the rise over that period of time.

McCord and others like her would like to crank the stress up even more. Essentially they have created a real-life experiment in organizational behavior: what happens to the human lab rats if you make them live with constant fear?

The "team, not a family" notion is not McCord's only appalling innovation. In 2018 she published a book, *Powerful: Building a Culture of Freedom and Responsibility*, that elaborated on her vision. In her book, McCord explains that employees should no longer expect their managers or anyone at the company to help them with career development or acquiring new skills. The company doesn't have time for that. "Managers should not be expected to be career planners. In today's fast-moving business environment, trying to play that role can be dangerous," she writes.

A company also should not bother putting a struggling employee on a performance improvement plan and giving them a chance to get better. Instead, just fire them right away, McCord says. McCord also advises HR managers not to worry so much about documenting workers' shortcomings before firing them. Just get rid of them! They won't dare to file a lawsuit. McCord explains this in a section of the book with this very reassuring title: "People Very Rarely Sue." Good to know. McCord also devotes a chapter to "The Art of Good Good-byes."

In McCord's version of reality, people are not supposed to mind getting fired. You can fire someone, tip their life (and the lives of their spouses and children) upside down, and yet there should be no tears. Everyone should remain friends. She actually seems to believe this happens. In her book, McCord describes running into a designer whom she once fired and recalls how they had "a great catch-up" that ended with a big hug. "I loved her then and still do!" McCord writes. She seems to assume that the jilted designer feels the same way about her. I'd give that one a little more thought.

McCord peppers *Powerful* with stories about firing people and takes pride in how well she performed—the executioner recounting how skillfully she swung the sword, how quickly and cleanly she lopped off the head. There were "hundreds," she once told an interviewer, adding that she doesn't like the word *fired* and prefers to talk about people "moving on." Many of the people she "moved on" were doing good work. Netflix just no longer needed them. McCord didn't understand why some of them got so weepy about it. Why couldn't they just move on?

It's hard to overestimate how influential the Netflix culture deck has become. Since 2009, it has been viewed nearly eighteen million times. Facebook's chief operating officer, Sheryl Sandberg, once said McCord's code "may well be the most important document ever to come out of the Valley." According to TechCrunch, a Silicon Valley news blog, the Netflix code has become "a cultural manifesto for the Internet's economic epicenter" and a "crystal ball into the future of daily life" in the modern workplace.

Yet the whole "team, not a family" thing is obviously stupid and even more obviously a lie designed to dress up an appalling corporate policy—we're cruel assholes who treat our workers poorly—as something desirable. Netflix claims to be operating a "high-performance culture," with standards so high that many people simply can't measure up. According to the culture code, Netflix is "like a pro sports team," which needs to "have stars in every position." In recent years Netflix started saying that while a lot of people get fired at Netflix, "there's no shame in being cut from an Olympic team."

Good. Fucking. Grief. Where to begin with such overweening self-regard? First of all, this is Netflix. They make some TV shows and provide streaming movies over the Internet. They're not putting a man on the moon or tinkering with the human genome to find a cure for cancer. Second, the company has nearly five thousand employees, and many are customer support call center reps, some of whom make as little as $14 an hour. These are not professional basketballers earning millions of dollars a year or members of the Olympic ice hockey team.

For the record, professional sports teams do not, in fact, have stars in every position. Moreover, the best pro sports teams succeed *exactly because* the players feel like a family. Listen to members of the legendary Boston Red Sox squad that won the 2004 World Series: "The group of guys, the family, it wasn't just a team," says one. "We're a family, and you go to battle with your brothers," says another. Here's Tom Brady of the New England Patriots: "So many of the guys I've shared that locker room [with] are really my family." In fact, "Lots of great sports teams really do feel like families," says Sam Walker, an expert on sports and leadership and author of *The Captain Class: The Hidden Force That Creates the World's Greatest Teams*. Walker says the "family feeling" might not be necessary, but that "Most of the elite teams I studied were close. Teams that tend to overcome huge odds are usually really tight-knit."

Hastings and McCord may think their culture is great, but Netflix workers don't exactly share their opinion. On Glassdoor, a website where employees anonymously rate employers, Netflix garners a score of 3.7 out of 5. That's lower than Google, Apple, and Facebook, even lower than Ford Motor Company, Johnson & Johnson, Procter & Gamble, and ExxonMobil.

The desk jockeys at Netflix complain about a bruising environment with high turnover and rapid burnout. One call center worker wrote on Glassdoor: "Everything, from the time you spent in the restroom, to the time you spent on a certain type of call, is broken down to the second and charted. Honestly the most hostile environment I've ever been in." To be sure, some happy Netflix employees rave about the company. But the gripes like these stand out: "The amount of people who got fired for the FIRST THREE WEEKS I was there was unbelievable." "The culture document is really a PR document."

One thing that Netflix doesn't seem to value is diversity. Only 4 percent of Netflix employees are black, and only 6 percent are Hispanic, while 49 percent are white, according to Netflix's most recent annual diversity report. (Another 24 percent are Asian, 4 percent are "other/multiple," and 13 percent are listed as "unidentified.") In Netflix's "tech jobs" category—meaning the coveted engineering positions, which tend to pay better—only 2 percent of workers are black, and 4 percent are Hispanic. In the top ranks it's even worse. Seven of the company's eight top execs are men, and all are white. Netflix may be a "team, not a family," but if so, the team looks like the South African rugby team before the end of apartheid.

Despites its obvious shortcomings, McCord's culture deck has spawned a host of imitators, with dozens of companies creating "culture codes" that borrow Netflix's ideas—as well as its hubris and self-regard. Cambridge-based HubSpot, where I worked, created a culture code that plucked parts of the Netflix deck verbatim, including the "team, not a family" line. Spotify's code includes a photo of McCord and a quote from her—"Culture enables success, but it does not cause success." Spotify's version of "team, not a family" is a claim that to protect the company's culture, "firing is also crucial." Patreon's culture deck echoes McCord's language about "high performance" and says only "world-class talent" gets retained. Financial start-up eShares claims the company is "managed like a professional sports team," with groups that are "loosely coupled, highly aligned," a phrase from McCord.

Culture codes have become a *thing*, and it's an icky, stupid, pointless thing. As Tom Peters once told me, "As soon as you put it down in writing and put it up on a wall, you're screwed. That's not culture." Harvard psychologist and author of *Presence* Amy Cuddy talks about "insta-culture"—the notion that a company can make up a code, go buy a Ping-Pong table, and voilà—they've got a culture. Real culture takes time.

You can peruse dozens of corporate culture decks online. If you are going to read through them, you should consider putting on a raincoat and a face shield because you're about to get splattered with buckets of sanctimonious new-economy corporate goo. They all say a lot of the same things. They're a team, and managers are coaches. They like ethics, honesty, empathy, transparency. They are remarkable, adaptable, passionate, curious, and fearless. They are the best of the best, yet they are "ego-less" and humble. They celebrate success and learn from failure. They like freedom and hate rules. Oh, and finally: they're all unique. Every one of them. There's a name for this kind of earnest but mindless marketing guff: I call it *meaningfullessness*. The people who write culture codes have mastered it.

A problem with "team, not a family" is that when companies embrace this notion they sometimes start to take a perverse pride in firing people. Firing someone used to be (and still should be) a rare, unfortunate occurrence, a measure of last resort that both the employer and employee would prefer to avoid. But now at some companies firing people has become a badge of honor, even something to brag about.

Contrary to what McCord would like to believe, some people suffer terribly when they get fired. Trust me, I spent months reading letters from people who had read *Disrupted* and wanted to tell me their stories. No one, not a single person, felt sanguine about getting fired. They were hurt. They were bitter. They took it personally. Steve Jobs once said in a commencement speech that no one wants to die, and that "Even people who want to go to heaven don't want to die to get there." Similarly, even people who had been miserable in their jobs and wanted to find better work still felt angry and hurt about being fired. The termination might have come as a relief, but it also felt like a final insult.

And the pain can last a long time. People don't just bounce back and get over it. Twenty-something Xavier (not his real name) got booted after only seven months from a company with a Netflix-inspired culture code. He hadn't done anything wrong. It's just that the company hired a new vice president, and the new guy wanted to free up some headcount. "I have no clue why they hired you in the first place," the VP told Xavier. The VP probably never gave this another thought, but Xavier says the experience "was a crushing blow for me, not just professionally, but personally. It sent me into an unbearable depression I had never experienced before. For a year, I was reeling."

A woman I'll call Renata was fired from the same company after only five months. It was her first job out of college, and she had been hired to work as a recruiter. Ambitious and eager to get ahead, she asked for extra assignments and thought things were going well. But one day, without warning, her twenty-something boss called her into a meeting and fired her. The reason? "You just don't seem excited enough," the boss said.

Renata had no idea what this meant. The boss didn't offer to give her a second chance, or to help her do better, or to find her a different role in the company. "She told me that she was doing me a favor, because recruiting was not my life passion, and now she was giving me an opportunity to explore a different field instead," Renata recalls.

Her boss told her to leave straightaway, without even clearing her desk. The company would mail her belongings to her. She should just take her coat and go. She stumbled out of the building, wondering what had just happened. "I was confused, and panicked," she says. "In the short term I was worried about how I was going to pay my bills. But I was also panicked for the long term." She worried about how the five-month job would look on her résumé and how she would explain what had happened to future employers. She feared that maybe she was not cut out for corporate life. "I felt like a total failure." Months later, even after she found a new job, the experience of being fired and the way her boss had carried out the execution still haunted her.

THIS ISN'T A CAREER; IT'S A TOUR OF DUTY

One big and influential fan of the Netflix "team, not a family" model is LinkedIn founder Reid Hoffman, one of the billionaire oligarchs of Silicon Valley. In 2014, when Hoffman was touting his book *The Alliance: Managing Talent in the Networked Age*, he even borrowed McCord's language when he published an article in the *Harvard Business Review* titled "Your Company Is Not a Family."

Like McCord, Hoffman has positioned himself as a management oracle who can teach non-techies how to mimic the success of Silicon Valley. He takes the Netflix code and pushes it further, imagining a new compact in which companies can hire and fire at will, and where there are no "careers," only short-term gigs.

Some tech start-ups use job insecurity and the fear of being fired as a management tool. In this effort they have enlisted a powerful weapon: stock options. Most workers forgo part of their salaries in order to get stock options. Pick the right company, and your options might one day be worth millions. But you need to survive for four years in order to get your full option grant. Most of us dread getting fired, because it means losing a paycheck. Get fired from a hot tech start-up, and you lose more than a paycheck. You might be giving up a paper fortune. That pot of gold becomes a powerful incentive.

As the dollars get bigger, so does the stress, especially when employers take advantage of the leverage they've gained. In the hands of a bad employer those options can make people incredibly vulnerable to abuse and exploitation. That is reportedly what happened at Uber. For several years after its founding in 2009, Uber was the hottest tech unicorn in the world. Getting a job at the San Francisco ride-sharing company was like winning a golden ticket. But Uber's managers took full advantage of that. Uber became a toxic, stressful place to work, with bullying, allegations of sexual harassment, and a notoriously cruel culture.

"It's a money cult" is how a former worker described Uber to BuzzFeed in 2017. "People are putting up with massive amounts of abuse, mental abuse." Workers tolerated the punishing grind because they didn't want to lose their stock options. "The equity, people see that as their future, their retirement, the reason they moved to America, or why they moved across the country," one former employee said.

In Uber's culture of fear, employees were overloaded with work, forced to come in during the middle of the night to handle emergencies, and sometimes humiliated by managers in front of their peers. Some suffered panic attacks. A few were hospitalized, BuzzFeed reported.

For Joseph Thomas the pressure was too much. Thomas was a thirty-three-year-old African American software engineer who got recruited into Uber. Thomas thought he'd arrived in the promised land, but within months became so stressed out that he committed suicide. He left behind two young sons and a wife, who blamed his suicide on the stress of his job. "Joe was shutting down," Zecole Thomas recalled in *USA Today*. "He was broken. He would say, 'I feel stupid, they're all laughing at me.'"

Zecole Thomas hired a lawyer and filed a complaint, blaming the company for her husband's death. When newspapers wrote about the lawsuit, Uber issued a statement saying that "no family should go through the unspeakable heartbreak the Thomas family has experienced." It's unclear whether the lawsuit has been resolved. Thomas and her attorneys would not comment when I contacted them.

Uber execs might have felt bad about the Joseph Thomas suicide, but the company did not announce any plans to ease up on its stressed-out workers. In an interview six months after Thomas shot himself, Uber's chief technical officer compared working at Uber to the way diamonds are formed, by being "compressed with heat and pressure for thousands of years. Those who can actually survive and thrive from it come out as diamonds."

Good grief. No one in their right mind believes this is a healthy way to run a company.

JOB INSECURITY AND YOUR BRAIN

Anim Aweh sees the victims of these Silicon Valley sweatshops in her practice as a therapist in the Bay Area. "Some people here are making a ton of money, but their work is demanding," says Aweh, a twenty-seven-year-old social worker who counsels young tech workers. She works a lot with people of color, who face unique challenges in notoriously undiverse Silicon Valley. "They're told to work long hours. They're competing against one another. It's a rat race. One woman I work with said, 'The expectation is that you should just work hard, not work smart. Just do, do, do, do—until you can't do anymore.'"

Somehow a myth has arisen that Millennials don't mind job insecurity, that they enjoy hopping to new jobs and even *prefer* the "team, not a family" arrangement. Well, no. In fact, a "family feeling" is something people, Millennials included, say they *crave* at work. In a 2015 survey of 2,200 employees, most said they wanted to work for a company "with a family feel, held together by loyalty and tradition," though only 26 percent said they felt that way in their current positions. The desire for a family feeling wasn't just the old folks but was "a consistent choice among all age groups," according to the Chartered Institute of Personnel and Development, a UK-based professional organization for HR people, which conducted the survey.

Data suggests that younger workers do not "accept the new psychological contract," and that job insecurity "appears to be a significant stressor" for Millennials, Washington State University organizational psychologist Tahira Probst found. "Newer workforce entrants still desire job security, despite a decline in the amount of job security offered by organizations."

A 2013 Pew Research Center report found Millennials value job security and stability even *more* than Baby Boomers do. Nearly 90 percent said they would stay in a job for ten years if they knew they would get annual raises and the chance to be promoted. Nearly

80 percent said they would take a pay cut in exchange for greater security and stability, according to research by Qualtrics and Accel Ventures.

Job insecurity has always existed, but for most people it was a temporary phenomenon. Your company was going through a rough patch or had merged with another company, and there were rumors of "downsizing," and for a while you worried about losing your job. In the era of "team, not a family," however, job insecurity looms over employees at all times.

You may have worked for a boss who used fear as a management technique, presumably in the belief that a certain amount of insecurity keeps people on their toes and boosts productivity. That's rubbish, according to Tinne Vander Elst, an organizational psychologist at Katholieke Universiteit Leuven in Belgium, who has studied job insecurity for the past decade. Her research shows job insecurity correlates with diminished creativity, lower overall performance and productivity, and higher levels of workplace bullying. Workers who experience job insecurity demonstrate worse health, higher rates of emotional exhaustion, and long-lasting depression. They are more prone to accidents and injury, and more likely to have ethical lapses. They will put in less effort, say bad things about the company, and spend their time looking for a job someplace else.

What's more, scientists say chronic, low-grade stress may be worse than stress that is more intense but doesn't last long. Our brains are wired to deal with stress that is intense but brief, like escaping from a predator or fleeing from a burning building. We're not wired to handle chronic, ongoing stress, even if it is relatively mild. Yet that's what we get in the "team, not a family" workplace. It's a human version of the unpredictable chronic mild stress protocol that researchers use on rats, the one mentioned in Chapter 5.

Some pretty alarming things happen to our brains when we live with an elevated fear response over longer periods of time. The fear impedes our memory and can even damage parts of the brain.

Two brain scans done at Mayo Clinic show the difference between a healthy brain and a brain during a period of stress and depression. The healthy brain glows with activity, represented by big patches of bright yellow and orange. The stressed-out brain looks shut down, with vast regions of deep blue and dead black, with only a few scattered spots of yellow.

What happens when brains shut down? In Pune, India, a twenty-five-year-old software engineer killed himself and left behind a note that said, "In IT there is no job security. I'm worried a lot about my family." In 2016, in Seattle, a stressed-out white-collar worker at Amazon leapt off a building, driven to attempt suicide by fear of losing his job. He'd asked for a transfer to a different department, and instead his boss had put him on a performance improvement plan, or PIP, which usually leads to getting fired. After that incident, grieving Amazon employees took to an anonymous app to vent about the stress of living with job insecurity. "I have cried, worked all nighters and have had health issues because I was scared I will be put in PIP," one wrote.

WHAT GOES AROUND COMES AROUND

In a strange but satisfying twist, Patty McCord, the Netflix HR chief, became the victim of the code she created. In 2012, Netflix CEO, Reed Hastings, booted McCord, who had devoted fourteen years of her life to the company and did not want to leave. She barely mentions the episode in her book and doesn't explain what happened. "It was time for me to go" is all she offers.

I thought her own firing might have been an epiphany and caused her to rethink the "team, not a family" approach. Well, no. McCord admits that when she got fired, "I found the thought of leaving painful," and "I was not immune to the emotion of the situation." But the experience didn't shake her faith. She now runs a consulting practice, helping companies get that *Netflix mojo*. She has worked with J. Walter Thompson, a giant advertising agency; BlackRock, a giant asset management company; Warby Parker, online seller of hip eyewear; and HubSpot, the software company where I once worked and where I first encountered the "We're a team, not a family" philosophy.

The funny thing is that even though McCord and Hoffman espouse the idea that people should jump to new jobs a lot, neither of them has been eager to bounce around very much. Hoffman founded LinkedIn in 2002 and remained involved until the company was acquired by Microsoft in 2016. In 2009 he joined Greylock Partners, a venture capital firm, and has remained there ever since. McCord worked at four tech companies over the course of thirteen years, then settled in for a fourteen-year run at Netflix, where presumably she would still be working today had she not been fired.

Also, it's not clear that the "new compact" can create a successful, sustainable business. Hoffman's company, LinkedIn, grew quickly for a few years but eventually began hemorrhaging money and was acquired by Microsoft. Netflix's revenues grew 30 percent in 2017, and the company turned a profit, but Netflix also burns more cash than it generates. The company has obligations of more than $28 billion, some of it debt raised by selling junk bonds, a risky strategy that "recalls the dot-com era," as *Crain's New York Business* put it in a May 2018 article. Uber, despite its claims about a culture that produces "diamonds," stumbled in 2017, specifically because of its culture. After a string of scandals, the board fired Travis Kalanick, the company's CEO and founder.

THE OLD GUYS

Not so long ago it was considered admirable for CEOs to care about the welfare of their employees and their families. CEOs bragged about providing employees with steady, secure employment. Some companies paid employees more than they needed to, and gave people a chance to move up inside the organization. They created bonus plans and profit sharing, and offered medical benefits and pensions. Firing someone was a last resort. Layoffs were tragedies, and companies tried to avoid them.

I did a quick survey of books by CEOs from the last century. Their views on management and hiring would be virtually unthinkable today. In his 1984 autobiography, Lee Iacocca describes the shame and anger he felt when he was fired from a top job at Ford, and the even greater agony he experienced when, as CEO of Chrysler, he had to lay off thousands of workers to save the company from bankruptcy. The move came at "enormous personal expense for a great many human beings," he wrote.

Henry Ford, in his 1928 autobiography, *My Life and Work*, declares that creating jobs and providing as many people as possible with the chance to make a good living was the whole point of building his company. It wasn't about money, and it wasn't even about cars—it was about people. Ford built a trade school where kids apprenticed at Ford and got jobs there when they graduated, and he ran a hospital whose mission was to provide good care to working-class people.

Ford once had his executives make up a list of jobs that could be done by disabled people, so that he could create work for them. What jobs could be done by a blind person? By a person with only one arm? "My ambition is to employ more and more men and to spread... the benefits of the industrial system. We want to build lives and homes," he writes.

Thomas J. Watson Jr., the CEO of IBM, believed the company's highest priority was its "job security" policy, and boasts that for twenty-five years "no one has lost an hour's time in layoffs." If you screwed up at one job, IBM would find you something else to do, Watson declares in his 1963 memoir, *A Business and Its Beliefs: The Ideas That Helped Shape IBM*. "We go to great lengths to develop our people, to retrain them when job requirements change, and to give them another chance if we find them experiencing difficulties in the jobs they are in."

Bill Hewlett and Dave Packard served food at the annual company picnic for HP employees and their families. They were proud of the "family atmosphere" at HP. They bought land near the company's various offices for employees and their families to use for recreation—woods for camping in California, a lake in Scotland with good fishing, an area in Germany that was "suitable for skiing," as Packard recalls in *The HP Way*, published in 1995. In that book Packard publishes a speech he gave to managers in 1960, which shows the stark contrast between his view of the workplace and that of people like McCord and Hoffman. Here's an excerpt (I've added the italics):

> We have always considered that we have a responsibility to our employees to plan our work so we can assure job continuity. *We do not intend to have a "Hire 'em and fire 'em" operation.* At times it seems the most efficient way is to hire a group of people, work them as hard as possible, and when the job is finished, send them home. Well, even if this is the most efficient way, we have never operated in this manner. *We feel it is our responsibility to provide opportunity and job security to the best of our ability.*

Today's Internet oligarchs might say that the world has changed since those books were written, that the digital age demands different rules of engagement. I think that's rubbish, invented by people who for the most part have no idea what they're doing. The tools we use have changed, but human beings haven't. Dignity, respect, stability, and security still matter. The things those old-time CEOs understood about business and about people are as relevant today as they were in the last century.

Just look at the results. In their heyday, Henry Ford, Dave Packard, and Thomas Watson ran companies that were much bigger and more important than Netflix and LinkedIn are today. Even now, long after Ford, Packard, and Watson have passed away, those companies endure—and in fact make more profit than Netflix does.

Maybe those old guys were onto something. And maybe, if you're trying to build a company that can last a long time, they are the ones you should listen to. Instead of telling workers, "We're a team, not a family," you might consider being a team *and* a family.

CHAPTER EIGHT

CHANGE: "WHAT HAPPENS IF YOU LIVE INSIDE A HURRICANE THAT NEVER ENDS?"

F eel free to be skeptical," a man named Brian Robertson declares to an assembled group of about two dozen twenty-somethings and me. "Challenge me. Be skeptical, dig in, ask questions."

I am sitting in a meeting room on the second floor of the Wah Ying social club on Clay Street in San Francisco's Chinatown, a place with knotty pine walls, Chinese paintings, and an American flag. We are here for a half-day "taster workshop" to learn about something called Holacracy, a New Age management methodology that Robertson invented and which draws on philosophy, psychology, sociology, biology, cybernetics, and God knows what else.

This is June 2017, a few days after my play date with the Lego lady at the coffee shop in Menlo Park. I'd left the meeting believing that Lego workshops must be the nuttiest things that businesspeople could ever do in the name of workplace transformation, but I was wrong. Holacracy is exponentially worse. It's the closest thing to pure madness that I have ever experienced.

Change represents the third of my four factors. Everything about work seems to be changing, all at once, from *where* we work to *how* we work. The biggest changes involve new methodologies like Agile and Lean Startup. Holacracy is like a version of those things if they were put into a blender, mixed with LSD, and packaged by Charles Manson. Despite that, Robertson claims that more than a thousand companies have adopted Holacracy. Reader, I pray that yours is not one of them.

Robertson is thirty-eight years old. He wears a blue polo shirt and sports a shaved head and neatly trimmed goatee. He talks about governance, autonomy, and purpose. He believes in empowering people so they become self-directed members of emergent, self-organizing systems.

The word *power* comes up a lot. Robertson seems to be obsessed with power and how power gets distributed. He concedes that hierarchical power structures have served humankind for as long as humankind itself has existed and that it seems like a pretty good system.

Every government, every army, every university, and every corporation for as long as there have been corporations—they have all been hierarchical. Yet Robertson believes that when it comes to organizing a company, everyone since the dawn of the Industrial Revolution has gotten it all wrong. He wants to fix that.

In 2009 he drafted a forty-six-page "Holacracy Constitution," which has since evolved, through nine more versions, into the current thirty-nine-page document known as version 4.1.1. The constitution contains a preamble and appendices and Roman-numeraled articles that are broken into sections that in turn are broken lettered paragraphs that in turn have phrases marked with lowercase Roman numerals, producing things like "Section 3.3.6 paragraph (e) section (iii)."

The constitution describes rules, roles, and procedures; defines things like circles, domains, and accountabilities; and explains the "Integrative Election Process" (contained in Section 3.3.6) and "Integrative Decision-Making Process" (Section 3.3.5) that you now will all use from this day forward. On the final page is the "Constitution Adoption Declaration," which apparently someone from your company is supposed to sign, and which actually says the following:

> THE RATIFIER(S) SIGNED BELOW HEREBY ADOPT THE HOLACRACY CONSTITUTION, ATTACHED HERETO AND INCORPORATED BY REFERENCE (THE "CONSTITUTION"), AS THE GOVERNANCE AND OPERATING SYSTEM WITHIN _____ _____ (THE "ORGANIZATION"), AND THEREBY CEDE THEIR AUTHORITY INTO THE CONSTITUTION'S PROCESSES AND ENDOW THE DUE RESULTS THEREFROM WITH THE WEIGHT AND AUTHORITY OTHERWISE CARRIED BY THE RATIFIER(S), AS FURTHER DETAILED IN SECTION 5.1 THEREOF.

Whenceforth I had inspected Robertson's website and found this document and all parts thereof, including those attached thereto and incorporated thereby, I declared that I would herewith track down the author who had heretofore created this masterpiece wherefrom so much human misery and suffering might spring.

Seriously, what kind of madman writes things like this? Who sits down and writes a constitution?

But now I'm here and I'm sorry to report that in person Robertson is a bit underwhelming and not particularly charismatic. To be sure, he's a decent enough speaker and seems to have had some coaching. He talks the way tech CEOs do at corporate events, where they get on stage and try to sound conversational but it all still seems practiced, as if, during rehearsal, some public speaking coach told them exactly when to use that gesture, and which words to emphasize. It's the style Steve Jobs used, where he would pace around the stage a little bit, trying to seem relaxed and natural, adding in a pause here and there. But you could tell Jobs was just reciting memorized lines, and despite his best efforts he always seemed kind of stiff. That's the tone Robertson is going for. He knows his talking points and can reel them off from memory. He has probably given this same talk a thousand times.

Part of me feels bad for the guy. He wants so badly to be a management guru, and he really seems to believe that he has made a huge and important discovery that goes beyond companies and delves into something profound about human nature itself. It occurs to me that Robertson maybe doesn't just want to be a management guru; he might aspire to be a regular guru, a cult leader. He wants to be Bhagwan Shree Rajneesh, with a fleet of Rolls-Royce limousines and a commune of hippie followers who dance around like idiots while wearing orange underpants. He wants to be Colonel Kurtz in *Apocalypse Now*, living in a jungle with an army of disciples who would kill or die for him.

He's not going to win any recruits today, I fear. We workshop attendees sit at long folding tables, and everybody seems kind of bored. There's a guy from Google and two women who are finishing doctorates in management science at Stanford and are planning to start a company. There's a young couple who run a small brewing company in Washington and have brought along three of their employees. Coffee, bottled water, and peppermints have been provided. The whole thing feels a bit down-market, frankly.

A handful of cult members—employees of Robertson's consulting firm, HolacracyOne—hover around at the periphery, while Robertson runs through his spiel, repeating word-for-word some of what I saw him say in a video on his website. It's a good rap, and he's got it down.

Robertson first came up with the ideas behind Holacracy and inflicted them on the employees of a software company he had started. Eventually he came to believe that the management methodology was more interesting than the software company, and he decided that instead of selling code he would make a living by teaching people a new way to run companies.

Robertson wrote the "Holacracy Constitution" and in 2015 published a book, *Holacracy: The New Management System for a Rapidly Changing World*. The name *holacracy* comes from *holarchy*, a term from a 1967 book, *The Ghost in the Machine*, by Arthur Koestler, who was trying to figure out how the mind and body are related to each other and posited that humans are composed of things called holons. Each holon is autonomous but also part of a greater whole. As though he was preparing a stew of bad ideas, Robertson also drew on the work of Ken Wilber, a messianic fringe figure who created something called integral theory, which purports to be "an architecture of the Kosmos." Robertson also borrowed ideas from Agile.

Holacracy purports to be not just an epic clusterfuck approach to running a company but also a pathway to personal transformation. The philosophy begins with a single central idea: there are no bosses. No one has power over anyone else, but everyone has power. People work in self-managed, self-organizing groups. The organization is flattened, with no top-to-bottom structure.

"Hierarchy is obsolete," Robertson tells us. Hierarchical structures have the virtue of being stable and simple, but our culture has outgrown them and needs something new. The answer, Robertson says, is self-organization. "Think about the human body. The human body has hundreds of trillions of cells. But there is no boss cell," he says.

This makes no sense, but anyway, we move on. Robertson tells us he began his quest to reinvent work because he was once a regular employee and found the traditional work culture to be stultifying. As he speaks he clicks on a remote, driving a PowerPoint presentation on a screen behind him.

"I like to talk about my purpose in life," Robertson says. "My purpose is to show people a radical new way to organize power." As he says this he waves his hand—and the remote flies out of his fingers and skids across the floor. Whoops. Colonel Kurtz would never make such a blunder.

Ignoring the flub, he picks up the remote and presses on, explaining that the biggest obstacle we might face as we try to implement Holacracy at our companies is that we may encounter people who don't like it and push back against it. "Managers measure their value based on how many people report to them, and now they've lost that identity," Robertson says. "It's scary."

More scary, to me, would be working in a company that adopts this insanity and knowing that in order to keep my job I have to go through the brainwashing and pretend to become one of the pod people.

EVERYWHERE YOU LOOK: CHANGE

To be sure, Holacracy exists at the fringes of the fringe and will probably remain there. Chances are you won't ever get exposed to it, but it's very likely that you will have to deal with Agile, or Lean Startup. That process—constant change, new directives, managers who latch on to flashy ideas and then discard them—takes a toll on people. The workplace has already changed in profound ways, and over the next ten years there will surely be more management fads that bring wholesale disruption to workplaces.

Kooky management ideas are just part of the change roaring at us. We have a new compact with our employers, which involves jumping to a new job every two years and for many people that means having to take charge of our professional development and figure out a way to save for retirement—things that our employers used to handle for us. We have a new work culture that celebrates overwork, exhaustion, and stress.

Many of us are relocating to new offices, as companies abandon suburban office parks and move into urban locations. People who used to work remotely from home now must report for duty at an office, like those thousands of workers at IBM who have started schlepping into the company's new "Agile hubs." Even the physical spaces in which we work have changed. Instead of working in quiet private offices, we get crammed like cattle into big open spaces, with no privacy and too much noise.

Countless studies show that these nightmarish hellholes called "open offices" destroy productivity and make people miserable. Yet companies keep inflicting them on us, coyly pretending that the goal is to "foster collaboration," when really it is to squeeze pennies out of overhead by packing more people into fewer square feet of floor space. In an even more extreme approach, some companies no longer provide workers with a fixed workspace at all and instead relegate them to "nomad" status. You just show up with a laptop and roam around looking for an open spot where you can work. UBS, a Swiss bank, brags that this trick has enabled it to support one hundred workers in a space that previously housed only eighty.

"Fuck that, fuck you, fuck this, this is bullshit" is how a top Apple engineering executive reportedly responded when he was shown the floor plans of the company's $5 billion ring-shaped "spaceship" headquarters in Cupertino, California, and realized his group would be put into open-office spaces. "Fuck this, my team isn't working like this," he said. Because his engineers are vital to the company—they design the chips that power the iPhone—Apple built a separate building for them, where they would not have to use the open-office plan, according to John Gruber, a blogger with tight connections at Apple.

The open-plan arrangement isn't just unpleasant. Researchers say open offices can make people stressed out and physically sick. Open offices might even be harming our brains. A Cornell study found workers in noisy, open offices had elevated levels of epinephrine, also known as adrenaline, after only three hours of exposure.

Things have become so bad that even some companies that pioneered the open-office plan have realized the errors of their ways. In July 2017 I traveled to Grand Rapids, Michigan, to visit the headquarters of Steelcase, the world's largest office furniture maker. Steelcase doesn't just design chairs and desks. They also operate a research division that studies sociological aspects of work. A few years ago its researchers started noticing that the move to tear down cubicles and set workers free, which Steelcase had championed, had ended up causing harm.

"The pendulum has swung too far," says Donna Flynn, who has a doctorate in anthropology and runs the WorkSpace Futures research group at Steelcase. "Right now there are a lot of unhappy people at work. We're seeing the reemergence of people seeing the value of privacy."

Flynn says the answer isn't just to stick everyone back into private offices and cubicles. The office of the future, she says, will incorporate lots of different environments—open spaces for socializing and working in teams, but also individual retreats offering peace and quiet. Steelcase has partnered with Susan Cain, author of the bestseller *Quiet*, which celebrates the virtues of introverts, to create a line of products called Susan Cain Quiet Spaces. "We need to create new forms of privacy for people," Flynn says.

Flynn, who previously worked at Microsoft, says companies (and workspace designers like Steelcase) also need to do a better job of adopting new technologies so that people don't feel as overwhelmed as they do right now. Technology has started to evolve at such a rapid pace that people can't keep up, which is creating a backlash. "There is a big tension emerging," Flynn says. "We're introducing sensors, big data, virtual reality, augmented reality, and there is so much opportunity for these technologies—but at the same time there is a force pushing for work to be more human, to have more authenticity, more social connection. It's two opposing ideas. How are we going to resolve that?"

Technology should be a tool in the service of mankind, but sometimes it seems that humans are made subordinate to technology. And sometimes new technology that is supposed to make us more efficient or more productive instead slows us down and drives us nuts. Part of the problem is that we have entrusted tech companies to solve this for us, and while techies in Silicon Valley are wizards with chips and code, they can be clueless about humans.

Thanks to technology, we work longer hours, tethered to mobile devices and the ubiquitous Internet that enable us to be on call at all times, expected to return emails at night and on weekends and to work wherever we might be. Some companies now offer "unlimited" vacation policies, but paradoxically in such arrangements a lot of people end up taking less holiday time, not more. Some people never take a vacation at all.

Technology also makes it possible to push workers to physical extremes that people could not have imagined a generation ago. A friend of mine in Boston works as a McKinsey consultant and jets off each week to engagements in Asia and Europe. He often puts in over a hundred work hours a week, and logs 250,000 travel miles annually. Another consultant friend once spent months commuting from San Francisco to Rio de Janeiro. He, too, logs a quarter million miles a year and spends more nights in hotels than at home.

On the one hand, it seems miraculous that people can "commute" from Boston to Shenzhen or from San Francisco to Rio de Janeiro. On the other hand, I worry that human bodies are not equipped to handle this. Both my friends are in their forties. The guy in Boston says he loves this lifestyle, but admits he won't be able to sustain the job for more than a few years. The guy in San Francisco has been a consultant for twelve years and says, "I'm spent. I want to get out." He's married and has two kids, and notes that at his firm "Most partners are divorced."

WHAT'S YOUR TENSION? WHAT DO YOU NEED?

Back in the Holacracy workshop, Robertson asks for volunteers who will participate in some role-play exercises so that we can see what a Holacracy meeting looks like.

Imagine a dashing hypnotist declaring, on stage before a live audience, that he's about to put a group of subjects into a trance. He waves his hands, recites his magic words, and looks fiercely into his audience's eyes—but it doesn't work, and they don't go under, but at the same time they feel bad for him, and they don't want to ruin it for everyone else, so they play along and pretend to be hypnotized.

If you can imagine that, then you have an inkling of what happens next in this sad upstairs meeting room at the Wah Ying social club. As far as I can tell, Holacracy is bonkers. There are no managers, but there is a role called lead link, which is kind of like a manager, only it's not a manager, except that it kind of is. People work in "circles" and talk about their "tensions," while a facilitator (played by Robertson) decides how to resolve disputes.

"What do you need?" Robertson asks.

"I want marketing to qualify leads before sending them to me," says the head of sales.

"Okay, and do you have the right to ask for that? Let's see. No, you don't. It's not in his circle. So we'll have to add an accountability. Okay, head of marketing, will it serve your purpose to provide the head of sales with more qualified leads?"

The head of marketing looks puzzled.

"Notice that the question I'm asking you is not, 'Are you okay with this?' I'm asking, 'Does it serve your purpose?' It doesn't matter if you don't want to take it on. If it serves your purpose, you have to do it."

"Okay," the head of marketing says.

"My job," Robertson says, "as referee, is to ask will it serve your purpose, and do you have a right to expect something. If the answer is, 'No, you don't,' then we say, 'Okay, let's figure out how we can get you what you need.'"

Next role-play: the head of sales wants to lower the price of the product so he can sell more stuff. The woman who runs finance wants to keep prices high, to protect margins. Someone else says let's do market research and figure out what other companies charge.

"So she says 'Do market research,' and does that serve your purpose?" Robertson asks the head of sales. "It does, so that's what we'll do."

On and on it goes. Pretty soon people in the role-play meeting start getting pissed off. I don't blame them. Just watching them is making me want to jump out a window.

Robertson asks everyone how they're feeling.

"I'm getting annoyed," a muscle-bound guy says. "Does that happen in real life? Because I'm getting really annoyed with you right now."

Robertson remains unflustered. No matter what objection someone raises, he always has an answer, and the answer is always that whatever problem you have, you can solve it with Holacracy. I start thinking about whether this would work in the real world and imagining certain colleagues at some of my past jobs who would use this system to interfere with their co-workers—not for any good reason but just because they're assholes, and no matter what rules the company makes, they'll find ways to use those rules against other people. Robertson seems to begin with a belief that people are good and that everyone wants to get as much done as possible. Some do, but a lot of people spend their time trying to *not* get things done and trying to block attempts to load them up with more assignments.

"What happens if someone says they want something from a colleague, and the constitution says they have the right to ask for it, and it serves their purpose, but nevertheless the colleague just says no?" I ask. "What happens then? If the other person is supposed to do it but they just refuse? Can you role-play a situation like that?"

They act out the scenario. In the role-play, Robertson, playing the role of referee, resolves the dispute by telling the naysayer that she has no choice and has to add the assignment to her workload, and that settles that. Two thoughts: I'm not sure how this is any different than what happens in a regular company, where your boss tells you to do something and you have to do it. Second, I'd like to believe, as Robertson seems to, that once the referee has made a decision, everyone will live with that decision and follow the orders. But based on people I've worked with, I doubt that would be the end of it. What really happens, I imagine, is that the woman who gets stuck with a new "accountability" leaves the meeting pissed off, then spends a few weeks conspiring with her allies, and they all come to the next meeting loaded up with demands to inflict on the asshat who won the last round.

A woman points out that Holacracy seems like it might make sense in a really small company, but if you tried to scale the system up to work across a big company there would be too many complications.

"So does that make you feel tension?" Robertson asks. "Well then that tension is something you can bring up in a meeting. You can make things smaller, or consolidate roles. You see how I do this? When people show up with a complaint, you present them with a disarming question. You say, 'What do you need?'"

I do see how he does this. Whatever objection you raise, he just turns it back into a question for you. You simply cannot get a straight answer out of him. A boss who did this would drive you nuts.

In another role-play, we learn about governance meetings, where people "tell their tensions" and the team tries to solve them. In Holacracy, teams have tactical meetings once a week and governance meetings once a month. Each employee might be on as many as six teams, which means you could end up going to twenty-four tactical meetings and four governance meetings every month.

"Okay, so this is going to feel slow and clunky at first," Robertson says. "That's what happens when you're adopting Holacracy. People are going to complain that it's too slow, that everything takes longer. They'll want to go back to the old way of doing things." But you mustn't do that, Robertson says. "The process gets faster," he assures us. "Once you get used to Holacracy, you'll all get faster at it. It's hard. It's like when you're first doing yoga. It takes daily practice."

I've heard Agile experts say the same thing, that when organizations first adopt Agile they often find that everything is taking longer. Work feels gummed up. People get frustrated. It's all part of the process, the Agile gurus say.

This governance meeting follows a set process. First, someone who has a "tension" makes a proposal. Then people present objections.

The referee, played by Robertson, decides if the objections are con-stitutional. In my notes from this point of the meeting I write: *This is fucking nuts*.

In our role-play the proposal is that someone wants to let frontline sales reps set prices and change prices whenever they want. Right away, one guy has an objection.

"Do you see any reason that it does us harm, or moves us back-ward?" Robertson, playing referee, asks. "Yes or no. And I'm not asking do you like it."

The guy says yes, the proposal will harm the company.

"Okay, do you *know* that it will cause harm, or do you *infer* that?" Robertson asks the objector, in a game-show host voice. "And if the proposal would cause harm, would the damage be small enough that it could be fixed quickly?"

The guy says yes, they probably could change back if they needed to.

"Okay, so you just told me that this is not a valid objection," Robertson says.

Another woman presents a different objection, but Robertson says that objection involves something that can't be decided in a governance meeting; that objection has to be resolved in a tactical meeting.

The whole meeting gets logged in a piece of software, using pull-down menus and boxes that need to be filled out. The proposer, the person who has a "tension," has to write out the proposal and must start with a verb in the present participle form: changing, allowing, removing. Each objection must be presented as a statement.

A woman (I'll call her Lucy) says that her objection to the proposal is that the change they're considering might solve the "tension" for the proposer, but it will create a new "tension" for Lucy—in other words, fixing one problem will cause a new problem.

Robertson says that's not a valid objection. "You have to sit on your tension and wait for the result," he says. "If solving her tension is going to cause a new issue for you, then let's fix that. But you have to wait your turn."

There's also an "integration" step, where the tensions and the objections get reconciled. The meeting is "time-boxed" to either ninety minutes or two hours, Robertson says. And everyone has to get through their tensions, and all of their objections.

I cannot imagine sitting through two hours of this. Fifteen minutes has already started eating my brain. At this point in my notes I find the following, written in all caps: *I WANT TO FUCKING SHOOT MYSELF NOW. IF I WERE IN THIS MEETING FOR REAL I WOULD START SMASHING FURNITURE.*

Robertson claims Holacracy cultivates "a kind of mindfulness" and becomes more than just a way to get work done. "Sometimes it's a stealth tool for personal development for people, which I think is cool," he says. "It has helped people with their personal lives and relationships with their spouses." In fact Robertson says he uses Holacracy at home with his wife. "If my wife brings up a tension, then it's her turn to process her tension, and I help her resolve a tension. Then I say, 'Okay, now can we address one of my tensions.'"

Robertson's company, HolacracyOne, has twenty employees. Robertson has certified fifty Holacracy trainers who work independently. More than one thousand companies have adopted Holacracy. Small pilot programs are running at Dannon, the yogurt company; Ernst & Young, the consultancy; and Starwood, the hotel chain.

Robertson admits that the transition to Holacracy can be painful. When Zappos, the online shoe retailer, insisted in 2015 that employees commit to using Holacracy or leave the company, nearly 30 percent walked out. The ones who remained were so unhappy that Zappos fell off the *Fortune* magazine "Best Places to Work" list, where for years it had been a top company. "Employees were shocked and frustrated by the numerous mandates, the endless meetings and the confusion about who did what," *Fortune* reported in 2016. The quarterly all-hands company meeting became "a quirky mix of circus, therapy session, and revival meeting." People were "confused, demoralized, and whipsawed by the constant pace of change."

On Glassdoor, one Zappos employee declared that "leadership is insane and completely disregards employees and reality in decision-making, but parties are fun."

For all its hippy-dippy hoo-ha about empowerment and freedom, Holacracy turns out to be doctrinaire and authoritarian. Everyone must follow the rules, and there are *lots* of rules. Instead of reducing internal politics and eliminating favoritism, Zappos got more of both. People resented being put into a social experiment and treated like human lab rats. They hated that the system itself was more important than the people working inside it. "Zappos is struggling with Holacracy because humans aren't designed to operate like software" is how Aimee Groth, a writer at Quartz, put it.

Instead of admitting failure, Zappos CEO and founder Tony Hsieh doubled down on Holacracy and added a new concept called Teal, which was created by Frederic Laloux, a Belgian business guru and former McKinsey consultant. Teal isn't just a management concept. Its proponents bill Teal as—drum roll—"the next stage in the evolution of human consciousness."

Zappos employees get "points" and "badges," which sounds more like going back to school than leaping forward into the next stage of human consciousness. To survive, you must join enough "circles" to create the equivalent of a full-time job. If you bounce out of a circle you might end up talking to "why coaches" in the "Hero's Journey" team, or you could go to "Transition Support," to join a new circle, and if that doesn't work, you're fired.

Is this madness really what work is going to become? Robertson says the old traditional hierarchical structures won't work in the digital age. "In the 1950s the way we organized a company was fine for then," he says. "But the world has changed radically, even in just the past twenty years. It's breaking the way we work. It's straining it. That sends people looking for a new approach to running organizations. Most CEOs have an intuitive sense that there has to be a better way to run a company. They see Holacracy, and they feel drawn to a new paradigm. It's more dynamic, more lean, more agile."

It sounds great to be lean and agile. But I suspect that most of these ideas are not going to make any company perform any better. Recently I spoke to a CEO whose predecessor had adopted Holacracy. The first thing the new guy did was throw it all out. "Holacracy," he says, "is the illusion that the natural state of things is reverse entropy. If you just leave things and people alone, they will become more ordered and efficient. There is some cosmological evidence to the contrary."

The poor bastards who worked at the company had spent months learning how to work in Holacracy, and now had to unlearn everything they'd learned and go back to the old way, which they had previously unlearned. We're perilously close to entering a dystopian future where one nutty work guru leads us down one path, then another nutty guru leads us back up and down another, and where the only thing that all of the nutty gurus agree upon is that all of this change is good for us.

CHANGE AS PSYCHOLOGICAL MAYHEM

In the early 1990s, Roger Stuart, an associate professor at the Ulster Business School, in Belfast, Northern Ireland, conducted a study to find out how workers were affected during periods of "radical organizational change." Stuart and four researchers interviewed sixty-three managers from two large industrial companies in the UK that were going through big reorganizations and downsizing. They didn't interview workers who had been let go, but rather the managers who were carrying out the downsizing orders.

They were stunned by what they found. Though in their outward appearance the managers seemed fine, when they were alone with an interviewer, in two-hour conversations, they broke down and began to pour their hearts out. They revealed they were suffering tremendous psychological pain. The anguished interviews turned into therapy sessions. Some managers asked if they could come back again to talk more. Stuart and his team tried to accommodate them.

"For more than a sizeable minority, their stress, worry, angst and grief were revealing not just of the 'emotional hiccups' characteristic of transition but of the trauma more usually associated with disasters or catastrophes or even abuse," Stuart wrote in a research paper titled "The Trauma of Organizational Change."

While it might seem overwrought to compare a corporate layoff or reorganization to "having one's home damaged, one's possessions lost and members of one's family injured in an earthquake," Stuart believed it was a fair comparison. "In fact, in terms of individuals' thoughts, feelings and behaviours, both phenomena can be experienced in much the same way," he wrote.

Stuart's account of the study offers an extraordinary and terrifying look at human suffering in a corporate setting. He depicts a world where CEOs, under pressure from management consultants, business gurus, and academics, push employees beyond their limits. Tellingly, his citations don't mention the usual business pundits like Drucker, but instead include Sigmund Freud and Elisabeth Kübler-Ross, as well as Robert Jay Lifton, a psychiatrist known for his studies of trauma related to war and violence, and Robert S. Laufer, a sociologist who studied PTSD in Vietnam combat veterans.

The interviews with managers make for harrowing reading. Stuart finds it significant that many use metaphors from war. One describes "the grenade approach to downsizing. They throw a grenade into a room and blow 20 percent of the people out." Another recalls the pain of having to circle names of workers in red or blue, to determine which ones would be let go and which would be kept. Says the manager: "It was a nightmare. We called it gas chamber management. It will stick in my memory."

Stuart argues that workers got stressed out because in addition to learning new things they also had to *unlearn* old things. The goal of this "unlearning and relearning" was to make "a quantum leap 'out of the old' and 'into the new.'" Does that sound familiar?

Moreover, companies were careful to put in place safeguards against accidents and physical injury but were not paying any attention to the psychological harm they were inflicting on workers. Stuart recommends companies perform "psychological debriefings" and engage in what he calls "grief leadership." To make his argument more persuasive to bottom-line-focused CEOs, he says companies should do these things not out of kindness but because it will help their business. Unless companies look after the psychological well-being of workers, whatever benefits might come from restructuring will be outweighed by the cost of achieving them.

Of course no one listened. Twenty years later, in 2011, Gary Rees and Sally Rumbles, management professors at the University of Portsmouth in the UK, became aware of a new workplace phenomenon. Stuart had studied what happened to workers during periods of change, like a reorganization or downsizing. But those were temporary phenomena. The reorg starts, takes place for six months or a year, and then it's done. Rees and Rumbles saw that companies now were engaged in ongoing "change initiatives" that overlapped and blended into one another, such that "for employees the context of work is continually stressful and uncertain." Metaphorically speaking, Stuart had interviewed hurricane victims right after the winds stopped howling, but Rees and Rumbles were asking a different question: what happens if you live inside a hurricane that never ends?

They surveyed HR directors at one hundred local companies that were going through "change initiatives" and found that living with constant change was taking a tremendous toll on workers. More than half of the HR people surveyed said their workers were stressed out and burned out. The companies were suffering, too. They were not getting any net benefit from doing all this changing. Rees and Rumbles published their results in a paper titled "Continuous Change and Organizational Burnout."

In the summer of 2017 I tracked down Rees and Rumbles, speaking to them via Skype at their office in Portsmouth. I asked them if things had perhaps changed since they published their research. They said yes, things indeed had changed—the situation had become even worse. "There's been an intensification of work," Rumbles told me. "Companies are creating incredibly stressful environments."

They said they saw the effects of the stress on their own students. Many of them work part-time while attending university. But the notion of "part-time" no longer exists. "They're expected to be connected twenty-four-seven," Rumbles said.

Rees added: "People have always been busy at work, but this is different. This is not business as usual. There is so much change, and at such a rapid pace, that it creates mayhem. Today a big organization might run twenty to thirty change initiatives at the same time. That's the difference between now and thirty years ago."

An even more distressing change is that HR people no longer even pretend to be concerned about workers. Most of the HR people whom Rees and Rumbles surveyed said they knew workers were suffering, but they did not intend to address this. Rees recalled: "They said, 'Yes, we have problems with the amount of change, and yes, we have problems with burnout.' We said, 'So what are you going to do about it?' Their answer was, 'Nothing.'" Twenty years ago HR people would have at least pretended to care, he said.

Rees and Rumbles urge companies to rethink the idea of constant change. For one thing, a lot of the change is pointless. A survey of 1,500 executives found that only 30 percent of "change initiatives" produce any lasting improvement, Rumbles said. "It's just change for the sake of change," she said. Companies would be better off if they changed less frequently, and at a more measured rate, and put more thought into it. They should also put rest periods between each change. A corporate change is "almost like a bereavement," Rumbles said. New ideas are more likely to take hold if a period of change is followed by a period of stability.

Their biggest recommendation echoes one that Stuart proposed in 1995, which is that companies should simply bear in mind that their employees are human beings. That "human factor" should be weighed alongside things like productivity gains and financial results, and factored into decisions. "There is a need to convey respect," Stuart writes. "We need to make efforts to *contact our humanity* and allow it a greater say in our interactions and relationships with others" (emphasis added).

Treating people humanely usually means slowing down. That is exactly what two European business professors, Heike Bruch and Jochen Menges, recommend in a 2010 *Harvard Business Review* article titled "The Acceleration Trap." They argue that slowing down is not just a matter of being kind to employees, but also that when companies run too fast, they end up getting nowhere.

In a survey of ninety-two companies, Bruch and Menges found half were what they called "over-accelerated" and caught in "the acceleration trap," meaning they were doing too much too fast. One thing Bruch and Menges included was the way companies are adopting "new management technologies or organizational systems," things like Agile and Lean Startup. Bruch and Menges warned CEOs to avoid "the habit of constant change, or perpetual loading." Do less, they said. Give workers time to rest. Alas, over email, Bruch tells me that in the years since her research was first published, "the share of companies affected by the acceleration trap seems to increase."

I asked Rees and Rumbles if they saw any hopeful signs that work might get better. Their answer was depressing. "No, I can't see how this is going to slow down. In fact, I think it's going to accelerate. I think employers are going to get even more aggressive," Rees said. Today almost any job can be shipped overseas, and companies recognize the leverage this gives them. "Employers don't need to change. In fact, they can ramp it up even more," Rees said.

For thirty years researchers have been warning businesspeople that the stress of workplace change can traumatize people as severely as serving in combat, surviving a natural disaster, or suffering the loss of a loved one.

As huge as the technological shifts of the past twenty years have been, even bigger transformations now hurtle toward us in the form of artificial intelligence and robotics. Klaus Schwab, the head of the

World Economic Forum, says we are entering the "Fourth Industrial Revolution," when the rate of change will continue to accelerate.

The first quarter century of the Internet age has already pushed many people past their breaking point, making them "disillusioned and fearful," with "a pervasive sense of dissatisfaction and unfairness," Schwab says. But the future, as he describes it, sounds absolutely overwhelming: "We stand on the brink of a technological revolution that will fundamentally alter the way we live, work, and relate to one another." There will be change of greater "scale, scope, and complexity" than our species has ever experienced.

How disillusioned and fearful might we be twenty years from now, in a world that today we cannot imagine? As miraculous as the future might be, our brains might not be wired for it.

CHAPTER NINE

DEHUMANIZATION: "THINK OF YOURSELF AS A MACHINE WITHIN A MACHINE"

One day in July 2008, a fifty-three-year-old employee at France Telecom wrote a letter to his trade union representative. The worker was a satellite technician, but the company had assigned him to a new job in a call center. He hated the work. It made him feel "like a mechanical puppet." He had pleaded with managers to move him to another role, but they refused. He wanted his union rep to know that he could not take this job anymore. After sending the letter, he walked to a train station and threw himself under a train.

This man was one of *dozens* of France Telecom workers who committed suicide because of work-related stress from 2008 to 2014. To dispel any doubt, some left notes saying they were killing themselves specifically and solely because of work. The suicides happened in waves, which sparked an outcry in Europe and led to the resignation of the company's CEO.

This wasn't happening by accident. Most of the suicide victims were fifty-something engineers and technicians. France Telecom wanted to get rid of them, but they were civil servants, and the law said they could not be fired. So the company devised a new plan: it would make these people so miserable that they would quit. One strategy involved assigning employees to work in call centers. They were subjected to intense surveillance and forced to recite scripts, like "talking robots," one worker wrote in a suicide note. Professionals accustomed to working with freedom and autonomy now were punished for minor tardiness and had to ask permission to use the bathroom, according to the *British Medical Journal*.

The tactic was to demean the workers and dehumanize them— to deprive them of their human qualities. To treat them like robots. They were tethered to machines and expected to behave like machines themselves. To be sure, committing suicide was an extreme response. Why didn't they just quit? Why do some people crumble under this kind of treatment while others carry on? Each victim might offer a different explanation. More interesting, however, is what their suicides reveal about the nature of the work they were doing. Precisely that kind of work and those kind of working conditions are becoming more common. Think of people who get relegated to work in gig-economy jobs. Or people who fulfill orders in Amazon warehouses, racing around picking boxes off shelves, too busy to take bathroom breaks. Or the thousands of people living lives of quiet desperation in call centers—monitored, measured, and managed by machines. Some call center workers rarely interact with an actual human manager, and usually it is only to be rebuked because the performance-monitoring software has "reported" them for doing something wrong.

Even for ordinary white-collar workers, the modern workplace abounds with dehumanizing policies and practices, some trivial, some more profound. In my quest to understand the epidemic of worker unhappiness, I've come across stressors like dwindling paychecks, job insecurity, and constant, unrelenting change. But this fourth and final factor of unhappiness in the workplace— dehumanization—might be the most dangerous of them all.

Much of the dehumanization is driven by technology. Twenty or thirty years ago, when computer technology first entered the work-place, the idea was just to give people tools that let them get their work done more efficiently. We had personal computers running word processors and spreadsheets to help us complete tasks that once required hours of painstaking effort. Back then, we used tech. Today, it feels like tech is using us.

Computers have become unfathomably more powerful, pervasive, and intelligent. Technology connects the supply chain to the sales department to the accountants in the finance office. Tech tracks the humans who work in customer service and support—and in some cases just handles customer support on its own, without any humans needed. Tech tells telemarketers if they're hitting their quotas and warns them if they're falling short. Tech decides which people should be hired and which should be fired. The company itself can come to feel like a kind of computer, a big thrumming electronic machine that we humans get plugged into.

Hoping to save money, companies now automate every aspect of their organization, from sales and marketing to customer support. They are even automating HR, a department that actually has the word "human" in its name. Ask a question about how to sign up for health benefits, and there's a good chance you'll be talking to a chatbot. Send out your résumé when you're job-hunting, and it may be screened by a software program, not a human being. To get to an interview with a human, you first need to impress the software. As companies rely on ever-smarter "applicant-tracking systems," job hunters keep figuring out new "hacks" to beat the filters. Some even employ their own AI arsenal to combat the AI arsenal used by companies. A program called VMock uses machine learning and artificial intelligence to scan your résumé and tell you how to make it better. VMock tells you which words to use and which to avoid, and even recommends which fonts to use and how to format the document. By 2025 more than a billion people will have interacted with an AI assistant, *Wired* reported in June 2018.

How do corporate executives measure employee morale? That, too, can be done by machine. Instead of walking around and talking to people, managers today use apps like TinyPulse to survey workers about their happiness, apparently unaware that impersonal electronic surveys might be part of what makes workers unhappy. When I was working at a start-up, we were surveyed like this relentlessly. Once, we were asked what the company could do to make us more happy. "More surveys," I wrote back to the machine.

Even the most basic thing we do—talking to each other— increasingly has become mediated by technology, thanks not only to email and text messaging, but to newer platforms like Slack and HipChat. Have you ever seen two people at work sitting side by side, or facing one another, communicating via text messages rather than actually talking to one another? Apparently, a lot of us now prefer this. The problem is that the electronic tools that purport to connect us can also have the effect of making us feel isolated and disconnected from one another—"alone together," as MIT sociologist Sherry Turkle puts it.

Those are the small things, the "lite" version of dehumanization. The more extreme version is playing out in workplaces like Amazon shipping centers. There, much of the work is done by robots, but the company still needs humans for some tasks. The twist is that Amazon expects those humans to behave as much like robots as possible. They get few breaks and must constantly race to hit quotas. They perform repetitive tasks and are monitored by software that scores their performance and dispenses penalties for infractions. "The result is a work environment that is profoundly dehumanizing," according to a report by the Institute for Local Self-Reliance, a nonprofit advocacy group.

For white-collar workers, taking a job at Amazon means agreeing to be plugged into what one former employee described to the *New York Times* as a "continual performance improvement algorithm," a vast invisible machine that monitors employees, measures their performance, and doles out data-driven punishment. Remarkably, a lot of Amazon professionals go along with this. They subsume their identities into the system and become one with the algorithm. Significantly, they actually call themselves "Amabots."

AN AUTOMATON CLASS

Uber manages its three million drivers almost entirely with software. Why not? The company makes no secret of the fact that it hopes one day (as soon as possible) to get rid of human drivers entirely and replace them with self-driving cars. For now, the ride-sharing company treats human drivers as poorly as it can and keeps them at arm's length. Software becomes a barrier between worker and employer. To the driver, what is Uber? Where is it located? What does it look like? Uber is a black box. Uber is an app on a smartphone screen.

Drivers rarely talk to actual human managers at Uber, except when being recruited, and sometimes not even then. They answer to a software "boss" that tracks their performance and deactivates them if their score falls below a certain point. Software entrepreneur David Heinemeier Hansson says Uber drivers and other gig-economy workers represent a new caste of people—an automaton class, who are "treated as literal cogs in transportation and delivery machines." The machine—the software—is the essence of the company, not the humans. The humans are ancillary to the machine. We are meat puppets, tethered to an algorithm.

Companies first embraced the idea of using software to manage workers because it saved money. Now they've discovered a secondary benefit, which is that software can creep into employees' psyches and exploit their vulnerabilities. Uber uses software to manipulate its drivers psychologically, using tricks learned from addictive video games. The company employs hundreds of social scientists who devise behavioral science techniques that push drivers to work longer shifts.

This represents a new twist on Taylorism and the notion of management science. Software-driven psychological manipulation started in the gig economy but soon it may be coming for the rest of us. "Pulling psychological levers may eventually become the reigning approach to managing the American worker," the *New York Times* reports. Companies already use psychological tricks on consumers, hoping to get them to buy products.

Sixty years ago, the psychologist Erich Fromm warned in *The Sane Society* that the combination of capitalism and automation could create deep psychological harm, leading to widespread alienation, depression, and a kind of cultural insanity. "In the next fifty or a hundred years . . . automatons will make machines which act like men and produce men who act like machines. The danger of the past was that men became slaves. The danger of the future is that men may become robots."

During the early days of the personal computer and then the dawn of the Internet, a lot of people believed the growing use of technology would be good for workers. Technology would empower us and give us more autonomy and freedom. It could democratize the workplace and give rank-and-file workers a greater voice in how the company was run.

But some started to worry—including some who had invented the new ways of working. In the 1990s Babson College business professor Thomas Davenport helped create something called business process reengineering. This was a strategy for using computer technology to restructure organizations. It was supposed to be a good thing, but when corporations embraced "reengineering," they just used it as an excuse to fire lots of people. Davenport, who was seen as the father of reengineering, was appalled. He decried the mass firings as "mindless bloodshed" carried out by managers who "treated the people inside companies as if they were just so many bits and bytes." He called it "the fad that forgot people," and said he regretted his involvement.

Things only got worse. In 2005, another Babson professor, James Hoopes, warned that technology "can be used not only to liberate human beings but to control them," and fretted that as managers relied more on technology, employees were being dehumanized. In 2018 I wrote to Hoopes and asked him where things stand now. "My worst fears are becoming realized," he replied. "But now I'd say it goes beyond the dehumanized employee to the dehumanized customer as well."

When I visited Hoopes at his office on the Babson campus outside Boston, he said he has become disappointed in how companies have used information technology to automate customer service and are forcing customers to interact with computer systems. They're also using technology to track how customers use products and gather information about them. But the biggest letdown stems from how technology gets turned against employees. "I would like to see information technology that was put at the service of employees, as a way to make work better, rather than information technology being put at the service of management to make work more efficient," he told me.

There is a lot of research about the harm caused by dehumanization in the workplace. For one thing, it leads to bullying and harassment. It may contribute to mental illnesses such as depression, anxiety, and stress-related disorders. It can cause "pervasive feelings of sadness and anger," and "leave its victims feeling degraded, invalidated, or demoralized," according to a 2014 study by Kalina Christoff, a psychology professor at University of British Columbia in Vancouver. Another study found that dehumanized workers feel shame and guilt, while also demonstrating diminished cognition.

There's one aspect of modern work that is especially harmful, and that's the ever-increasing use of electronic surveillance. Privacy laws make it illegal for the state to spy on us in most Western countries. (Supposedly, anyway.) But employers are bound by no such restriction in the US. And despite stronger privacy protection in the EU, the situation is not much better. You're an employee at will. They can snoop on you as much as they want. And they do— more and more each year.

AT WORK IN THE PANOPTICON

In the eighteenth century, British philosopher Jeremy Bentham designed an ingenious prison in which a single guard could control a large number of inmates. It was a circular building where a guard sat in a central tower and prisoners were placed in cells around the periphery. A viewing mechanism enabled the guard to watch any prisoner at any time. Since prisoners could not tell when they were being watched, they would have to assume that they were always being watched. Therefore they would behave. Instead of needing an army of prison guards, you could exploit the psychology of the inmates and get them to control themselves. Bentham called this the panopticon, from Greek roots meaning, roughly, "to see all."

The idea didn't really fly as a way to build prisons, but it is often used as a metaphor about power and control in modern society, most notably by French philosopher Michel Foucault. Researchers who study workplace surveillance often cite Foucault's work when they discuss the "panoptic effect" that surveillance exerts on employees.

Today electronic surveillance at work has become nearly ubiquitous and is enabled by an array of powerful tools. "Electronic performance-monitoring" systems track punctuality, break time, idle time—pretty much everything you do at work. Employers snoop through our email, most often using algorithms to scan for keywords but sometimes by having actual humans read through the messages. In 2007, an American Management Association survey found that 40 percent of companies had human beings reading through employee email. Keep that in mind next time you feel the urge to fire off a message bashing your CEO to a work buddy.

Companies monitor our social media activity, too. Some even spy on us through the cameras in our computers. They listen to and record our phone calls, and they track our location with ID badges, wristbands, and mobile phones. A Wisconsin company called Three Square Market has put RFID implants into employees' hands so they can swipe into the building just by waving their hand. Some collect biometric information about workers, like their voiceprints, iris scans, and fingerprints. A common application is requiring fingerprints for "time and attendance" systems, making employees prove when they clock in and clock out.

In Illinois, dozens of employers, including Intercontinental Hotels, are facing lawsuits from employees whose fingerprints were gathered and who claim the practice violated an Illinois law about biometric privacy. Companies also use voice biometrics with customers, with banks like Vanguard using voiceprints to authenticate account holders. Nuance Communications, which sells voice biometric technology, claims to have collected voiceprints from three hundred million people, who perform more than five billion authentications annually. In addition to gathering biometrics, companies also feel free to peer into our brains, subjecting workers to personality training and figuring out how to push their buttons. According to the *Wall Street Journal*, some organizations, like SPS Companies, a steel processor, now use AI-based tools to evaluate employee surveys and figure out how people really feel about work—as opposed to what they say.

Companies claim surveillance is necessary, that it boosts productivity and prevents theft, for example. But many companies plunge ahead just because the allure of new technology becomes impossible to resist. Those companies don't need a cost-benefit analysis, but "monitor their employees simply because they can," one study said. The same study argues that whatever benefits employers might gain from surveillance may be outweighed by the harm caused to workers.

The damage is significant. Surveillance creates a toxic and demoralizing environment, a digital sweatshop filled with stress, anxiety, depression, fatigue, anger, and even loss of identity. When the US National Association of Working Women surveyed female call center workers about surveillance in the 1980s, women frequently described their feelings about surveillance using images of rape or sexual abuse. Another study found a spike in health problems. In a survey done at AT&T comparing monitored to unmonitored clerical workers performing similar tasks, monitored workers reported significantly more physical ailments, like stiff necks, sore wrists, and numb fingers, as well as "racing or pounding heart" and acid indigestion.

Surveillance "can have a profound effect on employees' sense of dignity, their sense of freedom, and their sense of autonomy," Jennifer

Stoddart, the privacy commissioner of Canada, warned in a 2006 speech. "The working world of the future could be a very scary place if we don't hold the line on increasingly pervasive monitoring."

Now, as I write this twelve years later, we are surveilled in ways Stoddart could not have fathomed. Much of the surveillance technology comes from Silicon Valley. Tech companies also are among the most aggressive users of surveillance, tracking emails, chats, instant messaging, website visits. "It's horrifying how much they know," a former Facebook employee, who got fired for leaking information to a reporter, told the *Guardian*. Facebook employs a team of secret police, known internally as "rat-catchers," who hunt down workers suspected of leaking confidential information. "If anyone steps out of line, they'll squash you like a bug," the fired Facebook employee told the *Guardian*.

Apple reportedly plants moles throughout the organization to spy on workers—employees call them the "Apple Gestapo." Google and Amazon encourage employees to snitch on co-workers. Amazon even provides a software tool to make snitching easier. Workday, a Silicon Valley software maker, delivers a similar snitching tool as part of its bundle of HR programs, used by more than two thousand companies.

Many tech companies run a modern-day version of an old-fashioned sales boiler room—vast call centers where hundreds of workers, usually recent college graduates, bang away on phones, calling dozens of people every day. Basically, they're telemarketers. For some, the work can be soul-destroying, especially because of the way workers are monitored and surveilled.

Six months after graduating from a big California university with a humanities degree, a woman I'll call Athena got hired by Yelp, the online review website. She went in feeling excited to be working at a cool tech company with video games and a beer garden in a hip part of San Francisco, but almost immediately became disillusioned.

Her every move was monitored by software. Her calls were recorded. "I hated having to repeat the same task every two minutes for eight hours a day. It was dehumanizing. I became depressed. I would come home and go to sleep at eight o'clock. I started to dread going to work." She lasted about a month, just long enough to get her first (bad) performance review. "It was an incredible disappointment, a terrible experience," she says.

TAKE A SEAT. THE ROBOT WILL BE RIGHT WITH YOU.

The next time you look for a job, your first interview might not be with a human being—but with an AI-powered software system.

Instead of talking to a recruiter from the HR department, you sit in front of a computer, or even your smartphone, and answer questions that pop up on the screen. You use your device's camera to record your responses on video. You might also be asked to solve a puzzle or play a game. The whole thing takes about ten minutes. When you're finished, artificial intelligence algorithms zip through your video, sizing up how well you speak, which words you use, and even evaluating your tiniest facial expressions. Are you smiling? Blinking? Raising your eyebrows a lot? If the robot recruiter deems you worthy of actual human attention, you will be passed on to the next round of interviews. Fail to impress the software, and you'll receive a nice thank-you note.

This sounds like science fiction, even perhaps like the Voight-Kampff test from *Blade Runner*, the one used to identify replicants by asking them questions. But this stuff is happening today. A Utah tech company called HireVue provides this service to more than a hundred companies, including Unilever and Hilton Worldwide.

Companies like the AI system because it lets them look at far more job candidates—ten times as many as they might see using the old-fashioned in-person approach, HireVue claims. They also can zip through a lot of candidates in less time. At Hilton, the average "time to hire" went from six weeks to five days after the hotel chain started using HireVue's AI interview system. Another driver is diversity. Computers supposedly don't have unconscious bias that humans bring to the table. HireVue claims the software does a better job of picking job candidates than a human recruiter.

HireVue has been in business since 2004. At first the company provided a service that lets companies interview job candidates by recorded video. That saved companies money because they didn't have to send recruiters to college campuses to conduct first-round interviews. That also meant companies could look at a lot more candidates from more campuses. "It lets them really open up the aperture much wider," HireVue CEO Kevin Parker says.

But there was still a bottleneck. Human recruiters still had to look at all the videos, and there is only so much they can do. Sure, they could fast-forward through videos and make decisions. But to scale up even more, "We started asking, how can we use technology to take the place of what humans are doing?" Parker says.

HireVue assembled a team of data scientists and industrial and organizational psychologists, who took existing science on things like "facial action units" and encoded it into software. In 2016, HireVue began offering this service to its customers.

HireVue has more than seven hundred clients, including Nike, Intel, Honeywell, and Delta Airlines. Only about a hundred are using the AI-powered assessment service, though Parker says that part of the business is growing rapidly. So far, HireVue's AI system has evaluated more than a half million videos.

One HireVue client, a big bank, reviews a thousand videos each day. HireVue's business is taking on scale that previously would have been unimaginable. In the company's first twelve years it recorded a total of four million videos. Today HireVue records that many in a year. And this is just the beginning. A decade from now this stuff will be routine and commonplace, Parker says.

This brave new world means job seekers must learn a new set of skills. Consultants are already springing up to teach students how to impress their robot overlords. "The big challenge of the talk-to-the-box interview, or the AI interview, is that you can't get any feedback on whether what you're saying is interesting to the interviewer or not," says Derek Walker, course director at Finito Education, a London consultancy that offers career training and has started coaching new college graduates on how to do well in AI-based interviews.

All of the nonverbal give-and-take of a human-to-human interview goes away. For most people that can be really disconcerting. "This is completely alien to us as human beings," Walker says. "We're used to going back and forth, building rapport, and you can't do that with a box. So it's difficult to feel comfortable. Certain people find this a very nerve-wracking and disturbing experience."

It's so disconcerting that some good job candidates might get passed over because they don't perform well, he says. The trick is to practice. Walker works mostly with recent college graduates, helping them learn to feel comfortable in front of the camera.

Walker has spent thirty years in recruiting, including stints at Merrill Lynch, Barclays, and Saïd Business School at Oxford University, and for most of that time the field has remained largely the same. AI-based interviewing "is the first real major innovation for quite a long time," he says.

Today AI-based job candidate assessments are a novelty, but in a decade or two they could well be routine. There's a scary implication to this. HireVue's system can work up a rich profile of a job candidate and even evaluate their personality, by asking questions that measure traits like empathy. On top of that, HireVue recently acquired MindX, which uses psychometric games and puzzles to gauge someone's cognitive abilities. They can estimate your IQ and other reasoning abilities. In theory the system can infer things that you are not even aware of. It might know more about you than you know yourself.

This raises issues about the kind of information being gathered and who has control over that information. In 2017 and 2018 Facebook came under fire after revealing that companies like Cambridge Analytica in Britain had used online puzzles and quizzes to glean psychographic information about millions of Facebook users, and then employed that insight to manipulate people with targeted political ads.

They were using stupid little Facebook quizzes. Imagine how much more information you reveal about yourself in a job interview. HireVue's robot recruiting system is building a database of deep, rich psychographic information on millions of people. Moreover, the data is not anonymous. Your psychographic blueprint is connected to all of your personal information—name, address, email, phone number, work history, education. And they have you on video. Everything you say in an interview can follow you around for the rest of your life. If the AI determines that you're "not competitive" or "too independent," or have only "average intelligence," will this rule you out from certain jobs forever? If you slip and use the word *damn*, will the system mark you out as vulgar?

Parker says HireVue collects a lot of information, "but we safeguard it. We're very careful about that." HireVue stores the information but doesn't own it. The information is owned by the clients who pay HireVue for its service. "We never use it for any other purpose other than to help someone get an interview and a job," Parker says.

Fair enough. But the potential exists for this data to be compiled, sifted, sold, shared, stolen, and used in ways that we can't imagine. Will people even realize, when they sit down to apply for that bank teller job, what they are actually giving up? Even if they are aware, what choice will they have? Will they not apply for the job? Giving up privacy could become the price people pay to enter the workforce. Getting hired could mean letting Skynet delve into the deepest recesses of your psyche and figure out your IQ, your personality type, and all your quirks and foibles. A complete psychographic profile of you exists—the blueprint of your brain, every inch of your wiring—and you have no control over it. Apply for another job, and the system adds to your profile. Over the years, your profile becomes richer and more granular. Can you imagine what that information would be worth to a political party, or certain government agencies? And what they might do with it?

The whole process of recruiting and evaluating and hiring used to be haphazard and half-assed, with information strewn across different systems and kept in paper files. It's messy, but that messiness of the analog world was basically what we called privacy. Soon thousands of companies will be gathering profiles on millions of people. Anyone who gets that data can figure out what makes those people tick. We worry a lot, and rightly so, about humans being replaced by machines and about jobs being killed by automation. We also should worry about the humans who will have to work alongside artificial intelligence.

The machines determine who gets hired and sometimes (as at Uber) who gets fired. What will this do to humans, as a species? In the journey from analog to digital work, we are being pushed into bargains that we may not fully comprehend. In our quest to gain efficiency, to boost productivity, to do more with less, we may give up something much greater in exchange.

YOUR NEXT BOSS MAY BE A COMPUTER

Ray Dalio is the founder of Bridgewater Associates, the world's largest hedge fund. He's one of the richest people in the world. And if Dalio has his way, your next boss might be a computer. For several years Dalio has been trying to develop an AI-powered "automated management system" that could render human managers, with their gut instincts and "World's Greatest Boss" mugs, obsolete. The system is based on concepts and processes—known internally as the "Principles"—that Dalio uses to run Bridgewater. It's "like trying to make Ray's brain into a computer," an insider told the *Wall Street Journal*. The project is being led by computer scientist David Ferrucci, who helped create IBM's Watson artificial intelligence system, and has had various code names, including the Book of the Future, the One Thing, and the Principles Operating System, or PriOS.

Hedge funds like Bridgewater already rely on AI systems to make stock trading decisions. Teaching machines to make business decisions seems like the next logical step. In 2017, Dalio told *Business Insider* he expected to have a "thorough version" of PriOS running at Bridgewater by 2020. He compares PriOS to a GPS navigation system. Just as your GPS tells you where to make the next turn, PriOS will tell managers which decisions to make, like when to hire or fire someone, or even when to make a certain phone call, *Vanity Fair* reported in 2017. Dalio wants to share his invention with the world and told Bloomberg in 2017 that tech companies were eager to get their hands on it.

Using software to manage a company may not be so far-fetched. Even top executives might be replaceable, say researchers at Silicon Valley's Institute for the Future, who a few years ago coded up software called iCEO that could do the job of a big-company CEO. Devin Fidler, one of the researchers, wrote about the project for the *Harvard Business Review* in 2015 and warned, ominously, "It will not be possible to hide in the C-suite much longer."

Whether this will be good or bad depends a lot on who programs the AI and sets its parameters. Dalio wants to replicate in software the brutal, combative culture that he created at Bridgewater. For most of us that would be a nightmare. Even in the nasty world of hedge funds, the cult-like Bridgewater has earned a reputation for shocking levels of nastiness. "A cauldron of fear and intimidation" is how one former employee described the hedge fund in a complaint to a state labor board.

Dalio forces all Bridgewater employees to undergo psychometric testing. (He loves testing. When his kids were little, he had them psychometrically tested as well, to get "a road map for how they would develop over the years.") Security guards roam the halls. There are cameras everywhere. All meetings are recorded. People carry iPads with an app that lets them constantly critique each other using "dots"—live, on the fly, during every meeting— while an algorithm gathers up all the dots from all the meetings and generates a profile of each person's personality, which is used to assign them to particular jobs. Employees are encouraged to criticize each other and rat each other out. Some people are badgered to tears. "If there was a hell this would be it," says one Glassdoor commenter, adding that "it's a cult, basically," and a "human being experiment."

Working for the real-life Dalio sounds awful enough. But the AI-replicated version of him could be even worse. Imagine putting this clusterfuck of a culture into an AI-powered computer, then giving that computer to the nitwits you work for today and letting them run wild with it, and you have an idea of the kind of future that Ray Dalio wants the rest of us to inhabit.

It's amazing to me that anyone takes Dalio seriously in the first place. But the guy has a net worth of nearly $18 billion—he once earned $4 billion *in a single year*—and when you're worth that kind of coin, people listen to you. In 2017, Dalio published a memoir, *Principles*, which lays out his philosophy about life and work. The book has been a massive global bestseller.

In the book Dalio embraces the metaphor of man as a machine—but unlike, say, the philosopher Erich Fromm, who envisioned men behaving like machines but considered this a nightmarish abomination, Dalio thinks it's great. "Think of yourself as a machine within a machine," he intones. If you're managing people, imagine that you're operating a machine, trying to get the best outcome, he advises.

Principles grew out of a hundred-page manifesto, also called "Principles," that is given to all Bridgewater employees and contains 227 principles for becoming a better person. *New York* magazine once said the manifesto read as if "Ayn Rand and Deepak Chopra had collaborated on a line of fortune cookies."

The book's title also flicks at the notion of being "principled," which is not something you usually associate with hedge fund managers. The tome is nearly six hundred pages long, and it's only the first of a two-volume set Dalio plans. Clearly this man has a lot on his mind. To get a sense of how Dalio sees himself, consider that on page 2 of *Principles*, by way of explaining why he wrote the book,

Dalio says he wishes that Einstein and Churchill and Leonardo da Vinci had written down their "principles," too.

Dalio is a hero in a certain circle of finance and consulting professionals, but it's too early to say how ideas like his will play out in the wider world. Even if he fails to create an AI-powered boss, someone else will probably figure out how to manage people with computers.

The potential downsides are obvious—and in some cases, they are already happening. Consider the case of Ibrahim Diallo, a thirty-one-year-old software programmer in Los Angeles who lost his job when his employer's software system went haywire. The software determined that Diallo had been terminated. His manager knew this wasn't the case. But "the machine" kept shutting down the ID badge Diallo used to enter the building. It also prevented him from logging into his computer. Diallo's manager escalated the situation to a director. The director sent email to HR—and received back a computer-generated email saying Diallo was not a valid employee. Security guards escorted Diallo out of the building. "At first I was laughing. It was confusing and funny at the same time," Diallo told me.

It took three weeks to sort things out. Diallo returned to work but left the company a few months later. He says the experience taught him something: "Automation can be an asset, but there needs to be a way for humans to take over if the machine makes a mistake." The incident also revealed something about the human tendency to defer to machine intelligence and to invest computers with authority. We believe they are smarter than we are. Have you ever followed the directions on your satnav navigation app, even when the route seems to make no sense? If so, you know how this works. The good news is that usually it is right. Even if it's not, the worst that happens is you go down a wrong road and get delayed a little bit. In the case of Diallo, a guy lost his paycheck for a few weeks. But the stakes may get higher as we rely on AI to run our workplaces. And by most estimates AI is going to play an ever bigger role in our lives.

Sales of artificial intelligence software will grow from $8 billion in 2016 to $52 billion in 2021, according to IDC, a research firm. Sales of robotic systems will more than triple, from $65 billion in 2016 to just under $200 billion in 2021. By 2030 robots may wipe out eight hundred million jobs, roughly one-fifth of all jobs worldwide, according to McKinsey. By 2050, robots may replace one-third of American working-age men, Brookings Institution vice president Darrell West claims in his 2018 book *The Future of Work: Robots, AI, and Automation*.

Companies love robots and AI-powered management systems. They don't have accidents. They don't call in sick and don't have messy personal lives. They also don't collect paychecks or demand health insurance and pension plans. Someday, investors could create companies that might not need any flesh-and-blood humans at all. The workers would be robots, and the managers would be artificial intelligence software code. Futurists call these "autonomous organizations." For investors, this sounds like a dream scenario—except that the next step might be that even the investors will not need to be human. In 2016, a team of computer scientists in Hong Kong launched a hedge fund run completely by AI. "If we all die, it would keep trading," founder Ben Goertzel told *Wired*.

How can humans keep up? The answer so far has been for humans to try to be more like machines. We need a Plan B.

PART III

THE NO-SHIT-SHERLOCK SCHOOL OF MANAGEMENT

CHAPTER TEN

THE BATTLE FOR THE SOUL OF WORK

For most of 2017, I was traveling around the country and occasionally abroad, attending conferences and sometimes giving speeches. It was a crazy, tumultuous year. Trump was president. The stock market was booming. Yet famous CEOs were getting fired, retailers were vanishing like Spinal Tap drummers, and even some of the world's biggest companies were choked with fear. Stories kept popping up saying that in this way or that, Silicon Valley was starting to look the way it did in 1999 and 2000, right before the dotcom crash. Income inequality kept getting worse, and no one seemed to care.

In May 2017, I attended a conference in New York, called TechCrunch Disrupt, which was, as expected, mostly awful. On one side of a big hall there was something called "Startup Alley," where desperate start-up founders with generally terrible ideas had paid a thousand bucks to rent a booth in the hope of being discovered by a venture capitalist. On the other side was an auditorium where start-up bros assembled in panels to talk about the new economy. My favorite was a forty-year-old former IBM management consultant, a guy with a law degree and an MBA, who now had launched a company to sell sneakers online and thus had arrived dressed like a teenage skateboard kid: funky T-shirt over a white long underwear shirt, backward baseball cap, ankle-high red sneakers left untied, a giant ring on one hand, and on his left wrist a huge watch and a groovy-dude braided leather bracelet. TechCrunch Disrupt encapsulated everything that had gone wrong with the new economy—the bros and fake bros, the bullshit, the scammers, the hordes of people who wanted to cash in and get rich, by any means necessary.

But two extraordinary things happened at this show. First, Steve Case, the founder of AOL, got up and talked about Revolution LLC, his investment firm, which seeks out companies in cities like Detroit, Cleveland, Columbus, and Indianapolis. Case had been traveling around in a bus, holding pitch competitions, spraying money into those forgotten cities, hoping to spark local entrepreneurship and tap into idle workforces. "We've been destroying jobs in the heartland, and we're not focusing on putting up money to fund entrepreneurs in those places," Case said. "Rise of the Rest" was the name of his bus tour, and that would be the name for a $150 million seed fund he announced later in the year.

The second extraordinary thing I saw was a talk by Dan Teran, the CEO of a gig-economy start-up called Managed by Q, which provides cleaning crews for offices. Teran had defied the conventional wisdom of Silicon Valley by categorizing all of his workers as employees with full benefits, rather than forcing them to work as contractors. Teran was onstage with Oisin Hanrahan, the CEO of Handy, a rival cleaning company, which categorizes workers as contractors. They debated—politely—the relative merits of each approach. Teran was far more convincing. What's more, he was the first person from the new-economy world I'd ever heard talk about wanting to take care of employees and provide good jobs for people.

After the conference I tracked him down. Once I found Teran, I started finding others like him. It turns out that a quiet movement has been taking shape, led by people who see how things have gone wrong and believe that business might be the solution. Business could be a way to make money but also a way to transform society and lift people out of poverty. Each person I met introduced me to others, and so my journey into the world of work took an unexpected turn, and one that left me feeling more uplifted and hopeful.

These people work in different fields, but they subscribe to what UK business professor Sally Rumbles described to me in an interview as the "no-shit-Sherlock school of management." As she put it: "If you treat people the way you'd like to be treated, if you praise them, and thank them, what a surprise! They do a good job on the whole."

That sounds like common sense. Yet unfortunately the idea that a company might be good to its employees has become so unusual that some people do not even think it is possible. Recently at a party I was talking to a veteran tech CEO who has started and run several successful software companies. He asked me what I was working on, and when I told him I was writing a book about companies that treat workers well, he dismissed the idea as unrealistic: "You can't do any of that stuff when you're a venture-funded company," he said. The venture capitalist investors would not allow it. Once you go public, Wall Street won't tolerate it, either.

For half a century, bankers and venture capitalists have been told that they are the only ones who matter, that companies exist solely to deliver the biggest possible return to them. That's the gospel of shareholder capitalism, the doctrine created by Milton Friedman. In the second dotcom boom that doctrine has been pushed to new extremes by companies that have adopted a grow-at-all-costs, investors-take-all business model. It has been great for VCs and oligarchs, but everyone else gets shortchanged:

- CUSTOMERS get "minimum viable products" (translation: shoddy stuff) from companies whose mantra is "move fast and break things." Internet companies spy on customers, invade their privacy, and sell their data. For companies like Facebook, the users *are* the product. We exist only to be packaged up and sold to advertisers.

- COMMUNITIES should benefit when they are home to the headquarters of wealthy corporations, but instead communities get shortchanged as tech giants dodge taxes, finding ways to stash their enormous profits overseas in offshore accounts.
- EMPLOYEES should be happy and prosperous but instead get overworked in stressful work environments with toxic cultures. They face bias, discrimination, and sexual harassment, along with vanishing benefits and a new compact that provides no security and turns jobs into gigs.

The grow-at-all-costs business model makes employees miserable, and it does this almost by design. Worse, the model doesn't really work, at least not if you're trying to produce a healthy, profitable organization that can sustain itself. Some of the unicorn start-ups that have gone public in recent years seem less like companies than like investment vehicles, little wagons that venture capitalists slap together and roll down into the public markets, then fetch back loaded with gold. Unfortunately, these wobbly little wagons have a tendency to blow up. Zynga, maker of cheesy Facebook games, went public in 2011, but within months its business went south. Zynga's stock price collapsed from $13 to $3 and has remained at about that level ever since. Zynga remains in business, but I suspect its best days are behind it.

If that's what you're trying to do—if you want to grow fast, lose money, make as much money for yourself as possible, and run away—then by all means you should treat your employees poorly. Doing otherwise would be irrational. You should adopt the new compact proposed by Silicon Valley oligarch Reid Hoffman, and the "team, not a family" philosophy from Netflix. Those were invented to serve this smash-and-grab business model.

But if you're trying to build a company that can remain in business for fifty or one hundred years, you should do exactly the opposite. Recent academic research suggests that the way to build a truly successful company—one that outcompetes its rivals, turns a profit, and remains in business—is to treat your employees extremely well.

In a study of low-cost retailers, Zeynep Ton, a professor at the MIT Sloan School of Management, found that the most successful companies were not the ones who cut labor costs to the bone. The best companies "invest heavily in their employees. They view their workforce as a valuable asset to be enhanced, not as a big, scary expense to be kept under tight control," Ton writes in *The Good Jobs Strategy*, a book that explains her research into model companies like Costco, Starbucks, UPS, and Toyota. In her research, Ton found that the winning companies paid more than their rivals. They also *overstaffed*, hiring more people than they needed, so that they would create a little slack in the system.

HOW TO BE A GREAT PLACE TO WORK

You might also extract lessons from companies whose employees remain happy over time. Once a year, *Fortune* magazine teams up with a research organization, Great Place to Work, to produce a list of the hundred best employers in the United States. Over the past twenty years a few companies have made the list every year. *Fortune* calls them "the Legends." They include Cisco and SAS Institute from tech; REI and Nordstrom from retailing; TDIndustries in construction; Goldman Sachs in banking; Marriott and Four Seasons from the hotel business; and Wegmans and Publix, the supermarket chains.

What common DNA do they share? These companies operate in very different industries, and for the most part they have little in common with one another, except for two things: they are all incredibly successful, and they treat their employees exceptionally well. This doesn't mean putting out Ping-Pong tables and free candy, or running kooky New Age team-building games. Rather, this means paid sabbaticals, on-site child care, and reimbursement for college tuition.

All of the legends extend health benefits to part-time workers. Some even provide part-timers with perks like paid time off for sick days, vacations, and holidays. The lesson? Skip the Ping-Pong and the New Age guff about mission statements and culture codes, and give people things they actually value.

Notably, most of the legends are not publicly traded. They are privately held or owned by employees. If there exists a connection between being publicly traded and having unhappy workers, it is probably because IPOs enrich a few people at the top but don't do much for everyone else, and because once you go public big finance starts pushing management to take stuff away from employees in order to boost returns to investors.

Also, most of the legends are old. Eight of the ten mentioned above were founded before 1962. The youngest, Cisco, was founded in 1984. Maybe some old-time virtues still make sense, even in the new economy. "These companies are able to change and evolve, but they have their values baked in, and they live up to them," says Ed Frauenheim, director of research at Great Place to Work, which is based in Oakland, California.

Great Place to Work has been sifting through its annual data to identify traits that consistently great companies share, and boiled it down to these: "Trust, pride, and camaraderie," Frauenheim says, reciting it like a mantra. Great Place to Work doesn't just do research. It's also an advocacy group. The organization now has branches in fifty-eight countries and has a mission to help companies improve labor standards and workplace practices. There are lots of techniques and initiatives, but the short version is this: be good to people. Heck, be *great* to people. The payoff: "You get the best work out of people when you treat them with respect."

Lately the organization has been turning its attention to tech companies in Silicon Valley and San Francisco. They've noticed the same distressing trends that I have: the short-term tour of duty and new compact in Reid Hoffman's *The Alliance*; the team-not-a-family approach that Patty McCord of Netflix touts. Tech companies believe that their extreme version of shareholder capitalism will produce better returns. The companies are their laboratories. Workers are their lab rats. Whether they are correct remains to be seen. As Frauenheim puts it, "There's an experiment playing out."

Two opposing worldviews are vying for the soul of the corporation. On one side are oligarchs like Hoffman and HR experts like McCord. On the other side are people like Frauenheim and his colleagues at Great Place to Work, who believe that companies do better when they treat workers well, and, as Whole Foods Market founder John Mackey puts it in his book *Conscious Capitalism*, that "business can elevate humanity."

To be sure, work is changing. People no longer want to spend their whole lives working at the same company, and companies can no longer provide lifetime employment. Companies want more flexibility, an organization that draws more on a contingent workforce that can be dialed up or down as needs change.

"But even if you have non-traditional employees," Frauenheim says, "people still want a foundation of trust. They need a sense that they're being cared for, that the company is looking out for your best interest, that they're not going to cut you at a moment's notice." This isn't just about being kind for the sake of being kind. "Companies that create a consistently great workplace race ahead of their competitors," Frauenheim insists.

That said, it's also about being kind. And what's wrong with that? Why should anyone need to make a business case for following the Golden Rule? We're talking about pretty basic stuff, like treating fellow human beings with dignity and respect, and not discriminating against people because of their race, age, or gender. Are investors and business owners so far lost to humanity that the only way to get them to behave ethically and morally is to prove to them that this will make them a little bit richer?

Some companies don't need the business argument. Some do the right thing just because it's the right thing. They pay employees more than they have to and provide great benefits. If that means the company makes a little less profit, the founder becomes a little less rich, and the investors receive a slightly smaller return, then so be it.

MAKING THE WORLD A BETTER PLACE

For two seasons I worked as a writer on the HBO comedy series *Silicon Valley*. A running joke on that show was about how tech founders always talked about "changing the world" and "putting a dent in the universe," and "making the world a better place." We were kind of cynical about it, and rightly so, because most of the techies who talked like that were full of shit.

Companies really can make the world a better place, just not in the way that Silicon Valley thinks of it. Tech moguls tend to think that changing the world and making the world a better place mean making an app that has millions of users or a company that generates billions of dollars in sales.

But you don't have to touch millions of lives or make billions of dollars to change the world. If you employ ten people, and they all get good benefits and a decent wage and feel happy at work— then you just made the world a better place. If you pay taxes and help build schools and feed kids, you just made the world a better place.

The first guys on my list founded their company in 2004, and ever since then have been told that they're nuts, or lazy, or stupid, or naïve. Yet fourteen years later they're doing so well that executives and entrepreneurs from around the world travel to their headquarters in Chicago and pay good money to attend their seminars, where they explain their unconventional management philosophy. Last year I had the chance to become one of their students.

CHAPTER ELEVEN

BASECAMP: BACK TO BASICS

J ason Fried and David Heinemeier Hansson run a software company called Basecamp, in Chicago. By the rules of Silicon Valley, they are doing everything wrong. They have never raised venture capital. They will never go public. They are not obsessed with growth. They have no sales reps, and spend nothing on marketing. Their fifty-four employees work forty hours a week, maximum. In summer, everyone cuts back to thirty-two hours, so they can all have three-day weekends, but they still collect their full paychecks. Working fewer hours means that less work gets done, but Fried and Hansson don't care. They're not in a big hurry.

"People in Silicon Valley say we're not ambitious enough," Fried tells me one Thursday in June when we meet for breakfast near his office, at the very civilized hour of nine thirty in the morning. "I'm fine with that. We don't want to be a three-hundred-person company. We just wanted to build a company that we would want to work at."

The kind of company they want to work at would be generous to employees and build a sustainable business that could provide people with long-term employment. Basecamp pays workers top salaries and provides "the best benefits in the world," Fried says. Perks include

$100 a month for a gym membership, $100 for massages, and $100 toward a co-working space rental if you want one. Basecamp provides $1,000 a year for continuing education and will match charitable gifts up to $1,000 a year. The company offers profit sharing and a 100 percent match on pension contributions, and pays 75 percent of health-care premiums. Every employee gets three weeks of paid vacation, another week or so of holidays, and personal days. You get a one-month paid sabbatical every three years, sixteen weeks of maternity leave, and six weeks of paternity leave. If you've been with the company for more than a year, Basecamp picks up the tab for an annual vacation, with a budget that maxes out at $5,000. "We provide specialized trips for singles, couples, and families, all within the budget," Fried says.

You can work wherever you want, whenever you want. Basecamp's employees are scattered across the world, in Canada, Brazil, Hong Kong, Australia, and a bunch of European countries. Only fourteen are based in Chicago, and though they all have a place to work in the main office, most of them still work from home a few days a week.

Fried and Hansson won't say how much they earn, only that Basecamp turns a profit of "tens of millions of dollars a year," which they split between them. A few years ago a tech publication estimated Hansson's net worth at $40 million. He owns a collection of million-dollar exotic cars and pursues an expensive hobby, competing in car races like the 24 Hours of Le Mans. Hansson is thirty-eight and married, with two kids. He and his family divide their time between Malibu, California, and Marbella, on the Costa del Sol in Spain. That's partly because living in Europe makes it easier for Hansson to drive race cars on the European circuit. But that's not the only reason. "It's mostly because Spain is a really nice place to live," he admits.

Fried, forty-four, has curly hair, a close-cropped beard, and a runner's build. He and his wife have a young son and another baby on the way. He tries to spend as much time at home as he can, which means, among other things, no crack-of-dawn power breakfasts, no work dinners, no pulling all-nighters. Being able to ease into the day at nine thirty on a nice day in June is part of the reason he started his own company.

"The basic premise of being an entrepreneur," Fried says, "is freedom. That's why people start a business, for freedom."

These guys don't want to be the next Mark Zuckerberg. They think people who do are, well, kind of nuts. They spend a lot of time encouraging aspiring entrepreneurs to pursue a healthier approach to operating a company. It starts with treating your employees well and looking after them. It also means looking after yourself. Work fewer hours. Avoid stress. Find happiness.

They have written several books about their laid-back philosophy, including *Rework*, which sold more than half a million copies worldwide. They are working on a new book, *The Calm Company*, and produce a podcast, called *The Distance*, where they present stories about small business owners they admire, from a small family-owned brewery in Wisconsin to a forty-year-old company in Chicago that makes butter molded into the shape of animals.

Through their books and essays Fried and Hansson have created a second career as business gurus. They speak at conferences and even run seminars at the Basecamp office in Chicago, offering people a nuts-and-bolts look at how to get more done in less time.

That's what has brought me to Chicago. After breakfast, Fried and I will travel to the office where thirty-seven people are waiting. They have paid $1,000 each, and some have traveled thousands of miles, hoping to learn from Basecamp.

A SIMPLE LIFE AND A GREAT MARGIN

Fried studied finance at the University of Arizona and graduated in 1996. A few years later, as the web was taking off, he launched a web design shop in Chicago that built websites for corporate customers. The company was called 37signals. In the early 2000s, Fried hired

Hansson, who was then a college student in his native Denmark, to develop a project management tool that 37signals could use to keep track of the work it was doing for clients. Hansson (who is known among software hackers by his initials, DHH) wrote the first version of Basecamp in 2004.

As Hansson was writing Basecamp, he also created a web framework—a tool that helps coders save time when they are writing web applications, by providing standard ways to do certain tasks that most web apps have in common, like fetching information from a database. Hansson called his framework Ruby on Rails and made it available to anyone, free of charge, as an open-source product. The code was wildly successful and today runs on more than a million websites. It also made Hansson something of a legend among web developers.

Fried created Basecamp originally for his own use but then recognized there could be a market for the product. He was right, and sales took off. Soon 37signals stopped developing websites for other companies and turned into a software vendor. After seeing Fried give a talk at a tech conference, Amazon founder Jeff Bezos took an interest in the company and bought a small percentage of the ownership from Fried and Hansson. Basecamp has never taken any outside funding from anyone else.

By 2014, ten years after introducing Basecamp, 37signals had a strong business but was facing a crisis. The company was now selling five software products. To keep developing and modernizing all five products, they would have to hire a much bigger staff. But Fried and Hansson liked staying small, so they sold off four of the products and focused on Basecamp, which also then became the new name of the company.

Cutting out all those products made life simpler. "Our revenue dipped for a couple of years, but who cares? We don't have to hit any numbers. We're not worried about public markets. It doesn't matter. We could still pay great salaries, and not eliminate any benefits, and still have a great margin," Fried says.

Basecamp, the product, is a somewhat simple (some say "rudimentary") piece of software that lets teams work together on projects and keep track of what each member is doing. Basecamp has tried various pricing plans over the years. In one version customers paid only $29 a month. But in 2014, when the current version came out, Fried and Hansson simplified the pricing. You can pay $99 a month, or $999 per year. Doesn't matter how many employees you have. There's just one flat rate.

Basecamp could make more money if, instead of charging every company the same flat rate, it charged a price based on the number of people who used the product. That's what most software companies do, but "it would turn us into the kind of company that we don't want to be," Fried says. "Why is software pricing so complicated? Because people are trying to extract maximum value. I'm not interest in maximizing anything. Are we leaving money on the table? Yes, every day we are. But we don't want to be nickel-and-diming people. It all flows from what kind of company you want to be."

Basecamp has more than one hundred thousand paying customers. Fried and Hansson won't talk about revenues, but back-of-the-napkin math suggests the company could be generating between $50 million and $70 million a year.

MORE SIGNAL, LESS NOISE

The seminar starts at noon. Most of the attendees are from the United States, but one woman has traveled from Romania, and there are two guys who run a software development company in Norway. "We want to help our people become more productive, but have a calmer workday and not stress people out," Anders says.

Fried begins his presentation by explaining all of the things that Basecamp doesn't do. There are no scheduled meetings, and no shared calendars, and no chat apps like Slack, though the Basecamp app has chat and instant messaging built into it, and employees use those. Also, Basecamp employees don't use email. "There is zero need for email when you use Basecamp," Fried says.

There are no product sprints, no all-nighters, no keg parties, no Ping-Pong tables—and no noise. At the main office in Chicago people observe "library rules" and speak in hushed voices. The walls are covered in sound-absorbing material, the floors with thick carpeting. "I think an office should be more like a library and less like a kitchen," Fried says. "You go into some companies and everyone's running around with their hair on fire. There's too much distraction. The culture here is, keep it down."

Oddly enough, even though Basecamp sells office productivity software, its founders are wary of relying too much on technology tools.

"Look at group chat," Hansson says. "It's getting a lot of attention because of Slack. But people end up getting interrupted constantly. They feel more stressed. These tools are supposed to make work easier and more productive and calm, and instead you have all this frenzy and it ends up exacerbating problems without any specific payoff. Six months after adoption, a lot of people are getting *less* work done, instead of more. If you were at least getting something back, if you could say, 'Well, I'm getting 30 percent more work done,' then it might be worth it. But I'm not hearing that at all."

Same goes for shared online calendars. At most companies, people can read your calendar and request a block of your time. Pretty soon you find entire days given over to meetings. Basecamp bans the practice. If you really need to talk to someone, you can arrange to do it. But you can't just glance at someone's calendar and request a time slot.

That's partly because Fried and Hansson hate meetings. Fried believes collaboration often turns into "over-collaboration," and that most of it is bullshit anyway. He says brainstorming "is wildly overrated. There are tech companies where you have this weird thing and people are just brainstorming all the time. We brainstorm once a year, and then we spend the rest of the year doing it."

The goal at Basecamp is for every employee to get eight hours of uninterrupted work time every day. After that they should go home. "These people who say they're working eighty hours a week, why do we need eighty hours?" Hansson says. "Nobody needs eighty hours. Most of us can't fill forty hours."

Basecamp employees communicate entirely through the Basecamp software application. First thing Monday morning, the software asks employees a few "check-in" questions. What are you working on this week? What did you do this weekend? What are you reading? You don't have to answer all the questions. The idea is just to let everyone know what you're doing, and to share that information without having a meeting. At the end of the day the software sends another check-in question: What did you do today? The check-ins let the company's far-flung workforce, who are spread across many time zones, from Australia to the United States to Europe, keep track of each other.

Another rule: small teams, short projects. People work in teams of three on projects that last no more than six weeks. That means projects stay small. If a project gets too big, the team doesn't pull all-nighters or stress out trying to hit the deadline—they just remove a few features and do less. "We're always scoping things down rather than making them bigger," Fried says. At the end of each six-week cycle, the team decides what to tackle next.

The company's largest group is customer support, with sixteen people handling calls from customers. But everybody in the company has to work on the support desk. Typically they will put in one day every six weeks, "so everyone can hear directly from customers and understand the pain points, what frustrates or delights customers," Fried says.

The product itself doesn't change very often. Basecamp has cranked out three major versions in thirteen years. Fried says their model is the car industry, where companies offer new versions every six or seven years. They're especially fond of Porsche, whose flagship 911 sports car has retained the same basic shape since its inception in 1963.

Twice a year, in the spring and the fall, Basecamp flies all of its employees into Chicago for a week, mostly to socialize. Some teams also host separate get-togethers, renting a house in New Orleans or Florida where they can work alongside one another for a few days. But otherwise, most people work on their own. The company doesn't track how many hours people put in. "We could do that," Fried says, "but we don't."

He tries to know about people's lives outside of work and to cultivate a family feeling. People use the morning check-ins to post photos of their new babies and weekend ski trips. One guy in Australia, a woodworker, posts photos of cabinets he's working on. "People ask me, 'Why would you pay someone to write about what he did that weekend or take pictures of his cabinets?' But it's important," Fried says. "I work with these people. I want to know them."

Unlike a lot of Silicon Valley companies, Basecamp actually tries to hang on to workers, and Fried is proud of how well they've done. Seventy percent of the employees have been with the company for more than four years, and half have been there for more than five years. Ryan Singer, the head of strategy, joined fifteen years ago. "I might be able to make more money or get equity somewhere else, but it's not worth it if I have to sit in meetings all the time or can't travel when I want to," he says. "The main thing is, I'm in control of my time at Basecamp. Nobody can book time on my calendar. I have time to think, and flexible hours. I've also had the latitude to teach myself new skills and work in different departments, which keeps me challenged."

Some people in Silicon Valley don't quite know what to make of Basecamp. Others seem downright irked by their culture. "They tell us we're cute, we have a cute little lifestyle business," Fried says. "Our employees have longer tenure with the company. Our people are happier. They spend time with their families. They get to enjoy the summer months. People tell me, 'Steve Jobs could not have made Apple if he took Fridays off.' Well, I'm not trying to make Apple. And I don't care what Steve Jobs did."

In 2017, Fried and Hansson got into a prolonged Twitter debate with Keith Rabois, a well-known venture capitalist and minor Silicon Valley oligarch who insists workaholism is the only way to be successful. (To refresh your memory, Rabois is the guy who got in trouble at Stanford for shouting homophobic slurs. His other claim to fame is that in 2013 he resigned as chief operating officer at Square after being caught up in a sex scandal; he had encouraged his boyfriend to apply for a job at Square but never told anyone they were involved, and when they broke up, the boyfriend threatened to sue Rabois and Square for sexual harassment.) Rabois spends a lot of time on Twitter, often bullying people and hurling insults, a Trump-style tough guy. When Hansson published an essay arguing that workaholism is pointless, and also a con—a way for rich VCs to get richer by telling young kids to work themselves to death, Rabois pounced: "For lazy people who want to accomplish nothing, his post is perfect."

Fried and Hansson responded that they considered themselves successful. After all, they were running a tech company that had been profitable for eighteen years. Rabois responded, "I don't believe $30m companies are interesting."

Fried argued that "success" means staying in business, and that his local dry cleaner, which has been operating for twenty years, is a success. Rabois shot back: "Excellent. I don't object to persuading your dry cleaner to blog."

As the debate continued, Rabois became increasingly agitated— and more obnoxious. He said no one running a successful startup would have time to blog. He bragged about his successes and how much money he has made. He said people who haven't made a fortune should just keep quiet. "When you create a billion dollar company, or invest in 20+ of them, or have an 85x or more return from 2003-2013 u get to opine," he tweeted.

To a woman who wrote that she works hard but also takes vacations and believes she can still build a successful company, Rabois sniped: "Keep telling yourself that fiction. It probably makes you feel good."

When someone pointed out that Hansson created Ruby on Rails, a software program that is used by more than a million websites, Rabois scoffed that Ruby on Rails actually isn't very good technology.

Fried and Hansson probably did not win over any workaholics, but they did accomplish something else. By drawing out Rabois, they exposed the kind of preposterous, egomaniacal assholes who hold power and influence in Silicon Valley, and offered a warning to young entrepreneurs: take money from a venture capitalist, and you'll end up working for some smug, sarcastic, know-it-all prick like this guy, who will constantly tell you that you're not working hard enough while he spends his days getting into arguments on Twitter.

DO THE HUSTLE

Rabois is far from alone in championing workaholism. In 2017 I wrote an op-ed for the *New York Times* describing how Silicon Valley hucksters had started selling young people on a kind of prosperity gospel in which anyone—yes, that's right, even *you*—could start a company and get rich, as long as they were willing to give up their friends and family and personal lives, and work themselves to death. I was prompted to write the article after I came across the craziest start-up story I've ever heard. A young start-up founder who was running out of money was now making a desperate offer: if anyone would invest $250,000 in his company, he would donate one of his kidneys. I tracked the guy down to interview him by phone. As far as I could tell, "Kidney Boy," as I came to think of him, was sincere. I emailed Jason Calacanis, a well-known angel investor in Silicon Valley, and asked if the kidney offer would persuade him to take a look at the company. "That's the most dystopian thing I've heard in years," Calacanis wrote back. I took that as a no.

To me the story captured how crazy things have become in the world of tech start-ups. Offering to sacrifice body parts is probably the inevitable outcome of a culture where founders (usually young and male) are challenged by older bros to think of starting a company as something akin to going through Marine boot camp on Parris Island: *Do you want to succeed? How bad do you want it? I don't think you have what it takes!* People in Silicon Valley are not worried about workaholism. In fact, they celebrate it. Some think young techies aren't working hard enough. Michael Moritz, a famous venture capitalist at Sequoia Capital, recently wrote a piece in the *Financial Times* urging American tech workers to keep up with their counterparts in China, who work fourteen-hour days, six days a week, while taking hardly any vacation time and seeing their kids only a few minutes a day.

In the Valley, *hustle* has become a hot new buzzword. People wear *hustle* T-shirts, and attend *hustle* boot camps. Once a year, several thousand people pay $300 each to attend Hustle Con, a conference where expert hustlers teach wannabe hustlers how to hustle—which is in itself a hustle.

The best-known hustler is Gary Vaynerchuk, also known as Gary Vee, a tech entrepreneur and angel investor with a reported net worth of $50 million. Vaynerchuk's motto is "Crush It!" He has nearly two million Twitter followers, has published a string of bestselling books, and constantly produces videos and gives speeches.

On stage he turns into a cartoon Tasmanian Devil, almost a parody of a motivational speaker. Imagine a pint-sized Tony Robbins, unshaven, wearing a T-shirt and spewing F-bombs after consuming a dozen Red Bulls, and you get the idea. Vaynerchuk tells his acolytes that if they want to get the "bling" and fly on private jets, they need to be working eighteen hours a day. No personal life, no relaxing, no vacations. What's more, they must do this for years. One of his sayings is that before you can eat caviar, you have to eat shit. "I want you to eat shit for the next ten years," he says on stage. Personally, I'd pass on that deal. For reasons I don't understand, people worship him and flock to his events in droves.

In my *Times* op-ed I also discussed the Twitter spat that erupted after Rabois teed off on Hansson's essay about workaholism. Of course people tweeted a link to my article to Rabois, and of course he started tweeting about it, deriding my essay as "ludicrous" and "sophomoric."

When a scientist named Lenny Teytelman pointed out to Rabois that scientists have gathered data showing that nonstop work is destructive and counterproductive, Rabois fired back with insults, saying what would Teytelman know about how to build a great company? "When u succeed at something u get to offer an opinion," Rabois tweeted.

For the record, Teytelman studied math at Columbia, got a PhD in genetics and computational biology from UC-Berkeley, and then spent four years working in a renowned stem cell lab at MIT. He then founded a start-up that provides an online repository for working scientists. Yet here was Rabois, billionaire douchebag, telling a start-up founder with a doctorate in science that he lacked standing—in a debate about science and how to build companies.

RUNNING FASTER, GETTING NOWHERE

During a keynote speech at a Lean Startup conference, Fried asked his audience of six hundred techies how many ever got four straight hours of uninterrupted work time in a given day. He says about 10 percent raised their hands.

"It's not only tech. It's everywhere," Fried says. "We speak at a lot of conferences, and everyone is talking about this. 'I'm working longer hours, but I'm getting less done.' Expectations are out of control. Everyone is obsessed with growth, but nobody knows why."

The result is workers getting pushed beyond their limits and burning out. The problem starts with VCs like Rabois who sell young startup founders (mostly young, mostly male) on a macho nerd-commando lifestyle—which of course is great for the VCs, who do nothing yet reap the lion's share of the benefits when a company succeeds.

"These guys make being an entrepreneur sound like *The Hunger Games*," Hansson says. "People humble brag about how wiped out and exhausted they are. They're glorifying death marches. It's all about serving the VCs. But trust me, the VCs are not working 120 hours a week."

He and Fried say they can't stand the fawning coverage given to venture capital fund-raising and the way journalists breathlessly report that some money-losing unicorn company has raised another round of venture funding at an even more mind-boggling valuation.

"Why doesn't anyone ever ask these companies what happened to the money they raised in the last round?" Fried says. "These are business failure stories being held up as business success stories."

Yet even business schools now glorify the growth-at-all-costs, get-rich-quick-and-run business model. "You have students who have not even started anything yet and they're already talking about exit strategies. Business schools are not teaching people how to run a business and keep costs down and make more money than you spend. They're teaching students how to look for money, how to raise money, how to write your Series A contract, how to make an exit. An entire generation is being taught that this is how you run a business. It's obscene," Fried says.

The dysfunction originated in tech start-ups, but now, "these guys in Silicon Valley are being elevated to hero status," Hansson says. "They're the role models that everyone is looking up to and trying to emulate. And that's how the bullshit keeps spreading."

What's more, techies in Silicon Valley have become adept at shutting down dissent. Dare to disagree with them, and you'll get dismissed as a crank, or a Luddite, or someone who just doesn't "get it," the way Rabois sneered at Hansson and Fried on Twitter.

Because of that, "people are afraid to speak up," Hansson says. "Nobody wants to be the one who says the emperor has no clothes. But that's why it's so critical to get the message out there."

CHAPTER TWELVE

MANAGED BY Q: "EVERYBODY CLEANS"

Allan Erickson had just begun a new job, working the overnight shift for an office-cleaning start-up called Managed by Q, when his supervisor pulled him aside and pointed out a young guy who was working nearby, down on his knees, cleaning the underside of a desk.

"You know who that is?" the supervisor said. "That's Dan. He's the guy who signs the checks. He's the owner of the company."

Dan Teran, the CEO of Managed by Q, was twenty-six years old at the time. Erickson, ten years his senior, was so impressed that he put down his rag and went over and shook Teran's hand and introduced himself. "Why is he out here cleaning? I mean, he's the owner of the company," Erickson recalls. "You're not going to find the CEO of Uber out driving a car, or the CEO of McDonald's out flipping burgers."

At the New York-based Managed by Q, however, they have a policy: "Everybody cleans," Teran says. No matter what your title is, when you first get hired, you go out for a shift as a cleaner.

"Cleaning offices is really hard. I want people who are in corporate roles to have a very visceral understanding of how hard our people in the field are working," Teran says. Also, he says, "You really get to know what someone is made of when you see them scrubbing toilets." I don't think any of my former bosses would ever have done janitorial work, but thinking about it gives me tremendous pleasure, at least with some of them.

Teran, now twenty-nine, is not your typical start-up CEO. And his company, which he and everyone else just call Q—the name comes from the James Bond character Q, who develops the gizmos and gadgets for secret agents—is not the typical gig-economy start-up.

The biggest difference has to do with how Q treats its workers. Unlike almost every other gig-economy company, Q categorizes workers as proper employees. The company provides health insurance, a pension plan, and stock options. Starting pay is $12.50 per hour, and there's a generous paid-time-off policy. Most important, Q promotes from within, offering people who start out as cleaners the chance to get roles inside the corporate offices.

Conventional wisdom among Silicon Valley venture capitalists has been that gig-economy companies can't survive unless they categorize workers as contractors. That's how Uber categorizes its drivers, for example. By some estimates, using the contractor model cuts labor costs by 30 percent.

Teran is making a contrarian bet that the VCs are wrong. Being cheap on labor might help in the short term, but to Teran it would be a costly and even fatal mistake in the long run. It might seem paradoxical, but he believes spending more on labor will end up boosting his bottom line. Customer satisfaction will go up, and employee turnover will go down. Lower turnover means Q won't have to spend as much time recruiting, hiring, and training new workers to replace the ones who have left. "People think they have to choose between having a good business and being a good employer, but that's a false choice," Teran says.

Q affords this by keeping other costs low. Q leases office space on the eleventh floor of a building in New York's Soho neighborhood. A lot of tech start-ups spend a fortune building lavish offices, but at Q the decor is nothing fancy: wood floors, white walls, lots of big windows. People work side by side at long tables in a big open loft. A set of rolling bleachers can be moved around and assembled for meetings. There's a little kitchen at one side of the room. Teran works out of a small office with a couch, a few chairs, a big TV, and a couple of whiteboards. It's nothing fancy. "Frugality is a value of ours," Teran says.

Same goes in his personal life. Teran lives in a low-income co-op in Brooklyn that he bought when he was first out of college. "I don't need to live in a nice place," he says. "I'm characteristically very low maintenance. My father was a carpenter. He told me the number one way to accumulate wealth is to live within your means."

Another big influence on Teran's business philosophy was Zeynep Ton, a professor at MIT's Sloan School of Management and author of *The Good Jobs Strategy*, who argues that companies like Starbucks and Costco have succeeded because they provide better pay and benefits for workers. Building a reputation as a great place to work makes it easier to recruit new workers. It can even help companies attract new customers. "Part of the bet is that we will be able to service demand better by building a brand that's about being a great place to work," Teran says.

So far the bet seems to be paying off. Q's customer retention and employee retention are higher than the industry average. After four years, Q has nearly eight hundred employees—six hundred who work in the field and two hundred office workers. The company operates in five cities—New York, Los Angeles, Chicago, Boston, and the San Francisco Bay Area—and has 1,300 clients. Sales are on track to nearly double in 2018.

For Teran, this is just the start. His vision goes way beyond just running a cleaning business. In fact he says someday the cleaning business may represent only a fraction of Q's business.

SOCIAL JUSTICE MEETS SCALING UP

Teran studied international relations and urban public policy at Johns Hopkins University. "I literally never took a business course in college," he says. During his undergraduate years he worked as a community organizer in Baltimore and interned at a law firm in New York with Erin Brockovich on environmental cases.

In high school he volunteered for Habitat for Humanity and worked on a Navajo reservation in New Mexico and at an orphanage near Tijuana, Mexico. He was part of a youth group at his Catholic church that was active in social issues. "I got interested early on in social justice," he says. He thought about working in politics or the law, but then saw that "a business is an opportunity to have an impact, and the bigger the scale, the bigger the impact."

In 2014 he founded Q with a partner, Saman Rahmanian, who is no longer involved. For the first year, the company didn't have enough cleaners, so Teran had to kick in. "I was working all day in the office and then cleaning at night," he says.

Soon, Teran expanded into providing other services. Today, in addition to cleaners, Q provides companies with people who do maintenance and repair, and provide IT services; Q even provides office temps and receptionists.

Teran wanted to offer more, things like painting, plumbing, moving, and HVAC work. To do that, he launched Q Marketplace, which acts as a middleman, connecting customers to service providers. A customer in Chicago with a broken sink can do a search on the Q Marketplace website and find a local plumber who can come right away. It's not quite the same as services like TaskRabbit, where you can hire someone to run any kind of errands. The Q Marketplace vets all the service providers, and they're only dealing with people or companies that provide office services.

To distinguish between its two businesses, Q labels its original cleaning business Q Services. That group—the cleaning business—still generates 95 percent of Q's revenues, but eventually

Teran thinks Q Marketplace could become the larger part of the business.

Teran's ultimate goal is to handle every aspect of managing a physical space. He uses Amazon Web Services as a model. Instead of building and managing their own data centers, today most companies just fill out a few forms and rent computer power from Amazon Web Services. They might have no idea what kind of computers are being used, or who is running the servers. In the ultimate version of this, a law firm or ad agency could rent new offices, call Q, and never worry about the physical space again. Q would do everything and send you a single bill every month. Some chores, like cleaning, would be done by Q employees. Other things, like installing air-conditioning systems, would be done by contractors hired by Q. But the customer would not have to think about any of this. They could get everything they need just by clicking a few menus in an app.

One day, Teran hopes, Q will scale this out around the world, providing a global supply and demand platform for office services. "That sounds like science fiction, but it's going to happen," Teran says.

That's the audacious vision that Teran sold to venture capitalists. Billing itself as "the operating system for offices," Q has raised $70 million in venture capital funding. Some VCs passed on Q because Teran insisted on treating cleaners as full employees. Investors who got hung up on that issue were not seeing Teran's much more ambitious "operating system for offices" vision, one that will take a decade or even longer to build out. "There were people who didn't understand the bet we were making," he says.

Teran has assembled a management team of industry veterans whose résumés include MBAs and stints in management consulting firms and companies like Amazon, Huffington Post, and Github. In 2017, Q acquired Hivy, a tiny start-up developing office-management software that complements the software that Q Services has developed.

MIND THE GAP

One challenge of gig-economy companies is managing two different workforces—in Q's case, blue-collar people on the cleaning crews and white-collar start-up kids at headquarters. "There's a huge gulf," says Maria Dunn, director of people and culture. "I'm trying to teach the managers here how to talk to the field operators. It's two different worlds, but we're ferociously trying to bridge that gap. I think it will be critical to our success."

Dunn grew up in a blue-collar town north of Albany, New York, with a single mom who worked as a nurse. She waitressed to put herself through university and after graduation worked in HR for companies with blue-collar workforces before finding her way into the Manhattan tech start-up world. She was drawn to Q because of its pro-worker policies. "I think if you invest in people and make them a part of something, it's a better business model in the long term," she says.

Dunn joined Q toward the end of 2016 and found that while Q was offering great benefits to workers, the cleaning crews often didn't know about them. "People would say, 'Wait, you guys have a 401(k) plan? Oh my God, I didn't realize that.'" Some "operators"— that's what Q calls people who work on cleaning crews—knew that the company offered benefits but didn't dare bring it up. "You hire new engineers and they come in and say, 'Okay, what's your stock plan, what's your 401(k) plan'—but hourly rate workers can be hesitant, or even afraid to ask about them," Dunn says.

The company built a team to reach out to workers by organizing "squad assemblies" at the office to walk people through what's available. "We're basically waving the flag, telling people what the offerings are here, that there are additional forms of compensation in addition to the hourly wage," Dunn says.

Everyone who works thirty hours a week or more qualifies for health insurance. A base-level plan comes at no charge to the employee, but only covers that person. Other health plans require a contribution.

Also, Q offers a pension plan with a 50 percent match, and an employee stock purchase program.

Some blue-collar workers are almost suspicious when they get pitched on a pension plan. "We're telling them, 'Look, the company is setting up a savings plan for you, and you can contribute 6 percent but you'll get 9 percent,' and they're like, 'Wait, what's the catch?'" Dunn says.

For many of Q's workers the biggest motivator isn't the benefits. In a company survey, the biggest motivator of all turned out to be career growth—the chance to get promotions, to move up and make more money.

"For operators, the idea that they might come in here as a cleaner but end up working someplace with a desk and a laptop, that's very attractive to them," Dunn says. "People are looking for ways to grow, to move up."

Greg Brech joined Q as a cleaner, but from the beginning he was aiming higher. He was twenty-eight, living in San Francisco, and waiting tables when he saw an ad for a job at Q. "I brought up the page with the benefits and I thought it must be a scam. I figured it was too good to be true," he says.

The biggest draw was the health insurance benefits, but "the promise of moving up inside the company was important, and I knew I had the drive to do that." Brech had worked in an office before, and had started college but dropped out.

For over a year Brech worked as a cleaner. During that time he got promoted to become a mentor, a role that involves training new hires. He also moved back to New York, where he grew up, and was able to keep his job. When a recruiting job opened up, Q invited him to apply for the position, and he got it.

He sifts through hundreds of résumés a week, brings in ten to fifteen people for in-person interviews, and hires three or four. He tells the new hires how he began as a cleaner and got promoted to an office job. "If you do the right thing, you will move up," he tells them. "It's not something we just say to entice people."

Brech was one of the first people to make the leap from working in the field to a job at the head office, and he credits the company's welcoming environment for making a leap like that possible. "It feels like a family," he says.

That "family feeling" comes up a lot when you talk to Q employees. Tianna Green-Munroe started out as a cleaner but now works as an office coordinator at Q's main office in New York. "This is my home away from home. It's my second family," she says.

After about a year in the field, Green-Munroe got promoted to a job as a receptionist in the main office. Less than a year later she got promoted to office coordinator. In her late twenties, Green-Munroe is married and has an infant son. Insurance covered her during her pregnancy and delivery, and Q provided twelve weeks of paid maternity leave.

More important, she says, was the support she got from co-workers who sent flowers to the hospital and called every day during her leave to see how she was doing. They made a Q onesie for the baby and go crazy when she brings him to the office. All this might be hokey and old-fashioned, but it's hard to overestimate how much it means to people. "This job has really been life-changing for me," Green-Munroe says.

Same goes for Allan Erickson, the guy who was so taken aback when he saw Teran out working with a cleaning crew, crawling underneath desks. Erickson lives in the Bronx, and his work history includes a job as a baggage handler at JFK Airport and gigs at Baskin-Robbins and McDonald's. In two and a half years at Q he's had five promotions, and now he's a supervisor, managing thirty operators.

The one thing that seems to mean even more to Erickson than the promotions is that when he runs into Teran at the office, the boss takes a minute to chat with him. Teran asks about Erickson's son and even remembers the kid's nickname. "I damn near cried the first time he asked me that," Erickson says. "His plate is full, he's doing so much, but he's taking time to ask me how I'm doing, how my son is doing, to call my son by his nickname."

How can such a small gesture mean so much? Remembering the name of someone's kid, or sending someone flowers when they have a baby—these are common courtesies, and they take little effort or expense. Yet people are moved by these gestures, and I suspect it's because a lot of workers, especially the lower-income workers who toil in the front lines of many organizations, go through most of their work life feeling invisible. When a boss takes the time to actually *see* them, it blows them away. In terms of bang for the buck, these small gestures might represent one of the most powerful management techniques in the world.

Tom Peters saw a version of this practice in action at Hewlett-Packard in the late 1970s. In his legendary management book, *In Search of Excellence*, Peters gave the practice a name—MBWA, or "management by wandering around." He has been pounding the table about it ever since. The phrase is so well known that it even has its own Wikipedia page. Yet few managers do it, especially at new economy companies.

New research from Great Place to Work suggests that companies where front-line workers feel connected to the top brass produce *three times as much revenue growth* as do companies where the brass and the front-line people don't know each other.

Chris Nassetta, CEO of Hilton Hotels and Resorts, requires all top executives to spend a week working in the field as housekeepers, dishwashers, and bellhops. Nassetta worked with maintenance crews. At the end of his week the crew gave him a golden plunger as a sendoff present.

Hilton also has empowered front-line workers and gives them more autonomy. Frauenheim tells the story of a Hilton housekeeper who, while cleaning a room, noticed that the guests were celebrating their anniversary. She recommended the hotel send up a free bottle of wine with a note. "She created an incredible experience, and she gets to experience the joy of doing someone that favor," he says.

Another gap-closing company is Marriott. When the hotel chain opened its first properties in India, locals insisted the company should provide separate dining rooms for executives, so they would not have to eat alongside the maids and maintenance workers in the cafeteria. Marriott insisted that everyone eat together. "It was a way to break down barriers, and to generate better ideas, just by having executives talking to the front-line folks more," Frauenheim says.

Companies that close the gap also report better productivity. Their employees express higher intent to stay with the company and are more likely to be "brand ambassadors," who talk up the company to people they meet.

Building bridges between top executives and front-line workers isn't exactly rocket science. It's kind of common sense. What's more, it's not even difficult to do. Yet the payoff can be huge.

SELLING A LOT WITHOUT SELLING OUT

Teran's heroes include CEOs like Howard Schultz of Starbucks and James Sinegal of Costco, who stuck to genuine principles about elevating the lives of their workers while also managing to build huge, successful, global companies. It's easy enough to run a small company that feels like a family and treats employees well. But it's tough to hang on to worker-friendly values when a start-up grows up and becomes a big corporation. Yet that's what Teran hopes to do. He wants to build a global corporation that can impact the lives of thousands of employees and "become big enough that our ideas really matter," he says. Schultz and Sinegal are two rare examples of CEOs who have managed to pull this off.

Teran could make his life easier and might even increase his chances of success if he followed the playbook that Uber and most other gig-economy companies use: screw the workers, grow as fast as you can, operate at a loss, and cash out in an IPO. When he was first raising venture funding in 2013, it was "right as the Uber unicorn hype was reaching a fever pitch," Teran says, and "literally dozens of investors suggested that we were thinking about the business the wrong way." Teran wasn't swayed. Instead, "It served as a filter for the investors who we ultimately decided to work with and who shared our values."

Teran's decision early on to make all his cleaning crew workers full employees is starting to look somewhat prescient. In the last few years, some gig-economy companies have been sued by workers demanding employee status. The lawsuits damage a company's reputation and drain its bank account. They can even be fatal. When Homejoy, a start-up that provided home-cleaning services, shut down in 2015, its co-founders cited the cost of fighting four lawsuits brought by workers as a reason for going out of business.

Handy, another home-cleaning company, and one that often gets compared to Q, also was hit with a lawsuit by its contractor workers. The company remains in business, but the lawsuit led to bad publicity, including a blog post with the following headline: "Handy Sued for Being a Hellscape of Labor Code Violations."

Handy's legal problems prompted Slate, an online magazine, to publish a six-thousand-word exposé, which examined the company's shabby treatment of workers but also dug up dirt on other problems, including bad morale, lousy customer service, and a heavy-drinking frat boy culture that had gone off the rails. Slate revealed that the bros at Handy had invented a game called Wheel of Fellatio, "a makeshift Wheel of Fortune with sex acts instead of dollar amounts." A neighboring company had complained about a whiteboard at Handy that "managed to fit slurs toward women, black people and gay people into just five words."

Hoping to avoid lawsuits and reputational damage, some gig-economy companies, like Luxe and Instacart, have started shifting workers to the employee model preemptively. Meanwhile, VCs who were once crazy about funding gig-economy start-ups seem to have lost some enthusiasm for the space.

For now Q seems to be doing well. Its sales grew 71 percent in 2017, and Teran expects to nearly double in 2018. The Q Services division, which employs the cleaners, actually turns a profit, though the overall company still loses money. Q Marketplace remains a tiny part of the business, but will more than triple its revenues in 2018.

In the past two chapters I've shown you two companies that have created positive, human-centric cultures. But what about investors? You can't build companies without them. But most venture capitalists seem to view employees as their adversaries. In their mind, every dollar spent on labor reduces the return they will get on their investment.

But in the next chapter I'm going to introduce you to a pair of investors who are using their investment dollars to build companies that focus from the beginning on treating workers well.

CHAPTER THIRTEEN

KAPOR CAPITAL: CONSCIOUS CAPITALISTS

Kapor Capital is based in Oakland, east of San Francisco. That one fact says a lot about what makes this venture capital firm different from all of the top VC investors in Silicon Valley. Most of the VC powerhouses have their headquarters forty-five miles away, on a two-mile stretch of Sand Hill Road in Menlo Park, California. They are nestled into sleepy, leafy little office parks, clustered right next to one another, in dead-quiet, understated Northern California buildings. To visit them, you drive way up in the hills above Stanford University, where the parking lots are filled with Teslas, birds chirp in the eucalyptus trees, and skinny spandex-clad techies zip around on exotic carbon-fiber racing bikes that cost more than what some people pay for a car.

By contrast, to visit Kapor Capital, you drive across the Bay Bridge from San Francisco, drop down off the highway, and drive through a vast homeless camp under a freeway overpass on Martin Luther King Jr. Way, past buildings decorated with graffiti art and pawn shops, bail bond services, and payday lenders. Oakland sits across the bay from San Francisco, but they're remarkably different places. Oakland is a gritty, working-class city. It's also an African American city. For a long time black people were the biggest ethnic group in Oakland, and while demographics have shifted recently, African Americans still represent about a quarter of the population.

By setting up shop here in Oakland, Mitch Kapor and Freada Kapor Klein, the husband-and-wife team behind Kapor Capital, were sending a message—they were not part of that other world. Unlike those big venture capital firms over on Sand Hill Road, the Kapors are not trying to make as much money as possible by any means necessary. Instead, they have a social mission. Some call it impact investing. Or diversity-focused investing. Or mission-driven versus money-driven investing. The Kapors call their model "gap-closing investing," meaning they will only invest in companies that are "serving low-income communities and/or communities of color to close gaps of access, opportunity, or outcome," Freada says.

The Kapors moved from San Francisco to Oakland in 2012 and bought a vacant building in Oakland's Uptown neighborhood. In 2016 the onetime Pacific Telephone and Telegraph switching station opened as the Kapor Center for Social Impact, a nonprofit organization whose goal is to help underrepresented people of color get education in STEM (science, technology, engineering, and mathematics) and make careers in the tech industry. The center has a hundred-seat auditorium and a big roof deck that's great for parties. The Kapors make the center available to other organizations for conferences and workshops. The offices of Kapor Capital are housed inside the Kapor Center, along with another Kapor organization, the Level Playing Field Institute, a nonprofit that runs a summer math and science program for minority students.

In addition to making a statement about their priorities, the Kapors' move to Oakland has turned out to be a pretty smart investment. Oakland is on the rebound. New businesses are popping up—little coffee shops, brewpubs, farmers markets, and trendy restaurants catering to the young professionals. Once considered one of the most dangerous cities in America, Oakland now makes the *Forbes* list of

America's Coolest Cities, with Uptown, the neighborhood where the Kapor Center is located, finding itself on the *Forbes* list of America's Best Hipster Neighborhoods.

"Here in Oakland we have a different story than in San Francisco," Mitch says. It's a Thursday evening in the summer of 2017. We're eating takeout sushi in the Kapor Capital offices, while Dudley, the Kapors' big goldendoodle, sprawls out in the corner. "We have community engagement, and start-up weekends, and First Friday programs for Oakland entrepreneurs, where we get people together and talk about how you start a company."

Mitch is sixty-eight years old with a shock of white hair and some-times a white beard to match. He's a onetime meditation instructor who became a software entrepreneur and got rich, almost by acci-dent. Freada, sixty-six, is a small woman with curly black hair and intense dark eyes. She grew up in Biloxi, Mississippi, and once saw her older brother, age seven, get beaten up for being Jewish. You get the sense that she's been fighting ever since. In the early 1970s Frieda was a student activist and rape crisis counselor at UC-Berkeley. After graduation she founded an organization to combat sexual harass-ment in the workplace, wrote articles for a newsletter called *Feminist Alliance Against Rape*, and got a PhD in social policy and research from Brandeis.

As Freada told an interviewer in 2018: "Diversity is all that's ever mattered to me, for all the decades of my professional life."

THE RISE OF "IMPACT INVESTING"

In a way what's happening to Oakland is a metaphor for what the Kapors are hoping to do with the tech industry. Over the past ten or twenty years the industry has gone off the rails. The smash-and-grab, get-rich-quick, screw-the-workers business model has become deeply entrenched. That model has created a dysfunctional work-place culture where women are excluded or harassed, where "bros hire bros," where employees are treated poorly, and where people of color are unwelcome.

The industry's lack of diversity is not just unfair, but it's also bad business. Research by consulting firm McKinsey in 2015 found that companies in the top quartile for gender and racial diversity were 35 percent more likely to produce higher-than-average financial returns. More-diverse companies are better able to recruit top talent and have higher employee satisfaction, McKinsey claims. Whether diversity makes people *happier* remains a subject of debate. Certainly, people who previously were excluded and now can get jobs are happier. But a 2014 MIT study suggests that diverse workplaces have more friction than workplaces with homogeneous cultures. Sara Ellison, the MIT economist who led the study, used the analogy of a baseball team made up entirely of catchers. They wouldn't win many games, but they would probably get along great. In other words: diversity might not make everyone happy, but happiness in and of itself may not be the right goal.

For decades the Kapors have been trying to boost the diversity of the tech industry. They've launched educational programs to teach girls and underprivileged kids how to write code, for example. But things haven't gotten better; if anything, the industry seems to be moving backward. In 2012 the Kapors came up with the idea of yoking investment dollars to social change. This is not a new concept. Socially progressive mutual funds have been around for a long time.

What's different is that the Kapors are doing this with venture capital. Investing seed money means getting involved early and shaping a company's culture, sometimes from day one. By making early-stage investments the Kapors can buy themselves a seat at the table. It's not uncommon for venture capitalists to help start-ups assemble management teams and decide which executives to hire.

The Kapors believe "impact investing" might accomplish things that nonprofits and philanthropic organizations cannot. "The world runs on business," Mitch says. "We need to change working conditions.

We need to create more good work where people are treated well. Philanthropy is not going to solve that problem."

The Kapors are part of a mission-driven movement that is springing up at the edges of Silicon Valley and has been starting to get traction. Company founders and company funders alike are pushing back against the rich-get-richer business model that traditional venture capital firms have created over the past twenty years. A new generation of start-up founders are committing to building healthy and diverse corporate cultures, and they are supported by a handful of small venture capital firms that share their values.

Kapor Capital doesn't require that a company have a founder who is a woman or a person of color. They focus instead on the product or service the company creates. It has to be one that they consider "gap-closing" rather than "gap-widening." Here's a hypothetical example. A company that sells a really expensive service that helps rich kids do a little better on their SATs would be gap-widening; a service that helps poor immigrant kids get access to a good education would be gap-closing.

Traditional venture capitalists don't care about this. If anything, they prefer start-ups that sell stuff to rich people, for obvious reasons. That's why the tech industry has been producing so many "mommy start-ups," meaning companies started by young guys who want services to do things their moms used to do for them—like do their laundry (Washio, Cleanly, Rinse, FlyCleaners, Prim, Mulberrys) and bring them food (DoorDash, Instacart, Blue Apron, Maple, Sprig, Plated, and at least sixty others have been funded since 2011). There are start-ups that sell $500 "collectible" sneakers and one that uses robots to make pizza.

TECH'S BIG DIVERSITY PROBLEM

I saw the tech industry's diversity problems firsthand when I was a fifty-something guy struggling to fit in at a start-up where almost everyone was half my age. I've often been asked to talk about age bias and the plight of older workers, and I'm happy to do it—but bias based on race and gender is far worse—and all three are related.

One young woman I interviewed was the only black student in her computer science class and was ignored by her white male colleagues. Another person I spoke with, an African American guy, thought he did great in a phone interview, only to show up for the in-person interview and see the startled look in the young white guy's eyes. "It was like, 'Oh, I didn't know you were—um, sorry, I didn't know you were so *tall*.'" A friend I'll call Alex, an Ivy League graduate with twenty years of tech experience, shows up to pitch his start-up to VCs and can tell by their expressions that they're not going to fund him. Is it because he's black? Or because he's in his fifties? He can't be sure.

Every year, Apple, Google, and Facebook publish diversity reports, and every year they say the same thing: sorry, we still haven't made much progress. The numbers are appalling. In some tech companies black workers represent only 2 percent of the employee population; Latinos fare only slightly better. Only one-third of workers are female. There are fewer women working in Silicon Valley today than in the 1980s. In leadership ranks the imbalance is worse—management teams and boards of directors are loaded with white men. Somehow, over the past twenty years, Silicon Valley has gone backward.

It's even worse in the venture capital industry, where 1 percent of investment team members are black, and Latinos make up just over 2 percent, according to The Information, a Silicon Valley publication. Women represent only 15 percent of decision-making roles. VCs claim that they make decisions based entirely on the strength of the company's ideas, and without any regard for race or gender. But can you guess where the members of the White Man Club tend to put their money? "I can be tricked by anyone who looks like Mark Zuckerberg" is how Paul Graham, the founder of Y Combinator, a top Silicon Valley start-up incubator, once famously put it. Graham later claimed he was joking, but a glance through the roster of Y Combinator portfolio companies turns up an awful lot of nerdy young Zuckerberg clones.

As for why there are so few women in venture capital, Michael Moritz, a partner at Sequoia Ventures, once said that it's not because of gender bias but that "What we're not prepared to do is to lower our standards." The obtuseness, arrogance, and self-regard of that comment boggles the mind. When Moritz said that, Sequoia had *no* female investing partners.

Moritz is not some fringe character. He is a legend in the world of venture capital and worth a reported $4 billion. He helped launch some of the biggest tech companies in the world, including Google, Yahoo, and PayPal. He is also one of the VCs who kicked in $50,000 each to support the 2016 ballot measure that would sweep homeless people off the streets in San Francisco. Yet he is revered by his peers. Many of them feel the same way he does about hiring women and people of color; they're just polite enough not to say it out loud, in public.

I've heard various theories for how things got so bad in Silicon Valley. One is that venture capitalists and tech companies are lazy about recruiting. Instead of casting a wide net, they hire kids out of Stanford and Berkeley, where black and Latino students are underrepresented. There's the good-guy theory, which is when one guy tells another guy that a third guy is a "good guy," meaning he's one of us, go ahead and hire him. Another theory is that, just like Michael Moritz at Sequoia, techies really believe that diversity would hurt their performance. The men who run VC firms and tech companies pay lip service to diversity, but deep down they believe that their current arrangement—hiring young men, mostly white, and building "bro" cultures—actually delivers the best results.

Meanwhile the guys who run Silicon Valley came up with an excuse: we want to hire more women and people of color; we just can't find any qualified candidates.

I reached out to Mary Campbell, the president of Spelman College, a historically black college for women in Atlanta, Georgia, and asked her about this claim. Campbell explained that there's more to improving diversity than just recruiting. For one thing, Spelman's graduates in STEM fields are already in high demand, and they all find good jobs—just not in Silicon Valley. They're working at Boeing and in biotech companies, rather than the "bro culture" tech companies.

The bigger issue, Campbell said, is retaining black employees. Black graduates who go to Silicon Valley often feel unwanted or out of place, so they leave. To hang on to those people, Silicon Valley needs to become a place where those young people feel welcome. "It's about having a community, having a local church you can go to, having the chance to meet a spouse," Campbell says.

How can it be that these "innovative" tech companies in Silicon Valley seem like some of the most backward organizations in the world? This is basically segregation, only instead of taking place at the University of Alabama in 1963, it's happening in California in 2018.

The consequences aren't just moral failings—they're financial. Freada Kapor has consulted with most big tech companies and produced voluminous research. Contrary to the prevailing opinion among bro-CEOs, Kapor argues that diversity produces better returns. A 2017 study by the Kapor Center estimated that employee turnover related to cultural issues was costing the tech industry $16 billion a year. Yet not much progress has been made, she concedes. "Google spent $289 million on diversity over the course of two years, and you show me what changed," she says.

Mitch cites a lack of interest on the part of CEOs as part of the problem. Without that push from the top, nothing happens. "It's just not a top priority for Mark Zuckerberg," Mitch says. "He has a lot of other stuff going on. It's not really important to him. That's my conclusion. If this were important at the CEO level, then you would see companies taking more dramatic action." Also, these companies are making loads of money. "They're doing swell. So it's a case of, if it ain't broke don't fix it," Kapor says.

In recent years the Kapors started to dial back on trying to fix big tech companies. They believe they can have more impact by working with new start-ups. "We're focusing on young companies," Mitch says. "I think it's more likely that a new generation of companies can do better. If you bake in a commitment to diversity and inclusion right from the start, it will still be part of the company when you get large."

BREAKING THE CODE OF SILENCE

The Kapors have been activists, in one way or another, since the early 1970s, when Mitch was at Yale and Freada was at UC-Berkeley. They might have become just another kooky old hippie couple living in the Bay Area except that in the early 1980s Mitch became fantastically rich. This happened almost by accident. After graduation in 1971 he spent a decade bouncing around. He taught Transcendental Meditation. He worked as a DJ. In 1978 he bought an Apple II computer and taught himself to write programs, which landed him a job at VisiCorp, a tiny software developer near Boston.

In 1982, Mitch founded Lotus Development, named after the lotus position used in meditation, to sell a software program called Lotus 1-2-3, a spreadsheet that ran on the recently introduced IBM personal computer. Kapor expected Lotus would generate $1 million in sales in its first year. Instead, sales topped $53 million, making Lotus one of the biggest software companies in the world. Within a decade annual sales would approach $1 billion. The company went public. Eventually it was acquired by IBM for $3.5 billion. Mitch the meditation instructor became Mitch the multimillionaire.

Lotus became known for worker-friendly culture, with a goal to become the most progressive company in the United States. Mitch told the venture capitalist who funded the company, "There are some things that are as important as making money and one is how I treat people."

The company offered a generous pension plan. Lotus also provided a sabbatical program and on-site day care. It was one of the first big companies to offer benefits for same-sex partners, and it stuck to its guns even when big institutional investors dumped their shares in protest. Managers went through rigorous diversity training. "We had lots of female executives. There was incredible social awareness," recalls John Landry, a former chief technology officer.

Carrie Griffen spent seventeen years at Lotus, from 1983 to 2000, in a variety of communications and management roles. "We were happy at Lotus, not only because the company cared about its employees, but because the leadership fostered the right culture," she says. "People work hard when they're happy, and inspired, and when they are part of an honorable culture. That's the Lotus I remember."

Lotus is also where Mitch and Freada met; she joined the company in 1984 as the head of employee relations, after completing her PhD at Brandeis, though they did not become romantically involved until later, in the 1990s. Mitch left Lotus in 1986, because he didn't like running a big company, and frankly, he wasn't very good at it. Freada left in 1987 and created a consultancy offering training on workplace bias. But the progressive culture they set in motion continued.

After Lotus, Mitch went back to bouncing around. He developed a program called Agenda, which Lotus distributed. He moved to San Francisco and co-founded the Electronic Frontier Foundation, a digital rights organization that defends civil liberties.

Mitch began investing in start-ups and had a sharp eye for picking winners. He put seed money into Dropcam, which was acquired by

Google, and Twilio, which went public and now has a market value of nearly $4 billion. At that point, Mitch was just investing as an individual, but in 2009 he and Freada formed Kapor Capital. One of the first bets they made was on Uber. In October 2010, Kapor and twenty-eight other Silicon Valley techies threw together $1.5 million in a seed round for the ride-sharing company, reportedly at a valuation of $4 million. By 2017, Uber's valuation had skyrocketed to $70 billion. The early investors had made a killing. A stake that cost $20,000 in the seed round had ballooned in value to $40 million, by some estimates. (The Kapors won't say how much they invested in Uber or what their stake is worth today. They also point out that they made the investment in Uber before they committed to social-impact investing.)

The big win on Uber came with baggage. Uber had built a toxic culture that was the antithesis of everything the Kapors stood for. There was no diversity. Women were treated horribly. So while the investment added to the Kapors' bank account it also became a blot on their reputation. In February 2017 Uber was engulfed in scandal after Susan Fowler, a former engineer at the company, published an essay on Medium describing sexual harassment that had driven her to leave the company. Soon other women from Uber came forward with similar stories about an abusive workplace. Uber tried to put out the fire by creating a team to investigate the complaints, led by Eric Holder, the former attorney general of the United States.

Still, the Kapors were fed up. They published an open letter saying that carrying out an investigation wasn't going to be enough. They revealed that for years they had been working behind the scenes to get Uber to fix its "culture plagued by disrespect, exclusionary cliques, lack of diversity, and tolerance for bullying and harassment of every form." Freada had given a talk at Uber and consulted with some of its executives. At this point, Uber needed a massive overhaul, and the company should "hold Uber leadership accountable, since all other mechanisms have failed," they wrote.

In essence the Kapors were calling for Uber's board to fire the company's founder and CEO, Travis Kalanick. Some fellow investors considered the move a betrayal. In Silicon Valley there's an unspoken rule that investors should never do anything to hurt the valuation of the company, including criticizing management in public. In their open letter the Kapors said the code of silence needed to change. "As investors, we certainly want to see Uber succeed, but success must be measured in more than just financial terms," they wrote.

Other venture capitalists were quick to criticize the Kapors. Some started trying to poach companies away from Kapor Capital, warning founders not to take more money from them and to let other investors buy out the Kapors. These efforts failed. Kapor's portfolio companies stuck with the Kapors. "One prominent investor told one of our founders, 'They'll just turn on you like they turned on Uber.' The CEO's response was to tell the investor she would never accept their money and that the values we expressed were the reasons she approached us to be her first investor," Freada says.

"We broke the code by speaking," Freada says. "We were supposed to give them our advice, but quietly. But we were frustrated. We had spent many hours with them, trying to counsel them. And they were not listening. We had been unable to influence them. We felt we had to hold them accountable. Uber's culture was toxic."

A few months after the Kapors published their open letter, Uber's board pushed Kalanick out as CEO. Six months after that, when investment firm SoftBank bought a chunk of Uber, the company's valuation had dropped by about $20 billion. You can't blame the Kapors for all of that. Uber had many bigger problems than their open letter. But the incident had been a defining moment. It showed that the Kapors would not be afraid to speak up, even if it could hurt them financially. If any companies were scared away, they were probably not companies that Kapor would want to fund anyway, Mitch says.

"SAVING CAPITALISM FROM ITSELF"

Nine years after its inception, Kapor Capital remains a relatively tiny firm, with only six investment partners in addition to the Kapors. Three are women. Three are Hispanic and three are black. One partner is Benjamin Jealous, the former president of the NAACP (National Association for the Advancement of Colored People), who joined in 2013 and is now running for governor of Maryland. "Entrepreneurs from diverse backgrounds look at our team page, and they can find someone who looks like them, and they think, 'Hey, these people might have a sense of who I am,'" Mitch says. More than half of the companies they've invested in have been led by a founder who is a woman or a person of color.

Unlike most venture capital firms, which get money from pension funds and college endowments, the Kapors only invest their own money. (They have plenty to work with—their net worth has been estimated at $500 million.) Since 2012, Kapor Capital has invested only in companies that they consider to be "gap-closing" and that they believe can have social impact at a very large scale. That radically reduces the number of deals they look at, and it means ruling out promising opportunities in areas like self-driving cars, virtual reality goggles, and robots that make pizza.

What's more, an investment from Kapor Capital comes with strings attached. Companies must abide by a set of principles that Kapor calls the Founders' Commitment. That includes setting goals on diversity and inclusion, and producing a diversity and inclusion progress report every quarter. Companies must invest in training on how to mitigate bias, give employees opportunities to do volunteer work, and participate in diversity and inclusion workshops hosted by Kapor Capital. The firm announced the Founders' Commitment in 2016. But companies Kapor funded before 2016 have the option to sign on, and three-quarters have done so.

The principles are spelled out in the acronym GIVE, which stands for goals, invest, volunteer, and educate. The gist is that companies must set diversity goals and send in a quarterly report on how they're doing. They must attend training sessions hosted at Kapor Capital, invest in training for their employees, and give employees time to volunteer with underrepresented communities.

The result of the Kapors' efforts is a new generation of companies that have healthier, more inclusive workplace cultures and are making products and services that are "gap-closing." Kapor Capital funded Managed by Q, the subject of the previous chapter, and Honor, which provides home health-care services and, like Q, categorizes its workers as full employees. Those companies are "gap-closing" because they're creating good jobs for working-class people.

Others are gap-closing because they provide services for low-income people. LendUp provides credit cards and small short-term loans to people with low credit scores, who might otherwise rely on predatory payday lenders. Pigeonly, founded by an ex-convict, helps inmates stay in touch with family and friends while they are incarcerated, sending photos and making low-cost phone calls. Thrive Market is a members-only online grocer that charges 25 percent less than traditional supermarkets and offers free memberships to veterans, public school teachers, and low-income families. HealthSherpa helps people find affordable health insurance plans. Genius Plaza, founded by Ana Roca Castro, provides a bilingual curriculum for kids in low-income schools. The company now serves two million children in the United States and Latin America, and is growing rapidly; in 2017 its revenues tripled.

The Kapors are betting that gap-closing investments can deliver a good return to venture capitalists. They plan to publish a report on their fund performance in 2022, when the fund hits the ten-year mark. While it can take a while for start-ups to deliver returns, "we have many gap-closing companies across multiple sectors which are doing very well," Freada says.

In addition to investing, the Kapors are active philanthropists. In 2017, the Kapor Center launched an annual Impact Award, to honor people and companies that are doing a lot of work around inclusion in the tech industry. Freada founded and chairs a nonprofit, SMASH, which offers a summer math and science program for minority students. In 2015 she co-founded a "diversity war room" called Project Include, which offers start-up CEOs a set of principles that are similar to but even more detailed and comprehensive than the ones in the Kapor Capital Founders' Commitment.

Diversity-focused investment firms and start-up incubators are springing up around Silicon Valley. Outfits like NewME, Base Ventures, Cross Culture Ventures, Backstage Capital, and Precursor Ventures are run by people of color and lean toward investing in companies run by women and people of color. XFactor Ventures is a women-run firm that invests only in companies with at least one female co-founder. Social Capital, a VC firm with more than $1 billion under management, has taken a stand on diversity: "I want the firm to look like what the world looks like. That means hiring and backing minorities and women," says its founder, Chamath Palihapitiya, a former Facebook executive.

To be sure, even if you pooled all of the resources of the good-guy venture capital firms and advocacy groups, they would still be tiny compared to the $70 billion that venture capital firms invest each year in the United States. But the good guys seem to be punching above their weight and creating a kind of movement.

Even at some big tech companies, things may be getting a little better. Google has launched a program with Howard University that brings students from historically black colleges and universities to spend twelve weeks on the Google campus, studying coding. Google's size becomes a double-edged sword. On the one hand, Google has vast resources and can tackle any problem. On the other hand, Google has nearly ninety thousand employees, so boosting diversity in any meaningful way is difficult.

The stakes have never been higher. A few decades ago, the tech industry did not exert much influence on the world economy. Today, technology is transforming every company globally. "Every business is a tech business," Mitch says. The world's five biggest companies, in terms of market valuation, are tech companies. That's why the Kapors and others in the movement are feeling so urgent. They're racing to fix the tech industry before its dysfunction spreads. As Mitch likes to say, "We're trying to save capitalism from itself." He's only half joking.

In the past three chapters I've looked at entrepreneurs and investors who are trying to build worker-friendly companies with cultures that are more inclusive and create opportunities for a wider range of people. But how can their ideas spread into the wider world of work? To do that, you need to create a movement. You need to develop a new generation of young people who are not brainwashed with Milton Friedman's greed-is-good doctrine, and will push back against it, and demand that workers should share in the wealth their labor creates, and stand on equal footing with investors. You need to create a new ideology—a new form of capitalism. In the next chapter, I'll tell you about people who are doing that, under the banner of what's called the social enterprise movement.

CHAPTER FOURTEEN

THE SOCIAL ENTERPRISE MOVEMENT

O n the morning of September 11, 2001, Dennis Shaughnessy flew from Boston to Baltimore, where he was scheduled to give a presentation at a conference hosted by the Food and Drug Administration. Not long after his flight touched down at Baltimore-Washington International Airport, two other planes that took off from Boston's Logan airport flew into the towers at the World Trade Center in New York. A third plane hit the Pentagon, and a fourth crashed into a field in Pennsylvania.

Shaughnessy, who could see smoke rising from the Pentagon from the roof of his hotel, was pushed to an epiphany: "I asked myself, if I were one of the people on those planes, would I look back and say that I used my career to do the most good possible? If this had been my last day, would I be happy with what I'd done?"

He was forty-three years old, a corporate lawyer by training, and now a senior vice president at Charles River Laboratories in Boston. That company's recent IPO had made him wealthy, with "more money than I ever dreamed of. It would be nothing to Bill Gates, but to me it was a fortune," he says.

It's not hard to imagine a man like this driving up the East Coast on the morning after 9/11, passing New York City, and thinking that maybe he does not want to spend the rest of his life schlepping down to Baltimore to give presentations for a company that breeds mice and monkeys for clinical trials.

"I started trying to think about starting another phase of my life where I could do more good than I was doing at the time," he says. "I definitely decided that I was not going to work as a traditional business executive. And I thought there must be some way to bridge the gap between raging capitalism and sloppy, inefficient nonprofits."

In 2003 Shaughnessy convinced Northeastern University to let him start a program inside its business school. He would develop a curriculum, organize field trips to South Africa and India, and teach students about social entrepreneurship. By "social entrepreneurship" he meant the notion that companies could both turn a profit *and* be a force for social good. The notion of a social enterprise has been around since the 1970s, but for decades remained mostly the purview of theorists and academics. But in the past decade, as people like Shaughnessy and thousands of others have signed on, the movement has become more mainstream. What's more, the notion of what a social enterprise could or should be has broadened, so that it's no longer just about providing vaccines in far-off corners of the developing world, but also focuses on creating good jobs that pay well and providing employees with benefits and job security. As more and more students are exposed to these ideas about what a business should do, the hope is that better treatment of workers will get spliced into the DNA of American companies.

Shaughnessy launched the Social Enterprise Institute in 2007 with a shoestring budget that he provided out of his own pocket. The demand was tremendous. In SEI's biggest years, more than six hundred students enrolled in at least one course. Thanks to the high enrollment, the SEI was at one time ranked as the largest undergraduate social enterprise program in the United States.

Every summer Northeastern sends forty students to Cape Town, South Africa, and various cities in India for four-week courses in which they work alongside local entrepreneurs. In some years the program has made trips to Kenya, Ghana, Haiti, the Dominican Republic, Venezuela, and Cuba.

In South Africa, Northeastern students take classes at the Tertiary School in Business Administration (TSiBA), a free university in Cape Town. Teams made up of students from Northeastern and TSiBA are assigned to work with local entrepreneurs and come up with ideas that could improve or expand their businesses. At the end of the two weeks each team pitches to a group of judges, who determine which entrepreneurs will get funded.

Judges hear twenty-five pitches and choose five entrepreneurs who get seed funding from grants made by SEI. The investments are small, usually $5,000 or less. Over the years, SEI students have consulted with about two hundred entrepreneurs in South Africa, and fifty of those entrepreneurs received some funding. About a decade ago, SEI students worked with Luvuyo Rani, an entrepreneur who had opened an Internet café in one of the townships near Cape Town. Today his company, Silulo Ulutho Technologies, employs 170 people, and operates thirty-nine Internet cafes and training centers.

The SEI program also influences students who return to the States and start their own companies. Ali Kothari, who traveled to South Africa in 2015, now runs a Boston-based start-up, Eat Your Coffee, which makes caffeinated snack bars and has a half dozen employees. Kothari buys his coffee from Grounds for Change, a roaster that passes part of its revenues to nonprofits. That means Kothari's company has paid for kids in Nicaragua to go to school for a year and funded microloans for women entrepreneurs in Guatemala. Kothari says his experience at SEI "opened me up to the idea that there are multiple ways to run a business, and profit is not the only way to maximize shareholder value."

When Austen Moye came to Northeastern in the fall of 2015 he was enrolled as a chemistry major and planned to go to medical school. That plan ended after he took Shaughnessy's introductory course, Global Social Enterprise, during his first semester, and then signed up for another Shaughnessy class in the spring. By the time he returned for his sophomore year, Moye was majoring in business. He says it's because Shaughnessy changed his perception of what business was all about—and it was completely contradictory to what other business professors were teaching him.

"I took a course in finance, and literally the first thing the professor said in the first class session was that the purpose of business is to maximize profit," Moye said. "Then I went to Shaughnessy's class and he's saying that business can be used for social good, it can be used to improve people's lives."

Shaughnessy says all he hopes to do is get students excited about social entrepreneurship. "They come in and they have no idea what any of this is about, and then they say, 'Oh my God, this is amazing, what else can I read about this, where can I go with this?'"

He believes social enterprise has grown so large and gathered so much momentum that it is no longer just a movement. "This is the future of capitalism," he says. Shareholder capitalism has held sway for a half century but has run its course. "This cycle will burn itself out soon. I'm not sure when. Ten years, twenty years. But it can't last."

"A NEW KIND OF ORGANIZATION"

Hundreds of social enterprise programs have sprung up at universities around the world. They're sending thousands of young people into the world believing that capitalism can do something other than just help rich people get richer. The movement represents a counterweight to the shareholder-centric ideas that Milton Friedman proposed in his essay in the *New York Times Magazine* back in 1970 and aims to undo a half century of corporate capitalism that has produced so many toxic, dysfunctional outcomes. Oddly enough, the social enterprise movement originated in business schools—the same places that were preaching the bible of Milton Friedman and producing miniature Gordon Gekkos for investment banks and management consulting firms.

Terms like *social enterprise* and *social entrepreneurship* started kicking around in the 1970s, which was just as the Friedman doctrine began to be taught in business schools. That is probably not a coincidence. Nor is the fact that interest in social enterprise has suddenly soared in the past ten years, a period when the problems created by shareholder capitalism have become acute. Now these concepts, which once were confined mostly to some hopelessly naïve do-gooders at the fringes of academia and the business world, have become mainstream.

To be sure, there has always been a middle ground between hard-core capitalism and pure nonprofit organizations. Worker cooperatives have existed for centuries, for example. And philanthropies and nonprofits have been around for as long as there have been rich people. But the modern concept of a social enterprise and social entrepreneurship involves creating a new kind of organization, a sort of hybrid. It's an organization that bridges the gap between for-profit and nonprofit organizations, and might blur the boundaries between those two worlds.

One idea has been for nonprofits to become more like for-profit corporations. Maybe they could do some for-profit work on the side, generating revenue to sustain their philanthropic mission. Another approach is to create for-profit companies that tackle social missions, like mitigating poverty, that once were within the purview of non-profits and philanthropies. An example of the latter is Samasource, a San Francisco company that outsources tasks for companies like Google to workers in impoverished countries. Workers need only a laptop and a bit of training, and can do things like content moderation, scanning websites for objectionable photos. Samasource was founded in 2008 and claims to have lifted sixty thousand people out of poverty.

An early pioneer in social enterprise was Gregory Dees, a professor whose academic career involved stints at Yale School of Management, Harvard Business School, Stanford Graduate School of Business, and Duke University's Fuqua School of Business. In 1998, while at Harvard, Dees published an article in the *Harvard Business Review* titled "Enterprising Nonprofits," in which he suggested nonprofits could behave more like for-profit companies, perhaps by creating for-profit side ventures that supported the organization. In 2001, while at Stanford, Dees published an essay titled "The Meaning of Social Entrepreneurship," which would become one of the most widely read articles in the field and remains a kind of bible for people interested in social enterprise.

At Duke, Dees co-founded the Center for the Advancement of Social Entrepreneurship, whose current director, Cathy Clark, ranks among the most influential academics in the field. Other influential figures include Gordon Bloom, who has founded social entrepreneurship laboratories at Princeton, Harvard, and Stanford; and Alex Nicholls and Dr. Peter Drobac at the Skoll Centre for Social Entrepreneurship at the University of Oxford.

In recent years the movement has been booming, according to Jessica Lax, a director at Ashoka, a nonprofit that supports social entrepreneurs and people it calls "change makers." According to Ashoka, in 2012 there were more than 1,200 colleges and universities offering programs in social enterprise, up from only eighteen in 1994. Ashoka was founded in 1980 by Bill Drayton, a onetime McKinsey consultant and federal government bureaucrat, who, like Dees, also has been called "the godfather of social entrepreneurship." The organization now has more than four hundred employees in ninety-eight countries.

Universities are adding programs not because employers request this but because "students are knocking down their doors," Lax says. "They're not happy with the state of corporate social responsibility, and they're also not happy with how a traditional nonprofit works. They're pushing for another way."

WIRPS: WELL-INTENTIONED RICH PEOPLE

Academics have developed the intellectual underpinnings of the movement, but equally important are people I call WIRPs— well-intentioned rich people. Bill Gates is probably the best-known WIRP, but WIRPs are everywhere and most are not household names.

That social enterprise center at Oxford, the one that employs Alex Nicholls and other top scholars, was built by Jeff Skoll, who made a fortune at eBay. In 2004 Skoll created the Skoll Foundation, which organizes an annual world forum around social entrepreneurship and launched an annual set of Skoll Awards for Social Entrepreneurship. Another WIRP—John Wood, who got rich at Microsoft—operates one of the biggest and best-known social enterprises in the world, a nonprofit called Room to Read, which has built a thousand schools and ten thousand libraries in the developing world.

Jay Coen Gilbert seems like an unlikely figure to lead a revolution. He graduated from Stanford in 1989, spent two years working at McKinsey, then in 1993 founded a sneaker company, AND1, which he sold in 2005 for a cool $250 million. Most guys in this situation— still young, suddenly wealthy—either go off and do crazy rich-guy things, or they start another company and try to turn their millions into billions.

Instead, Gilbert launched a nonprofit whose goal is to smash up the form of capitalism that has existed for the past half century—and which rewarded him so handsomely—and replace it with something new. Instead of shareholder capitalism, we would have *stakeholder* capitalism. Instead of only caring about investors, companies would care about the environment, the community, and—perhaps most important—their employees.

With two co-founders, Gilbert created an organization called B Lab, which developed a kind of do-gooder certification program. Just as the Royal Family in the UK have a crest for products that meet their approval, B Lab offers to certify that a company is a B Corporation.

To get the certification, companies go through an assessment that includes a deep dive into how much they contribute to employee well-being as well as compensation and benefits, training, health and safety, and flexibility. If you want to be a B Corporation, you have to prove that you treat your workers well.

What CEO would bother with such nonsense? Well, twelve years after B Lab's founding, nearly 2,500 companies have gained B Corporation certification—that's compared to 205 companies in 2009. These aren't all a bunch of tiny food co-ops and shops that make clothes out of hemp. We're talking about some big names, like Patagonia, Warby Parker, Ben & Jerry's, and Athleta.

There are good reasons to get the do-gooder seal of approval. For one thing, it helps with recruiting. In addition, a lot of customers care about this stuff, too, and prefer to do business with companies that treat workers well. Finally, and cynically, some companies probably go along for the halo effect, and because it might generate a little bit of buzz around their brand.

Gilbert says the B Corporation movement is catching on because we're going through a historical inflection point. Capitalism isn't collapsing—but it is evolving. Little by little, the world is figuring out that shareholder capitalism leads to a dead end, and so they're dumping it. Taking care of the community and your own employees is not a form of philanthropy but rather a form of enlightened self-interest. Just as a century ago Henry Ford started paying his factory workers $5 an hour in part so that they could afford to buy his cars, people who run B Corporations believe that treating workers well ultimately benefits them—and that a form of capitalism that impoverishes the vast majority of people does not make any sense for anyone. B Lab and others in the social enterprise movement are redefining what it means for a company to be successful.

This new form of capitalism sounds great for employees and the community, but maybe not so much for investors. Nevertheless, a lot of investors are getting on board, apparently agreeing with Mitch and Freada Kapor that investor money can be used to drive good behavior. A decade ago, when the Rockefeller Foundation coined the term *impact investing* to describe a business model that would generate both a financial return and a social or environmental impact, the idea seemed a little nuts. But today there are so many impact investors that there's also an organization to track them, called the Global Impact Investing Network, and even more remarkable, GIIN claims to have twenty thousand members.

The spiritual ancestor of impact investing is Grameen Bank, a microfinance organization founded in 1983 in Bangladesh by Muhammad Yunus, who was awarded a Nobel Peace Prize in 2006. Many impact investors are small or midsize investment firms, like Acumen, Good Capital, Root Capital, and Kapor Capital, which I wrote about in a previous chapter. But now even big Wall Street banks like Goldman Sachs and J.P. Morgan operate impact investing groups.

So the pieces are falling into place. We have an academic infrastructure, a generation of idealistic young people, and piles of money looking for a home. And these things are coming together just as the problems caused by shareholder capitalism are becoming so painful and so obvious that they can no longer be ignored.

No wonder social enterprise has captured the imagination of a new generation of young people. "It's a growing movement," says Jessica Lax at Ashoka. "More and more people want to make the world a better place."

Twenty or thirty years ago, that might have meant joining the Peace Corps or working for a nonprofit or NGO. Today it's just as likely to involve starting a business. And the people you're trying to help don't need to be halfway around the world; they might be your neighbors.

Appalachia in the Eastern United States has become a focus of social enterprise work, as organizations are trying to build companies to create jobs to replace those lost in the coal industry. An organization called Mountain Association for Community Economic Development has been funding new companies like a bakery, café, and training center in West Virginia that provides training and jobs for women who are returning to work after recovering from drug addiction or being incarcerated.

Greyston, a bakery and foundation in Yonkers, New York, created an "open hiring" policy, which means they hire without regard for background, providing work for former inmates and homeless people. The company cranks out thirty-five thousand pounds of brownies each day for customers like Whole Foods and Ben & Jerry's. The company philosophy: "We don't hire people to bake brownies. We bake brownies to hire people."

Indeed, the people helped by a social enterprise might not even be poor. Even a company that makes pricey down parkas and fleece jackets beloved by rich people can be a social enterprise. In 2015 Forbes estimated Patagonia was generating $750 million a year in revenues. By now annual sales of its swanky sportswear ("Patagucci," some call it) may be approaching $1 billion. Yet Patagonia is also a certified B Corporation, in large part because of the way the company treats its employees.

Patagonia is headquartered in Ventura, California, just a few blocks from the beach, and is famous for its flexitime policy, which lets employees skip out for an afternoon to go surfing or hiking, or to pick up a kid after school. Bigger benefits include on-site child care, generous paid maternity and paternity leave, and fully paid health insurance premiums. The office is closed every other Friday, so people can spend more time at home.

Patagonia's billionaire founder, seventy-nine-year-old outdoorsman Yvon Chouinard, likes to say that he never wanted to become a businessman. And it's sometimes hard to tell whether Patagonia exists in order to make money or because Chouinard saw a way to provide an enviably comfortable life for two thousand lucky employees who share his love of the outdoors. The answer might be both.

In the first pages of his memoir, *Let My People Go Surfing*, Chouinard says Patagonia is an experiment. He, too, is a kind of mad scientist, testing out theories about organizational behavior on actual human subjects. Since founding Patagonia in 1973, he has been trying to invent a new kind of company—and a new kind of capitalism. The old kind, the one centered around shareholders, has become a dead end. "We believe the accepted model of capitalism that necessitates endless growth . . . must be displaced," he writes.

But what would take its place? He imagines a more virtuous and more enlightened form of capitalism that distributes value to all stakeholders: customers, community, and employees. That system would not only be more kind and more fair. It would also be more sustainable. It would have the advantage of not ending with the pitchforks and revolution that Nick Hanauer, the Seattle billionaire and Amazon investor, keeps warning about.

One of Chouinard's big goals has been to influence other companies. The best way to do that was to build Patagonia and to prove that his model works. Patagonia has now been in business for forty-five years, and sure enough, people are starting to pay attention— including some people in Silicon Valley.

CHAPTER FIFTEEN

CAN ZEBRAS FIX WHAT UNICORNS HAVE BROKEN?

Here's an interesting thought experiment. What's the last really big, wildly profitable company that Silicon Valley has produced, the kind of company that grows like crazy and throws off so much profit that it seems like it's printing money? As far as I can tell, the last tech company that fits this description is Facebook—which was founded in 2004. That was fourteen years ago. Since then, the bros and VCs in Silicon Valley have been swinging and missing over and over again.

To be sure, Twitter (founded in 2006) managed to eke out tiny profits in two recent quarters, but this came after years of losses that totaled billions of dollars. Zynga (founded in 2007) and Groupon (founded in 2008) squeaked out minuscule full-year profits in 2017, but again after years of massive losses. Grubhub, the food delivery company, turns a modest profit, but Grubhub comprises two merged companies which were founded in 1999 and 2004, respectively—meaning it is actually older than Facebook.

The tech industry used to produce big, money-gushing companies all the time. But in the past ten or fifteen years, something has gone wrong. In that time period, Silicon Valley has become obsessed with unicorns: private companies that grow like crazy and achieve valuations of more than $1 billion. The start-up term *unicorn* was coined in 2013, but the hunt for them began long before that, back in the early 2000s, when the second dotcom boom began. In the current boom, VCs have become very good at creating unicorns. Today there are hundreds of them. Some have gone public, and some remain private. Many provide really terrific services. But as magical as these companies may be, there's one thing unicorns seem unable to do—turn a profit.

Tesla, Spotify, Dropbox, Box, Snap, Square, Workday, Cloudera, Okta, Blue Apron, Roku, MongoDB, Redfin, Yext, Forescout, Docusign, Smartsheet—they're all publicly traded, and they all lose money, and in some cases a lot of it, sometimes for years and years, long after they go public. Other unicorns like Uber, Lyft, Airbnb, Slack, Pinterest, WeWork, Vice Media, Magic Leap, Bloom Energy, and Postmates remain privately held, but reportedly don't turn a profit. As I write this, a tech start-up called Domo is attempting to offer shares to the public even though the company lost $360 million over the past two years, on sales of just $183 million, meaning Domo loses two dollars for every dollar it took in.

This is madness. It's not sustainable. But what if we could come up with something else?

That's what four women tech entrepreneurs—Jennifer Brandel, Astrid Scholz, Aniyia Williams, and Mara Zepeda—began to wonder in 2017. Since the tech world seems to like metaphors, the four women proposed a new one. Instead of building unicorns, why not be more like zebras? In an essay on Medium, titled "Zebras Fix What Unicorns Break," they explained the analogy. Zebras are herd animals and band together to help each other. Zebras might not run as fast as unicorns, but they have stamina and are built for the long haul. Just as zebras are black and white, a zebra company would do two things at the same time: turn a profit *and* improve society. They launched an organization, Zebras Unite, and invited like-minded people to join.

Sure, the metaphor is a bit of a stretch. But you get the idea.

As Zepeda explained to me, she and her co-authors want to build companies that deliver sustainable prosperity, not flashy start-ups that grow fast, lose money, and fizzle out. They want to build companies that cooperate rather than compete, and "deliver value *to* users, not extract value *from* them," she wrote.

That sounds incredibly sane and healthy. The problem is, VCs won't fund companies like that. They still want the unicorns and the rapid growth. The unicorn model does not create sustainable, healthy companies—but it does deliver to investors the biggest possible return in the shortest possible time. Silicon Valley VCs actually have more incentive to create bad companies than good ones. If you're a woman entrepreneur pitching a company that will grow slowly, turn a profit, and create a sustainable business, nobody on Sand Hill Road wants to take a meeting with you.

Since that's the case, the founders of Zebras Unite said, let's opt out and find a new way to fund the companies we want to build. "We need new corporate structures," Zepeda tells me in an interview. One model she admires is the "steward-owned" company, where shareholders are actively involved with the organization as management or employees. The business model is actually an old one, pioneered by Bosch and Zeiss. But now a German organization, Purpose Network, and its affiliated investment group, Purpose Ventures, are exploring ways to apply this model to start-ups and to create companies that "maximize purpose instead of profit," according to their website.

As for the zebras, so far more than four thousand people have expressed interest in joining Zebras Unite, and one thousand have become active community members. In November 2017, Zebras Unite held a conference in Portland, Oregon, called DazzleCon ("dazzle" is the actual name for a herd of zebras) which drew two hundred attendees. Zepeda tells me the Zebra movement is expanding, and now has more than twenty international chapters.

To be sure, Team Zebra is tiny compared to Team Unicorn. The VC industry pumped nearly $150 billion into start-ups worldwide in

2017 and is on track to invest even more in 2018, according to the National Venture Capital Association. Big-shot VCs would probably say the folks on Team Zebra are hopelessly naïve—if they even thought about them at all. Nevertheless, the fact that Team Zebra even exists seems like a sign that Silicon Valley might be starting to wake up from its long fever dream.

Meanwhile others have started pushing for reform, including some who possess a lot of clout. Paul Tudor Jones, a billionaire hedge fund manager, has little in common with the sandal-wearing types who showed up at DazzleCon, yet he too thinks the corporate world is in terrible danger and needs a massive overhaul. The problem is not just the way companies are structured—it's the overall economic system. "Capitalism may need modernizing," Jones told CNBC in June 2018. For half a century, corporate America has been ruled by the gospel of shareholder capitalism, as proclaimed by Milton Friedman. But that model, which puts investor returns above all else, has run out of gas, Jones said. Jones runs a foundation, Just Capital, that focuses on social-impact investing and measures the values of companies not just on profits but on how well they treat their workers.

Here's the thing. When a billionaire hedge fund guy starts sounding the alarm about income inequality, and saying that capitalism itself needs to be reinvented—well, I suggest we should pay attention.

A good start would be to push successful companies to be better citizens. In Silicon Valley, city officials in Mountain View (home to Google) and Cupertino (home to Apple) say they might start taxing big companies on a per-employee basis to mitigate problems like traffic congestion and the lack of affordable housing. The Californians were inspired by city officials in Seattle, who passed a measure that would tax big companies $275 per employee to help address the city's growing homeless population. Unfortunately, Seattle later canceled the tax after Amazon and other employers howled. (Amazon, the biggest employer in Seattle, would have paid $12 million per year, which is a pittance, considering the company generates billions of dollars in profit each year, and that its founder and CEO, Jeff Bezos, is worth $140 billion.)

If public officials can't force companies to help out, employees might. Workers in Silicon Valley are making noise about unions, in part to push companies to behave more ethically. "We want people to be afraid of the political power of their employees," Maciej Ceglowski, head of an activist group called Tech Solidarity, told Quartz in 2017. In 2018, four thousand Google employees protested the company's involvement in a military drone program, and a dozen resigned; Google agreed not to renew the contract. Employees at Microsoft and Amazon also have organized protests, demanding that their employers stop providing technology to U.S. Immigration and Customs Enforcement.

There are other hopeful signs for worker welfare. In France, the former CEO and other top executives of France Telecom, who dehumanized workers and drove them to suicide, will be forced to stand trial for their actions. If nothing else, the trial may encourage companies to curb abusive, exploitative practices and treat workers with more respect. In California, the founder of Theranos, Elizabeth Holmes, has been indicted for fraud, after the health-care unicorn failed to produce a promised revolutionary blood-testing technology. The case could serve to curb some of the excesses of unicorn culture, including its penchant for hype and its tendency to overlook aggressive rule-bending and corner-cutting.

The push to make companies better reaches beyond Silicon Valley. Sara Holoubek, founder of a New York City consulting firm called Luminary Labs, promotes a concept she calls Human Company Design. In Oakland, consultants at Great Place to Work and their colleagues at Great Place to Work offices around the world keep promoting the virtues of investing in employees and providing good jobs with long-term security.

The founders of Zebras Unite and all the others mentioned in this chapter reject the values and principles that have come to define what I call the Age of the Unicorn. Someday I believe we will look back on the past 10 or 15 years as an example of what happens when a generally good system—capitalism—is hijacked by bad actors and pushed and perverted to unsustainable extremes.

The unicorn business model has not produced any great companies, but it has enabled venture capitalists and various other hustlers to become unimaginably wealthy. In a way, this might seem like the most miraculous invention ever dreamed up by the wizards of Silicon Valley—a system that produces nothing of value yet generates tremendous amounts of wealth. It's like a perpetual motion machine, or a gizmo that turns dogshit into dollars. The truth, however, is that these billionaire grifter bros have not actually invented anything new. They've just put a modern-day spin on an old idea, creating "an enormous multivariate kind of Ponzi scheme," tech investor Chamath Palihapitiya declared in 2018.

In the service of chasing unicorns, the bros also spawned the brutal "new compact" built upon exploiting workers. After all, why treat workers well when you don't expect the company to be sustainable, and all you're trying to do is grow fast and cash out before it falls apart. The problem is that millions of ordinary human beings have become collateral damage to that model—not just workers in Silicon Valley but those in other industries whose employers are copying Silicon Valley.

What most offends me is how the people running this new-age Ponzi scheme keep pretending with such straight faces that this way of doing things actually represents the natural order of things—a tide that cannot be held back. Sure, they say, some workers will get chewed up during periods of rapid economic change, but this is what progress looks like.

It's complete bullshit, yet astonishingly enough, a lot of us have gone along with it. But now some people are starting to wake up. Eventually the scheme will collapse, as schemes always do. It remains to be seen how wide the damage will be, and how long it will take us to recover. But maybe, this time, instead of making the same mistakes all over again, we will dust ourselves off and start building a future that all of us actually want to inhabit, with companies that do in fact make the world a little bit better—for everyone.

SEVEN RULES FOR BUILDING A SANE, HEALTHY, HAPPY CULTURE AT WORK

Let's say you want to be a zebra rather than a unicorn—you'd rather be more like Yvon Chouinard at Patagonia and less like Jeff Bezos at Amazon. How do you do it? First, toss out the books coming out of Silicon Valley today, and look for lessons from the past. In their books, Henry Ford, Thomas J. Watson Jr., David Packard, and Tom Peters described a management philosophy from the second half of the last century that was almost exactly the opposite of what we have today. The approach they espoused became the underpinning of the golden age of American industry.

Second, forget the ping-pong and free beer and the kindergarten decor and focus on what people really want and value. Below are seven rules to help you build a sane, healthy, happy culture at work.

- SPEND MORE ON HUMANS. Companies that invest in their employees tend to outperform their competitors, says MIT professor Zeynep Ton, author of *The Good Jobs Strategy*. That means paying better salaries and devoting more money to training and development—an upfront investment that pays off over the long term, Ton adds. Software maker Basecamp figures out what companies in San Francisco are paying for various positions, then matches the top of the range for its own workers, who are in Chicago and other locations around the world. Make workers real employees rather than contractors. Provide good health benefits, and a retirement savings plan.

- SLOW DOWN. Doing too much too fast, working in constant sprints, launching concurrent change initiatives—these things overwhelm workers and actually hurt productivity. Fall into an "acceleration trap" and you'll look like a car stuck in snow, spinning your wheels and getting nowhere. Do less. Give workers a rest between change initiatives.

- CREATE SAFETY. Companies where employees feel safe, both physically and emotionally, tend to outperform the stock market by up to 200 percent, according to Great Place to Work. Part of feeling safe means feeling welcome. To get the best work out of your employees, get rid of fear. Remember the story of Gregory Berns, the scientist at Emory University who put people into an MRI scanner and studied their brains while zapping their feet with electric shocks? The lesson he learned: scared people make terrible decisions. They can't think straight. Provide job security, and the chance for workers to learn new skills and earn promotions.

- USE LESS TECH. How many of the apps we use at work were installed just because everyone else is using them? (That's right, Slack, I'm looking at you.) Before you adopt some new app or service, decide exactly what you expect to get from it. Audit your apps. If they're not delivering what you expected, tear them out. Some of your programs might actually be hurting productivity. Out they go! Also, be careful which processes you automate. When your employees need information from HR, make sure they talk to a human rather than a chatbot. Yes, it costs money to hire HR people. But it's still less expensive than losing employees who leave because talking to a chatbot makes them feel that the company doesn't care about them.

• CLOSE THE GAP. Companies where front-line workers feel connected to top management produce three times as much revenue growth, according to Great Place to Work. At Managed by Q, the "Uber for janitors" in New York, that means sending office workers out to clean toilets and scrape gum off desks. At Hilton, it means C-suite occupants spend one week a year working as bellhops and room cleaners. Imagine how much more humanely Amazon might treat its workers if Jeff Bezos and his lieutenants spent one week a year packing boxes in an Amazon shipping center.

• TURN A PROFIT. Everything begins with making a profit. Throw out the notion of growing as fast as you possibly can, without regard for making a profit—or "blitzscaling," as Silicon Valley guru Reid Hoffman calls it in his latest book. Abandon the "grow fast, lose money, cash out" mentality. That business model creates an incentive to treat workers as poorly as possible. If possible, bootstrap your company and don't take any venture capital funding at all. Embrace the discipline of turning a profit and using that money to fund growth and to treat employees well. Resist the urge to go public. The IPO might make you rich, but it will also give you a new boss—Wall Street. And if you think your old boss was an asshole, wait until you see this one.

• OBEY THE GOLDEN RULE. Keep in mind what business professor Sally Rumbles calls the "no-shit-Sherlock school of management," which holds that "if you treat people the way you'd like to be treated, if you praise them, and thank them, what a surprise! They do a good job on the whole." There's a reason why some version of the Golden Rule appears in pretty much every religion and ethical system ever created—because it works. Sure, a lot of things have changed since the Internet was invented—but people haven't.

Two years ago, I set out on this journey to write about kooky management fads, and to find out how work had gone wrong and why so many people were miserable. The short answer is that a half century of shareholder capitalism has led companies to treat employees badly—to steal their pensions, cut their pay, erase their benefits, and treat them like disposable widgets. In the last twenty-five years, in the age of the Internet, the damage has accelerated. Silicon Valley has taken a flawed philosophy and pushed it to new extremes, and then exported that style of working to the rest of the world.

Maybe the pendulum will start to swing back in the other direction. With this book I hope to give the pendulum a little nudge. I've been thrilled to meet so many people who reject shareholder capitalism and the new compact, and who believe that although business has changed, some old-fashioned commonsense virtues actually still work. To be sure, those people remain in the minority, but they're out there. They're starting new companies. They're building a new kind of capitalism.

Let's hope their ranks keep growing.

ACKNOWLEDGMENTS

The most satisfying aspect of writing *Lab Rats* was the chance to meet so many fascinating, thoughtful people. I'm indebted to the many who shared their stories with me and agreed to let me include those stories in this book. In most cases I've used pseudonyms in order to protect their privacy. I'm also indebted to the many scientists and researchers who took time to explain their work to me, including Dr. Gregory Berns, Gary Rees and Sally Rumbles, and Mitchell Kusy and Elizabeth Holloway.

At the headquarters of Steelcase I spent a day talking to a dozen incredibly interesting people who provided me with far more information than I could use in this book. I regret that I could barely scratch the surface, but I still hope to tell their stories. I'm grateful to others whose stories did not go into the book but whose perspectives informed my research, reporting, and writing.

My wife, Sasha, offered emotional support and encouragement, especially in the many months when I was holed up in my office. My daughter, Sonya, helped assemble the bibliography and thus gained her first (but I suspect not her last) professional publishing credit. My son, Paul, restored my sanity with a few much-needed ski days and mountain bike rides and never complained that I was not there to help him with his homework as much as I should have been. I'm sorry to have been away so much. And I am forever grateful for your love and support.

There is no greater gift for a writer than to be blessed with a really great editor, and with this book, as with *Disrupted,* I've had the good fortune to work with the best editor I've ever known—the brilliant, thoughtful, compassionate, and generous Paul Whitlatch. I'm happy to work with so many wonderful members of the Hachette Book Group family, including Mauro DiPreta, Michelle Aielli, Lauren Hummel, Sarah Falter, Michael Barrs, Odette Fleming, and art director Mandy Kain, who designed the cover. Production editor Melanie Gold and copy editor Lori Paximadis made enormous improvements in the manuscript. Once again, Elisa Rivlin contributed a sharp legal review as well as wise suggestions on the manuscript. Gary Morgen from Hachette's technology group oversaw development of a new author portal and also became a pal during his trips to Boston. David Lamb went above and beyond the call of duty by modeling for the cover. Thanks also to Emily Donaldson, who assembled the bibliography.

For the UK edition, I've had the good fortune to work with Mike Harpley, a gifted editorial director at Atlantic Books in London who also edited *Disrupted*. As with the last book, Mike managed to translate my text into actual English. But this time around Mike also contributed new ideas that will make the book more relevant to UK readers. I'm grateful to Mike and to everyone else at Atlantic Books who have been such cheery and supportive companions.

Finally, I would like to express my gratitude and affection for my agent, the incomparable Christy Fletcher, and her associates at Fletcher & Co., including Sarah Fuentes and Erin McFadden. Paradoxically, while writing a book about workplace misery and dysfunction, I have enjoyed the company of the best and nicest colleagues I've ever known, people whose friendship I cherish. I'm thankful for each and every one of you.

SELECTED BIBLIOGRAPHY

BOOKS

Bush, Michael C., et al. *A Great Place to Work for All: Better for Business, Better for People, Better for the World*. Oakland, CA: Berrett-Koehler Publishers, 2018.

Chang, Emily. *Brotopia: Breaking Up the Boys' Club of Silicon Valley*. New York: Portfolio/ Penguin, 2018.

Chouinard, Yvon. *Let My People Go Surfing: The Education of a Reluctant Businessman*. London: Penguin Books, 2006.

Ciulla, Joanne B. *The Working Life: The Promise and Betrayal of Modern Work*. New York: Three Rivers Press, 2000.

Dalio, Ray. *Principles: Life and Work*. New York: Simon and Schuster, 2017.

Drucker, Peter F. *Concept of the Corporation*. 3rd ed. New York: Routledge, 2017.

Ford, Henry. *My Life and Work*. New York: Garden City Publishing Co., 1922.

Fraser, Jill A. *White-Collar Sweatshop: The Deterioration of Work and Its Rewards in Corporate America*. New York: W. W. Norton and Company, 2001.

Fromm, Erich. *The Sane Society*. New York: Open Road Integrated Media, 2013.

Hogler, Raymond L. *The End of American Labor Unions: The Right-to-Work Movement and the Erosion of Collective Bargaining*. Westport, CT: Praeger, 2015.

Hughes, Chris. *Fair Shot: Rethinking Inequality and How We Earn*. New York: St. Martin's Press, 2018.

Iacocca, Lee, and William Novak. *Iacocca: An Autobiography*. New York: Bantam, 2007.

Karlgaard, Rich. *The Soft Edge: Where Great Companies Find Lasting Success*. San Francisco: Jossey-Bass, 2014.

Korschun, Daniel, and Grant Welker. *We Are Market Basket: The Story of the Unlikely Grassroots Movement That Saved a Beloved Business*. New York: American Management Association, 2015.

Kusy, Mitchell, and Elizabeth Holloway. *Toxic Workplace! Managing Toxic Personalities and Their Systems of Power*. San Francisco: Jossey-Bass, 2009.

Laloux, Frederic. *Reinventing Organizations: A Guide to Creating Organizations Inspired by the Next Stage of Human Consciousness.* N.p.: Nelson Parker, 2014.

Mackey, John. *Conscious Capitalism: Liberating the Heroic Spirit of Business.* Brighton, MA: Harvard Business Review Press, 2014.

McCord, Patty. *Powerful: Building a Culture of Freedom and Responsibility.* Arlington: Missionday, 2018.

McDonald, Duff. *The Golden Passport: Harvard Business School, the Limits of Capitalism, and the Moral Failure of the MBA Elite.* New York: HarperCollins, 2017.

Packard, David. *The HP Way: How Bill Hewlett and I Built Our Company.* New York: Harper Business, 2006.

Peters, Thomas J., and Robert H. Waterman. *In Search of Excellence: Lessons from America's Best-Run Companies.* New York: Harper Business, 2012.

Pfeffer, Jeffrey. *Dying for a Paycheck: How Modern Management Harms Employee Health and Company Performance—and What We Can Do About It.* New York: HarperCollins, 2018.

————. *The Lean Startup: How Today's Entrepreneurs Use Continuous Innovation to Create Radically Successful Businesses.* New York: Crown Business, 2011.

Ries, Eric. *The Startup Way: How Modern Companies Use Entrepreneurial Management to Transform Culture and Drive Long-Term Growth.* New York: Currency, 2017.

Sacks, David O., and Peter A. Thiel. *The Diversity Myth: Multiculturalism and Political Intolerance on Campus.* Oakland, CA: Independent Institute, 1998.

Schor, Juliet B. *The Overworked American: The Unexpected Decline of Leisure.* New York: Basic Books, 1992.

Schultz, Ellen E. *Retirement Heist: How Companies Plunder and Profit from the Nest Eggs of American Workers.* New York: Penguin Group, 2011.

Scott, Kim. *Radical Candor: Be a Kick-Ass Boss Without Losing Your Humanity.* New York: St. Martin's Press, 2017.

Sloan, Alfred P., Jr. *My Years with General Motors.* New York: Doubleday, 1963.

Stewart, Matthew. *The Management Myth: Debunking Modern Business Philosophy.* New York: W. W. Norton and Company, 2009.

Taylor, Frederick W. *The Principles of Scientific Management.* New York: Cosimo Classics, 2006.

Thiel, Peter, and Blake Masters. *Zero to One: Notes on Startups, or How to Build the Future.* New York: Currency, 2014.

Ton, Zeynep. *The Good Jobs Strategy: How the Smartest Companies Invest in Employees to Lower Costs and Boost Profits.* Boston: Houghton Mifflin Harcourt, 2014.

Vance, Ashlee. *Elon Musk: Tesla, SpaceX, and the Quest for a Fantastic Future.* New York: Ecco Press, 2015.

Watson, Thomas J., Jr. *A Business and Its Beliefs: The Ideas That Helped Build IBM.* New York: McGraw-Hill Companies, 2003.

ARTICLES

Chapter 1: Unhappy in Paradise

Adams, Susan. "Most Americans Are Unhappy at Work." *Forbes*, June 20, 2014. https://www.forbes.com/sites/susanadams/2014/06/20/most-americans-are-unhappy-at-work/#123252d2341a.

Berns, Gregory. "In Hard Times, Fear Can Impair Decision-Making." *New York Times*, December 6, 2008. https://www.nytimes.com/2008/12/07/jobs/07pre.html.

Curtin, Sally C., Margaret Warner, and Holly Hedegaard. "Increase in Suicide in the United States, 1999-2014." National Center for Health Statistics Data Brief no. 241, April 2016. https://www.cdc.gov/nchs/products/databriefs/db241.htm.

Green, Francis, and Nicholas Tsitsianis. "Can the Changing Nature of Jobs Account for National Trends in Job Satisfaction?" Department of Economics Discussion Paper 04/06 at the University of Kent, Canterbury, England, 2004. https://www.kent.ac.uk/economics/documents/research/papers/2004/0406.pdf.

Kellaway, Lucy. "Why Is Work Making Us Miserable?" *Financial Times*, January 22, 2017. https://www.ft.com/content/98d74346-de67-11e6-9d7c-be108f1c1dce.

LaBier, Douglas. "Another Survey Shows the Continuing Toll of Workplace Stress." *Psychology Today*, April 23, 2014. https://www.psychologytoday.com/us/blog/the-new-resilience/201404/another-survey-shows-the-continuing-toll-workplace-stress.

Levanon, Gad. "Job Satisfaction Keeps Getting Better." Conference Board, September 6, 2017. https://www.conference-board.org/blog/postdetail.cfm?post=6391.

Ma, Alexandra. "A Psychological Ailment Called 'Hikikomori' Is Imprisoning 500,000 Japanese People in Their Homes—and It's More of a Threat than Ever." *Business Insider*, January 14, 2018. http://www.businessinsider.com/hikikomori-worrying-mental-health-problem-traps-japanese-at-home-2018-1.

National Center for Health Statistics. "Health, United States, 2015: With Special Feature on Racial and Ethnic Health Disparities." U.S. Department of Health and Human Services. https://www.cdc.gov/nchs/data/hus/hus15.pdf.

Oswald, Andrew, and Jonathan Gardner. "What Has Been Happening to Job Satisfaction in Britain?" Unpublished paper, University of Warwick, Coventry, England, 2001. https://warwick.ac.uk/fac/soc/economics/staff/ajoswald/sat90supdate.pdf.

Pratt, Laura A., Debra J. Brody, and Qiuping Gu. "Antidepressant Use Among Persons Aged 12 and Over: United States, 2011–2014." National Center for Health Statistics Data Brief no. 283, August 2017. https://www.cdc.gov/nchs/data/databriefs/db283.pdf.

Tavernise, Sabrina. "U.S. Suicide Rate Surges to a 30-Year High." *New York Times*, April 22, 2016. https://www.nytimes.com/2016/04/22/health/us-suicide-rate-surges-to-a-30-year-high.html.

Chapter 2: The New Oligarchs

Biddle, Sam. "Happy Holidays: Startup CEO Complains SF Is Full of Human Trash." ValleyWag, December 11, 2013. http://valleywag.gawker.com/happy-holidays-startup-ceo-complains-sf-is-full-of-hum-1481067192.

Biello, David. "Climate Change Drives (Micro)Evolution in Finland." *Scientific American*, February 23, 2011. https://blogs.scientificamerican.com/observations/climate-change-drives-microevolution-in-finland.

Byers, Dylan. "Pacific: Elon Musk Is Humiliating Himself." *CNN Money*, May 25, 2018. https://amp.cnn.com/money/2018/05/24/technology/pacific-newsletter/index.html.

della Cava, Marco. "An Uber Engineer Killed Himself. His Widow Says the Workplace Is to Blame." *USA Today*, April 27, 2017. https://www.usatoday.com/story/tech/news/2017/04/27/is-uber-culture-to-blame-for-an-employees-suicide/100938330.

DeMay, Daniel. "Amazon Worker Leaps from Building at Seattle Campus." *SeattlePI*, November 28, 2016. https://www.seattlepi.com/local/article/Amazon-worker-leaps-from-building-at-Seattle-10640986.php.

Durden, Tyler. "Are Tesla's Self-Proclaimed 'World's Safest Cars' Actually Among the World's Deadliest?" ZeroHedge, May 29, 2018. https://www.zerohedge.com/news/2018-05-29/are-teslas-self-proclaimed-worlds-safest-cars-actually-among-worlds-deadliest.

Friend, Tad. "Tomorrow's Advance Man." *New Yorker*, May 18, 2015. https://www.newyorker.com/magazine/2015/05/18/tomorrows-advance-man.

———. "Sam Altman's Manifest Destiny." *New Yorker*, October 10, 2016. https://www.newyorker.com/magazine/2016/10/10/sam-altmans-manifest-destiny.

Hoffman, Reid. "If, Why, and How Founders Should Hire a 'Professional' CEO." Reid Hoffman website, February 9, 2017. http://www.reidhoffman.org/if-why-and-how-founders-should-hire-a-professional-ceo-2.

Kantor, Jodi, and David Streitfeld. "Inside Amazon: Wrestling Big Ideas in a Bruising Workplace." *New York Times*, August 15, 2015. https://www.nytimes.com/2015/08/16/technology/inside-amazon-wrestling-big-ideas-in-a-bruising-workplace.html.

Lemann, Nicholas. "The Network Man: Reid Hoffman's Big Idea." *New Yorker*, October 12, 2015. https://www.newyorker.com/magazine/2015/10/12/the-network-man.

Miller, Michael E. "'Tech Bro' Calls San Francisco 'Shanty Town,' Decries Homeless 'Riffraff' in Open Letter." *Chicago Tribune*, February 18, 2016. http://www.chicagotribune.com/bluesky/technology/ct-tech-bro-letter-san-francisco-homeless-20160218-story.html.

Mims, Christopher. "In Self-Driving-Car Road Test, We Are the Guinea Pigs." *Wall Street Journal*, May 13, 2018. https://www.wsj.com/articles/in-self-driving-car-road-test-we-are-the-guinea-pigs-1526212802.

Mishel, Lawrence, and Jessica Schieder. "CEO Pay Remains High Relative to the Pay of Typical Workers and High-Wage Earners." Economic Policy Institute, July 20, 2017. https://www.epi.org/publication/ceo-pay-remains-high-relative-to-the-pay-of-typical-workers-and-high-wage-earners.

Osnos, Evan. "Doomsday Prep for the Super-Rich." *New Yorker*, January 30, 2017. https://www.newyorker.com/magazine/2017/01/30/doomsday-prep-for-the-super-rich.

Packer, George. "No Death, No Taxes." *New Yorker*, November 28, 2011. https://www.newyorker.com/magazine/2011/11/28/no-death-no-taxes.

Peterson, Hayley. "'Seeing Someone Cry at Work Is Becoming Normal': Employees Say Whole Foods Is Using 'Scorecards' to Punish Them." *Business Insider*, February 1, 2018. http://www.businessinsider.com/how-whole-foods-uses-scorecards-to-punish-employees-2018-1.

"Pirate Bay Founder: Mark Zuckerberg Is 'Basically the Biggest Dictator in the World.'" *Business Insider Nordic* online. Last modified November 27, 2017. http://nordic.businessinsider.com/pirate-bay-founder-mark-zuckerberg-is-basically-the-biggest-dictator-in-the-world-2017-10.

"SF Tent on Sidewalk Prohibition Has Been Enforced 152 Times." Fox KTVU online. Last modified September 12, 2017. http://www.ktvu.com/news/sf-tent-on-sidewalk-prohibition-has-been-enforced-152-times.

Sinton, Peter. "The Villa That Oracle Built/Ellison Proceeds with Dream Digs Despite Market Setbacks." *SFGate*, March 27, 2001. https://www.sfgate.com/bayarea/article/the-villa-that-oracle-built-ellison-proceeds-2938199.php.

Smith, Noah. "Homelessness Is a Tragedy the U.S. Can Afford to Fix." *Bloomberg*, May 21, 2018. https://www.bloomberg.com/view/articles/2018-05-21/ending-homelessness-is-a-job-for-the-federal-government.

Stanford, Kyle. "The State of the U.S. Venture Industry in 15 Charts." PitchBook, January 26, 2018. https://pitchbook.com/news/articles/the-state-of-the-us-venture-industry-in-15-charts.

Welch, David. "Famed Short-Seller Jim Chanos Says Tesla Headed for 'Brick Wall.'" *Bloomberg*, December 13, 2017. https://www.bloomberg.com/news/articles/2017-12-13/famed-short-seller-jim-chanos-says-tesla-headed-for-brick-wall.

Wong, Julia Carrie. "Facebook Worker Living in Garage to Zuckerberg: Challenges Are Right Outside Your Door." *The Guardian*, July 24, 2017. https://www.theguardian.com/technology/2017/jul/24/facebook-cafeteria-workers-wages-zuckerberg-challenges.

Chapter 3: A Very Brief History of Management Science (and Why You Shouldn't Trust It)

"Agile working guide published." NHS Employers, accessed September 4, 2018. http://www.nhsemployers.org/news/2013/09/agile-working-guide-published.

Lashinsky, Adam. "How 'The Lean Startup' Turned Eric Ries into an Unlikely Corporate Guru." *Fortune*, February 22, 2018. http://fortune.com/2018/02/22/lean-startup-eric-ries.

Lepore, Jill. "Not So Fast: Scientific Management Started as a Way to Work. How Did It Become a Way of Life?" *New Yorker*, October 12, 2009. https://www.newyorker.com/magazine/2009/10/12/not-so-fast.

"Poor Man's Agile: Scrum in 5 Simple Steps." Hacker News. Last modified March 22, 2013. https://news.ycombinator.com/item?id=5406384.

"Who Should the Scrum Master Report To?" Illustrated Agile. Last modified May 8, 2014. http://illustratedagile.com/2014/05/08/scrum-master-report.

Wieczner, Jen. "GE CEO Jeff Immelt's Retirement Pay May Be a Lot More Than You Think." *Fortune*, June 12, 2017. http://fortune.com/2017/06/12/ge-ceo-jeff-immelt-net-worth.

Chapter 4: Who's Afraid of Silicon Valley?

Egan, Matt. "How Decades of Bad Decisions Broke GE." *ABC News*, November 20, 2017. https://www.local10.com/money/how-decades-of-bad-decisions-broke-ge.

Immelt, Jeffrey R. "How I Remade GE." *Harvard Business Review*, September–October 2017 Issue. https://hbr.org/2017/09/inside-ges-transformation.

Isidore, Chris. "Why Ford Fired Its CEO." *CNN Money*, May 22, 2017. http://money.cnn.com/2017/05/22/news/companies/ford-ceo-fields-hackett/index.html.

Rittenhouse, Lindsay. "CEOs Are Dropping Like Flies." *TheStreet*, September 23, 2017. https://www.thestreet.com/slideshow/14309542/1/dollar-tree-ceo-resigns-joining-30-others-from-these-companies.html.

Safdar, Khadeeja. "J.Crew's Mickey Drexler Confesses: I Underestimated How Tech Would Upend Retail." *Wall Street Journal*, May 24, 2017. https://www.wsj.com/articles/j-crews-big-miss-how-technology-transformed-retail-1495636817.

Chapter 5: Building the Workforce of the Future (or: Sorry, You're Old and We'd Like You to Leave)

Butler, Sarah. "Green's 'main purpose' in BHS sale was to avoid pension liability, says watchdog." *Guardian*, June 27, 2017. https://www.theguardian.com/business/2017/jun/27/sir-philip-green-main-bhs-sale-pension-regulator-report.

Everett, Cath. "IBM's Agile Approach to Working—Exemplar or Warning to Others?" Diginomica, August 22, 2017. https://diginomica.com/2017/08/22/ibms-agile-approach-working-exemplar-warning-others.

Gosselin, Peter. "Federal Watchdog Launches Investigation of Age Bias at IBM." ProPublica, May 17, 2018. https://www.propublica.org/article/federal-watchdog-launches-investigation-of-age-bias-at-ibm.

Gosselin, Peter, and Ariana Tobin. "Cutting 'Old Heads' at IBM." ProPublica, March 22, 2018. https://features.propublica.org/ibm/ibm-age-discrimination-american-workers.

Hiltzik, Michael. "IBM's CEO Writes a New Chapter on How to Turn Failure into Wealth." *Los Angeles Times*, January 29, 2016. http://www.latimes.com/business/hiltzik/la-fi-mh-ibm-s-ceo-writes-a-new-chapter-20160129-column.html.

Isidore, Chris. "IBM Tells Employees Working at Home to Get Back to the Office." *CNN Money*, May 19, 2017. http://money.cnn.com/2017/05/19/technology/ibm-work-at-home/index.html.

Kessler, Sarah. "IBM, Remote-Work Pioneer, Is Calling Thousands of Employees Back to the Office." *Quartz*, March 21, 2017. https://qz.com/924167/ibm-remote-work-pioneer-is-calling-thousands-of-employees-back-to-the-office.

Kozlowski, Rob. "IBM Computes $500 Million Contribution for Non-U.S. Pension Plans This Year." *Pensions and Investments*, March 1, 2017. http://www.pionline.com/article/20170301/ONLINE/170309978/ibm-computes-500-million-contribution-for-non-us-pension-plans-this-year.

Kunert, Paul. "Missed Opportunity Bingo: IBM's Wasted Years and the $92bn Cash Splurge." *The Register*, December 22, 2017. https://www.theregister.co.uk/2017/12/22/ibm_bernstein_analysis.

Ladah, Sam. "Building IBM's Workforce of the Future." IBM Think Blog, July 12, 2017. https://www.ibm.com/blogs/think/2017/07/workforce-of-the-future.

Simons, John. "IBM, a Pioneer of Remote Work, Calls Workers Back to the Office." *Wall Street Journal*, May 18, 2017. https://www.wsj.com/articles/ibm-a-pioneer-of-remote-work-calls-workers-back-to-the-office-1495108802.

Chapter 6: Money: "Garbage at the Speed of Light"

Allen, Katie. "Technology Has Created More Jobs than It Has Destroyed, Says 140 Years of Data." *Guardian*, August 18, 2015. https://www.theguardian.com/business/2015/aug/17/technology-created-more-jobs-than-destroyed-140-years-data-census.

Battelle, John. "A Total Rethink of How Work Should Work." NewCo Shift, November 16, 2016. https://shift.newco.co/a-total-rethink-of-how-work-should-work-5dc3980ea52.

Bellafante, Ginia. "A Driver's Suicide Reveals the Dark Side of the Gig Economy." *New York Times*, February 6, 2018. https://www.nytimes.com/2018/02/06/nyregion/livery-driver-taxi-uber.html.

Belvedere, Matthew J. "Facebook Co-Founder Hughes: The Digital Economy Is 'Going to Continue to Destroy' Jobs in America." CNBC, February 20, 2018. https://www.cnbc.com/2018/02/20/facebook-co-founder-chris-hughes-wants-500-per-month-in-basic-income.html.

Brennan, Collin. "Millennials Earn 20% Less than Boomers Did at Same Stage of Life." *USA Today*, January 13, 2017. https://www.usatoday.com/story/money/2017/01/13/millennials-falling-behind-boomer-parents/96530338.

Bureau of Labor Statistics. "Employment, Hours, and Earnings from the Current Employment Statistics Survey (National)." Databases, Tables and Calculators by Subject, for date range 2000-2017, accessed June 1, 2018. https://data.bls.gov/timeseries/CES3000000001.

——. "Service-Providing Industries." Industries at a Glance, accessed June 8, 2018. https://www.bls.gov/iag/tgs/iag07.htm.

Center on Budget and Policy Priorities. "Chart Book: The Legacy of the Great Recession." June 5, 2018. https://www.cbpp.org/research/economy/chart-book-the-legacy-of-the-great-recession.

Davidow, Bill. "The Internet Is the Greatest Legal Facilitator of Inequality in Human History." *Atlantic*, January 28, 2014. https://www.theatlantic.com/business/archive/2014/01/the-internet-is-the-greatest-legal-facilitator-of-inequality-in-human-history/283422.

Dean, James. "Amazon Staff 'Chewed Up and Spat Out by a Brutal Culture.'" *Times* (London), August 18, 2015. https://www.thetimes.co.uk/article/amazon-staff-chewed-up-and-spat-out-by-a-brutal-culture-c3zxz2dhbmj.

DeSilver, Drew. "U.S. Income Inequality, on Rise for Decades, Is Now Highest Since 1928." Pew Research Center Fact Tank, December 5, 2013. http://www.pewresearch.org/fact-tank/2013/12/05/u-s-income-inequality-on-rise-for-decades-is-now-highest-since-1928.

Elliott, Larry. "Rising Inequality Threatens World Economy, Says WEF." *The Guardian*, January 11, 2017. https://www.theguardian.com/business/2017/jan/11/inequality-world-economy-wef-brexit-donald-trump-world-economic-forum-risk-report.

Felton, Ryan. "U.S. Labor Agency Files Amended Complaint Against Tesla for Alleged Worker Rights Violations." Jalopnik, March 30, 2018. https://jalopnik.com/u-s-labor-agency-files-amended-complaint-against-tesla-1824214422.

Friedman, Milton. "The Social Responsibility of Business Is to Increase Its Profits." *New York Times Magazine*, September 13, 1970.

Garfield, Leanna. "Amazon Just Visited New Jersey—and the State Is Offering a $7 Billion Incentive to Land HQ2." *Business Insider*, April 13, 2018. http://www.businessinsider.com/amazon-headquarters-hq2-new-jersey-economic-incentive-2017-10.

Ghosh, Shona. "Electrocution, Cardiac Pain, and a Miscarriage: Amazon Warehouse Investigation Reveals 600 Ambulance Calls for Injured Workers." *Business Insider*, June 1, 2018. http://www.businessinsider.com/ambulances-called-600-times-amazon-uk-warehouses-2018-6.

Giang, Vivian. "A New Report Ranks America's Biggest Companies Based on How Quickly Employees Jump Ship." *Business Insider*, July 25, 2013. http://www.businessinsider.com/companies-ranked-by-turnover-rates-2013-7.

Green, Dennis. "A New Study Found That 700 Amazon Employees in Ohio Are on Food Stamps." *Business Insider*, January 15, 2018. http://www.businessinsider.com/amazon-employees-on-food-stamps-in-ohio-2018-1.

———. "The Retail Apocalypse Is Disproportionately Affecting Women—and Nobody Knows Why." *Business Insider*, December 18, 2017. http://www.businessinsider.com/women-are-losing-more-jobs-from-the-retail-apocalypse-2017-12.

Green, Dennis, and Mike Nudelman. "More than 8,000 Store Closures Were Announced in 2017—Here's the Full List." *Business Insider*, December 17, 2017. http://www.businessinsider.com/list-stores-that-closed-this-year-2017-12.

Hanauer, Nick. "The Pitchforks Are Coming . . . for Us Plutocrats." *Politico Magazine*, July/August 2014. https://www.politico.com/magazine/story/2014/06/the-pitchforks-are-coming-for-us-plutocrats-108014.

Hernández, Gabrielle Orum. "The New Short-Term Solution: Inside the Growing Legal Gig Economy." *Corporate Counsel*, May 23, 2017. https://www.law.com/corpcounsel/almID/1202787084603.

"Is Uber already harming the traditional taxi?" BBC News, May 15, 2015. https://www.bbc.co.uk/news/magazine-32743777

Jackson, Gavin. "How UK incomes are becoming more unequal — in six charts." *Financial Times*, February 1, 2017. https://www.ft.com/content/fc4a3980-e86f-11e6-967b-c88452263daf.

Kelly, Kevin. "The Roaring Zeros." *Wired*, September 1, 1999. https://www.wired.com/1999/09/zeros.

Lawson, Sarah. "'Constant Stress' at Amazon Centers Making Workers Sick, Says U.K. Union." *Fast Company*, August 18, 2015. https://www.fastcompany.com/3050040/constant-stress-at-amazon-centers-making-workers-sick-says-uk-union.

Long, Heather. "Ahead of Davos, Even the 1 Percent Worry About Inequality." *Washington Post*, January 22, 2018. https://www.washingtonpost.com/business/economy/ahead-of-davos-even-the-1-percent-worry-about-inequality/2018/01/21/551392d0-fd2f-11e7-ad8c-ecbb62019393_story.html.

———. "U.S. Has Lost 5 Million Manufacturing Jobs Since 2000." *CNN Money*, March 29, 2016. http://money.cnn.com/2016/03/29/news/economy/us-manufacturing-jobs.

——— "Number of Postal Employees Since 1926." United States Postal Service. Last modified March 2018. https://about.usps.com/who-we-are/postal-history/employees-since-1926.pdf.

Osnos, Evan. "Doomsday Prep for the Super-Rich." *New Yorker*, January 30, 2017. https://www.newyorker.com/magazine/2017/01/30/doomsday-prep-for-the-super-rich.

Pew Research Center. "The American Middle Class Is Losing Ground." Social and Demographic Trends, December 9, 2015. http://www.pewsocialtrends.org/2015/12/09/the-american-middle-class-is-losing-ground.

"Real Gross Domestic Product (GDP) of the United States of America from 1990 to 2017 in Billion Chained (2009) U.S. Dollars." Statista. Accessed May 31, 2018. https://www.statista.com/statistics/188141/annual-real-gdp-of-the-united-states-since-1990-in-chained-us-dollars.

Shambaugh, Jay, and Ryan Nunn. "Why Wages Aren't Growing in America." *Harvard Business Review*, October 24, 2017. https://hbr.org/2017/10/why-wages-arent-growing-in-america.

Smith, Craig. "Exclusive: Amazon Workers Sleeping in Tents near Dunfermline Site." *Courier* (UK), December 10, 2016. https://www.thecourier.co.uk/fp/news/local/fife/325800/exclusive-amazon-workers-sleeping-in-tents-near-dunfermline-site.

Stewart, Nikita, and Luis Ferré-Sadurní. "Another Taxi Driver in Debt Takes His Life. That's 5 in 5 Months." *New York Times*, May 27, 2018. https://www.nytimes.com/2018/05/27/nyregion/taxi-driver-suicide-nyc.html.

Swift, Art. "Labor Union Approval Best Since 2003, at 61%." Gallup, August 30, 2017. http://news.gallup.com/poll/217331/labor-union-approval-best-2003.aspx.

Topping, Alexandra. "Union membership has plunged to an all-time low, says DBEIS." *Guardian*, June 1, 2017. https://www.theguardian.com/politics/2017/jun/01/union-membership-has-plunged-to-an-all-time-low-says-ons.

Townsend, Matt, Jenny Surane, Emma Orr, and Christopher Cannon. "America's 'Retail Apocalypse' Is Really Just Beginning." *Bloomberg*, November 8, 2017. https://www.bloomberg.com/graphics/2017-retail-debt.

Wattles, Jackie. "Macy's Is Closing 68 Stores, Cutting 10,000 Jobs." *CNN Money*, January 4, 2017. http://money.cnn.com/2017/01/04/news/companies/macys-job-cuts-stock/index.html.

Welch, David. "Hertz's 101-Year-Old Business Nearing Twilight in Uber Age." *Bloomberg*, August 9, 2017. https://www.bloomberg.com/news/articles/2017-08-09/in-age-of-uber-a-101-year-old-business-approaches-its-twilight.

Werber, Cassie. "Machines Are Destroying Some Jobs, but Also Creating Better Ones Through 'Creative Destruction.'" *Quartz*, August 19, 2015. https://qz.com/483006/machines-are-destroying-some-jobs-but-also-creating-better-ones-through-creative-destruction.

Chapter 7: Insecurity: "We're a Team, Not a Family"

All Things Considered. "How the Architect of Netflix's Innovative Culture Lost Her Job to the System." National Public Radio, Planet Money Special Series, September 3, 2015. https://www.npr.org/2015/09/03/437291792/how-the-architect-of-netflixs-innovative-culture-lost-her-job-to-the-system.

DeVallance, Evan, et al. "Effect of Chronic Stress on Running Wheel Activity in Mice." *PLoS ONE* 12, no. 9 (2017): e0184829. https://doi.org/10.1371/journal.pone.0184829.

Diallo, Ibrahim. "The Machine Fired Me. No human could do a thing about it," Blog post. https://idiallo.com/blog/when-a-machine-fired-me.

Ferenstein, Gregory. "Read What Facebook's Sandberg Calls Maybe 'The Most Important Document Ever to Come out of the Valley." TechCrunch, January 31, 2013. https://techcrunch.com/2013/01/31/read-what-facebooks-sandberg-calls-maybe-the-most-important-document-ever-to-come-out-of-the-valley.

Frisbee, Jefferson C., Steven D. Brooks, Shyla C. Stanley, and Alexandre C. d'Audiffret. "An Unpredictable Chronic Mild Stress Protocol for Instigating Depressive Symptoms, Behavioral Changes and Negative Health Outcomes in Rodents." *Journal of Visualized Experiments* 106 (2015): 53109. https://doi.org/10.3791/53109.

Hastings, Reed. "Culture." Netflix, August 1, 2009. https://www.slideshare.net/reed2001/culture-1798664.

Hoffman, Reid, Ben Casnocha, and Chris Yeh. "Your Company Is Not a Family." *Harvard Business Review*, June 17, 2014. https://hbr.org/2014/06/your-company-is-not-a-family.

Jays5672. "I Worked As a Customer Service Representative for Netflix for Two Years." Reddit, November 2017. https://www.reddit.com/r/AMA/comments/79s8z0/i_worked_as_a_customer_service_representative_for.

Jiang, Lixin, Tahira M. Probst, and Wendi L. Benson. "Organizational Context and Employee Reactions to Psychological Contract Breach: A Multilevel Test of Competing Theories." *Economic and Industrial Democracy* 38, no. 3 (2015): 513–534. https://doi.org/10.1177/0143831X15579288.

Kim, Eugene. "Hundreds of Amazon Employees Used an Anonymous App to Vent About How the Recent Suicide Attempt Was Handled." *Business Insider*, December 11, 2016. http://www.businessinsider.com/amazon-employees-share-thoughts-about-suicide-survivor-2016-12.

McGonigle, Bryan. "Officials: Dow Chemical Explosion Caused by Mechanical Failure." Wicked Local North Andover, April 4, 2017. http://northandover.wickedlocal.com/news/20170404/officials-dow-chemical-explosion-caused-by-mechanical-failure.

Netflix. "Inclusion and Diversity." Accessed May 31, 2018. https://jobs.netflix.com/diversity.

O'Donovan, Caroline, and Priya Anand. "How Uber's Hard-Charging Corporate Culture Left Employees Drained." BuzzFeedNews, July 17, 2017. https://www.buzzfeed.com/carolineodonovan/how-ubers-hard-charging-corporate-culture-left-employees.

Overfelt, Maggie. "Millennial Employees Are a Lot More Loyal than Their Job-Hopping Stereotype." *CNBC*, May 10, 2017. https://www.cnbc.com/2017/05/10/90-of-millennials-will-stay-in-a-job-for-10-years-if-two-needs-met.html.

Reyes, Emily Alpert. "Millennials Value Job Security More than Baby Boomers Do, Survey Says." *Los Angeles Times*, December 10, 2013. http://articles.latimes.com/2013/dec/10/business/la-fi-mo-survey-millennials-job-security-20131210.

Saba. "Employees Want a 'Family Feel' at the Heart of Their Organisation's Culture, Finds Latest Employee Outlook Survey." News and Media, June 3, 2015. https://www.saba.com/press/news/employees-want-a-family-feel-at-the-heart-of-their-organisations-culture-finds-latest-employee-outlook-survey.

Shinde, Shalaka. "'In IT There Is No Job Security': 25-Year-Old Techie Commits Suicide in Pune." *Hindustan Times*, July 13, 2017. https://www.hindustantimes.com/pune-news/job-insecurity-drives-techie-to-suicide-in-pune/story-7p1ZwoRb5XtrUCreZVe1kN.html.

Siegel, David. "The Culture Deck: How People Work Is as Important as What They Do." Medium: TheStartup, June 12, 2014. https://medium.com/swlh/the-culture-deck-c4126ec63b18.

Silver, Sara. "Netflix Is Helping the City's Production Boom but Is Burning Through Cash." *Crain's New York Business*, May 14, 2018. http://www.crainsnewyork.com/article/20180514/FEATURES/180519967.

Stuart, Ruth. "Developing the Next Generation." CIPD Research Report, June 2015. https://www.cipd.co.uk/Images/developing-next-generation_tcm18-10268.pdf.

Vander Elst, Tinne, Anja Van den Broeck, Nele De Cuyper, and Hans De Witte. "On the Reciprocal Relationship Between Job Insecurity and Employee Well-Being: Mediation by Perceived Control?" *Journal of Occupational and Organizational Psychology* 87, no. 4 (2014): 671–693. https://doi.org/10.1111/joop.12068.

Wakefield, Jane. "The Man Who Was Fired by a Machine." BBC.com, June 21, 2018. https://www.bbc.com/news/technology-44561838.

Chapter 8: Change: "What Happens If You Live Inside a Hurricane That Never Ends?"

Aouf, Rima Sabina. "Apple Park Employees Revolt over Having to Work in Open-Plan Offices." Dezeen, August 10, 2017. https://www.dezeen.com/2017/08/10/apple-park-campus-employees-rebel-over-open-plan-offices-architecture-news.

Bray, Chad. "No Laptop, No Phone, No Desk: UBS Reinvents the Work Space." *New York Times*, November 3, 2016. https://www.nytimes.com/2016/11/04/business/deal-book/ubs-bank-virtual-desktops-london.html.

Broussard, Mitchel. "Some Apple Park Employees Said to Be Dissatisfied with Open Office Design." MacRumors, August 9, 2017. https://www.macrumors.com/2017/08/09/apple-park-employees-open-office.

Bruch, Heike, and Jochen I. Menges. "The Acceleration Trap." *Harvard Business Review*, April 2010 Issue. https://hbr.org/2010/04/the-acceleration-trap.

Holacracy website. Homepage, accessed May 31, 2018. https://www.holacracy.org.

Reingold, Jennifer. "How a Radical Shift Left Zappos Reeling." *Fortune*, March 4, 2016. http://fortune.com/zappos-tony-hsieh-holacracy.

Rogers, Christina. "A Pioneer of the Open Office Helps Ford Rethink the Car." *Wall Street Journal*, November 29, 2016. https://www.wsj.com/articles/a-pioneer-of-the-open-office-helps-ford-rethink-the-car-1480441096.

Rumbles, Sally, and Gary Rees. "Continuous Changes, Organizational Burnout, and the Implications for HRD." *Industrial and Commercial Training* 45, no. 4 (2013): 236–242. https://doi.org/10.1108/00197851311323538.

Schwab, Klaus. "The Fourth Industrial Revolution: What It Means, How to Respond." World Economic Forum, January 14, 2016. https://www.weforum.org/agenda/2016/01/the-fourth-industrial-revolution-what-it-means-and-how-to-respond.

Stuart, Roger. "Experiencing Organizational Change: Triggers, Processes, and Outcomes of Change Journeys." *Personnel Review* 24, no. 2 (1995): 3–88. https://doi.org/10.1108/00483489510085726.

———. "The Trauma of Organizational Change." *Journal of European Industrial Training* 20, no. 2 (1996): 11–16. https://doi.org/10.1108/03090599610110420.

Chapter 9: Dehumanization: "Think of Yourself as a Machine Within a Machine"

American Management Association. "The Latest on Workplace Monitoring and Surveillance." Accessed May 31, 2018. https://www.amanet.org/training/articles/the-latest-on-workplace-monitoring-and-surveillance.aspx.

Associated Press in London. "Millions of Voiceprints Quietly Being Harvested as Latest Identification Tool." *Guardian*, October 13, 2014. https://www.theguardian.com/technology/2014/oct/13/millions-of-voiceprints-quietly-being-harvested-as-latest-identification-tool.

Ball, Kirstie. "Workplace Surveillance: An Overview." *Labor History* 51, no. 1 (2010): 87–106. https://doi.org/10.1080/00236561003654776.

Beyer, Elizabeth. "Why One-Third of American Working-Age Men Could Be Displaced by Robots." *MarketWatch*, May 14, 2018. https://www.marketwatch.com/story/why-one-third-of-american-working-age-men-could-be-displaced-by-robots-2018-05-14.

Brookings. "The Future of Work: Robots, AI, and Automation." Event held May 14, 2018. https://www.brookings.edu/events/the-future-of-work-robots-ai-and-automation.

Buchanan, Jeff. "Wisconsin Company Offers to Put RFID Chips in Employees' Bodies." Xconomy, July 26, 2017. https://www.xconomy.com/wisconsin/2017/07/26/wisconsin-company-offers-to-put-rfid-chips-in-employees-bodies.

Burt, Chris. "Nuance Voice Biometrics Solution Hits Milestone." BiometricUpdate.com, January 31, 2018. https://www.biometricupdate.com/201801/nuance-voice-biometrics-solution-hits-milestone.

Christoff, Kalina. "Dehumanization in Organizational Settings: Some Scientific and Ethical Considerations." *Frontiers in Human Neuroscience* 8 (2014): 748. https://doi.org/10.3389/fnhum.2014.00748.

Copeland, Rob, and Bradley Hope. "The World's Largest Hedge Fund Is Building an Algorithmic Model from Its Employees' Brains." *Wall Street Journal*, December 22, 2016. https://www.wsj.com/articles/the-worlds-largest-hedge-fund-is-building-an-algorithmic-model-of-its-founders-brain-1482423694.

Davenport, Thomas H. "The Fad That Forgot People." FastCompany, October 31, 1995. https://www.fastcompany.com/26310/fad-forgot-people.

Diallo, Ibrahim. "The Machine Fired Me." June 20, 2018. https://idiallo.com/blog/when-a-machine-fired-me.

Fagan, Kaylee. "Employee Burnout Is a Huge Problem in the Tech Industry. This Survey Shows Which Companies Have It the Worst." *Business Insider*, June 3, 2018. http://www.businessinsider.com/employee-burnout-tech-companies-silicon-valley-blind-survey-2018-5.

Feloni, Richard. "The World's Largest Hedge Fund Is Developing an Automated 'Coach' That Acts Like a Personal GPS for Decision-Making." *Business Insider*, September 25, 2017. http://www.businessinsider.com/ray-dalio-bridgewater-automated-management-system-2017-9.

Fidler, Devin. "Here's How Managers Can Be Replaced by Software." *Harvard Business Review*, April 21, 2015. https://hbr.org/2015/04/heres-how-managers-can-be-replaced-by-software.

Griffin, Matthew. "No Humans Required, the Fully Autonomous AI Running a Wall Street Hedge Fund." *Fanatical Futurist*, March 7, 2017. https://www.fanaticalfuturist.com/2017/03/no-humans-required-artificial-intelligence-is-running-wall-street-hedge-funds.

Hansson, David Heinemeier. "Exponential Growth Devours and Corrupts." Medium: Signal v. Noise, February 27, 2017. https://m.signalvnoise.com/exponential-growth-devours-and-corrupts-c5562fbf131.

Hoopes, James. "The Dehumanized Employee." CIO, February 4, 2005. https://www.cio.com.au/article/165305/dehumanized_employee.

Levin, Bess. "Billionaire Hedge-Fund Manager Ties *W.S.J.* to 'Fake' News Epidemic." *Vanity Fair*, January 3, 2017. https://www.vanityfair.com/news/2017/01/ray-dalio-wall-street-journal.

Metz, Cade. "The Rise of the Artificially Intelligent Hedge Fund." *Wired*, January 25, 2016. https://www.wired.com/2016/01/the-rise-of-the-artificially-intelligent-hedge-fund.

Moise, Imani. "What's on Your Mind? Bosses Are Using Artificial Intelligence to Find Out." *Wall Street Journal*, March 28, 2018. https://www.wsj.com/articles/whats-on-your-mind-bosses-are-using-artificial-intelligence-to-find-out-1522251302.

Samuel, Henry. "Why Have 24 France Telecom Workers Killed Themselves in the Past 19 Months?" *Telegraph*, October 4, 2009. https://www.telegraph.co.uk/finance/news bysector/mediatechnologyandtelecoms/6259384/Why-have-24-France-Telecom-workers-killed-themselves-in-the-past-19-months.html.

Schatzker, Erik. "Ray Dalio Says He's Ready to Give Away Bridgewater's Secrets." *Bloomberg*, September 17, 2017. https://www.bloomberg.com/news/articles/2017-09-17/ray-dalio-says-he-s-ready-to-give-away-bridgewater-s-secrets.

Scheiber, Noam. "How Uber Uses Psychological Tricks to Push Its Drivers' Buttons." *New York Times*, April 2, 2017. https://www.nytimes.com/interactive/2017/04/02/technology/uber-drivers-psychological-tricks.html.

Solon, Olivia. "'They'll Squash You Like a Bug': How Silicon Valley Keeps a Lid on Leakers." *Guardian*, March 16, 2018. https://www.theguardian.com/technology/2018/mar/16/silicon-valley-internal-work-spying-surveillance-leakers.

Stoddart, Jennifer. "Finding the Right Workplace Privacy Balance." Presentation at the Ryerson University Workshop on Workplace Privacy, Toronto, Canada, November 30, 2006. https://www.priv.gc.ca/en/opc-news/speeches/2006/sp-d_061130.

Turner, Camilla. "Robots Interviewing Graduates for Jobs at Top City Firms as Students Practice How to Impress AI." *Telegraph*, April 21, 2018. https://www.telegraph.co.uk/news/2018/04/21/robots-interviewing-graduates-jobs-top-city-firms-students-practice.

VMock website. Homepage, accessed May 31, 2018. https://www.vmock.com.

Waters, Sarah. "Suicide Voices: Testimonies of Trauma in the French Workplace." *Medical Humanities* 43, no. 1 (2017): 24–29. https://doi.org/10.1136/medhum-2016-011013.

Yerak, Becky. "Mariano's, Kimpton Hotels Sued over Alleged Collection of Biometric Data: 'It's Something Very Personal.'" *Chicago Tribune*, July 21, 2017. http://www.chicagotribune.com/business/ct-employers-biometrics-lawsuits-0723-biz-20170720-story.html.

Chapter 13: Kapor Capital: Conscious Capitalists

Dizikes, Peter. "Study: Workplace Diversity Can Help the Bottom Line." Massachusetts Institute of Technology Public Release, October 7, 2014. http://news.mit.edu/2014/workplace-diversity-can-help-bottom-line-1007.

Hunt, Vivian, Dennis Layton, and Sara Prince. "Why Diversity Matters." McKinsey and Company, January 2015. https://www.mckinsey.com/business-functions/organization/our-insights/why-diversity-matters.

Kokalitcheva, Kia. "Google's Diversity Efforts Fall Flat." *Axios*, August 9, 2017. https://www.axios.com/googles-diversity-efforts-fall-flat-1513304728-60fd8127-a0c0-485e-9bf4-a89d6337fc8e.html.

Scott, Kristyn A., Joanna M. Heathcote, and Jamie A. Gruman. "The Diverse Organization: Finding Gold at the End of the Rainbow." *Human Resource Management* 50, no. 6 (2011): 735–755. https://doi.org/10.1002/hrm.20459.

Chapter 14: The Social Enterprise Movement

Tropeano, Joe. "Appalachian Transition in Action." Social Enterprise Alliance, January 17, 2017. https://socialenterprise.us/2017/01/17/appalachia-maced.

Chapter 15: Can Zebras Fix What Unicorns Have Broken?

Coren, Michael J. "Silicon Valley Tech Workers Are Talking About Starting Their First Union in 2017 to Resist Trump." *Quartz*, March 24, 2017. https://qz.com/916534/silicon-valley-tech-workers-are-talking-about-starting-their-first-union-in-2017-to-resist-trump.

"FAQs Purpose Economy." Purpose. http://purpose-economy.org/en/faqs/.

Le, Phuong. "Seattle Divided as Leaders Halt Tax on Companies Like Amazon." Associated Press, June 13, 2018. https://apnews.com/606ff14719bb4cf4a397cf2d79008992.

Margaritoff, Marco. "Google Halts A.I. Drone Deal with Pentagon Following Staff Protests." *The Drive*, June 4, 2018. http://www.thedrive.com/tech/21281/google-halts-a-i-drone-deal-with-pentagon-following-staff-protests.

National Venture Capital Association. "U.S. Venture Capital Industry Pacing for Another Record-Breaking Year in 2018," Press release, April 10, 2018. https://nvca.org/press-releases/u-s-venture-capital-industry-pacing-another-record-breaking-year-2018/.

Sorkin, Andrew Ross. "New Goldman Sachs Fund Will Track Paul Tudor Jones's Feel-Good Companies." *New York Times*, June 11, 2018. https://www.nytimes.com/2018/06/11/business/dealbook/goldman-sachs-paul-tudor-jones.html.

United States Department of Justice. "Theranos Founder and Former Chief Operating Officer Charged in Alleged Wire Fraud Schemes." Press release, June 15, 2018. https://www.justice.gov/usao-ndca/pr/theranos-founder-and-former-chief-operating-officer-charged-alleged-wire-fraud-schemes.

Zepeda, Mara, Jennifer Brandel, Astrid Scholz, Aniyia Williams, "Zebras Fix What Unicorns Break." Medium, March 8, 2017. https://medium.com/@sexandstartups/zebrasfix-c467e55f9d96.

INDEX